# Ministering to
## Twenty-First Century
# Families

## OTHER BOOKS BY DENNIS RAINEY

*The New Building Your Mate's Self-Esteem* (coauthor)

*Moments Together for Couples* (coauthor)

*Parenting Today's Adolescent* (coauthor)

*Two Hearts Are Better Than One* (coauthor)

*Starting Your Marriage Right* (coauthor)

*The Tribute and the Promise* (coauthor)

*Building Your Marriage*

*Managing Pressure in Your Marriage* (coauthor)

*One Home at a Time*

# Ministering to
# Twenty-First Century
# Families

*Eight Big Ideas*
*for Church Leaders*

## DENNIS RAINEY

Charles R. Swindoll, *General Editor*
Roy B. Zuck, *Managing Editor*

WORD PUBLISHING
NASHVILLE
www.wordpublishing.com
A Thomas Nelson Company

MINISTERING TO TWENTY-FIRST CENTURY FAMILIES

Swindoll Leadership Library

Unless otherwise indicated, Scripture quotations used in this book are from the New American Standard Bible (NASB). Copyright © 1960, 1962, 1963, 1971, 1972, 1973, 1975, 1977, 1995 by the Lockman Foundation. Used by permission.

Scripture quotations identified KJV are from the King James Version of the Bible.

Scripture quotations identified NIV are from the Holy Bible, New International Version, copyright © 1973, 1978, 1984, International Bible Society. Used by permission of Zondervan Bible Publishers.

Published in association with Dallas Theological Seminary (DTS):

General Editor: Charles R. Swindoll
Managing Editor: Roy B. Zuck

The theological opinions expressed by the author are not necessarily the official position of Dallas Theological Seminary.

*Library of Congress Cataloging-in-Publication Data*

Rainey, Dennis, 1948–
Ministering to twenty-first century families / by Dennis Rainey
Charles R. Swindoll, general editor
Roy B. Zuck, managing editor
p. cm.4—(Swindoll leadership library)
Includes bibliographical references and indexes.

ISBN 0-8499-1359-4

1. Pastoral Theology. 2. Family—Religious Life. I. Swindoll, Charles R.
II. Title. III. Series

BV4320.R35   2001                                   2001026269
259'.–dc21                                              CIP

*Printed in the United States of America*

01 02 03 04 05 06 BVG 9 8 7 6 5 4 3 2 1

# DEDICATION

I dedicate this book to three groups of pastors whom God has used greatly in my life. First, two pastors dramatically shaped my life spiritually. You men will never know how your lives impacted mine.

*H. D. McCarty*

*Alan Harrison*

Second, twenty-six pastors and their wives serve families worldwide by being part of our FamilyLife Conference Speaker Team. You are our friends and comrades in a "family reformation."

| | |
|---|---|
| *Charles and Karen Boyd* | *Robert and Judith Maddox* |
| *Dan and Julie Brenton* | *Ray and Robyn McKelvy* |
| *Karl and Junanne Clauson* | *David and Shari Meserve* |
| *Doug and Patty Daily* | *Johnny and Lezlyn Parker* |
| *Kyle and Sharon Dodd* | *Brett and Carol Ray* |
| *Michael and Cindy Easley* | *Mark and Lisa Schatzman* |
| *Dennis and Jill Eenigenburg* | *Jeff and Brenda Schulte* |
| *Doug and Susan Grimes* | *Clarence and Brenda Shuler* |
| *Dick and Nancy Hastings* | *Rick and Judy Taylor* |
| *Bruce and Janet Hess* | *Roger and Joanne Thompson* |
| *Alan and Theda Hlavka* | *J. T. and Enid Walker* |
| *Dan and Kathie Jarrell* | *Dave and Ann Wilson* |
| *Dave and Peggy Jones* | *John and Susan Yates* |

Third, I dedicate this book to three pastors and their wives who have led our church. Thanks for your compassionate shepherding and instruction of Barbara and me and our family.

*Bill and Carolyn Wellons*

*Bill and Anne Parkinson*

*Robert and Sherard Lewis*

# CONTENTS

## Part 3: Unique Families

## Part 4: A Time for Courage

# CONTENTS

# FOREWORD

I love the church. In fact I've devoted the majority of my life to advancing the cause of Christ through the outreach of the local church. It's a magnificent plan! Think of churches as mission outposts set up all over the world. In neighborhoods, towns, and villages across the globe, the church meets to carry out the mission of the Master. As a pastor, I lead one of those outposts, called Stonebriar Community Church, in Frisco, Texas. There are many others in our region, our country, and around the world equally devoted to the Savior.

Most of the people in a local church are united in a smaller group called a family. In other words the church is a "family of families." And of course *the local church is only as strong as its strongest families.* Show me a healthy, vibrant local church, and I'll show you an assembly filled with healthy, vibrant, fully functioning families.

My longtime friend Dennis Rainey is devoting his life to one cause— the strengthening of families. He understands that churches are comprised of families, and that healthy families are the best contributors to the welfare of any church. Healthy families are able to give more of their time, energy, effectiveness, and resources to the Lord's work. When families break down, churches step in to offer help and healing. When there are no effective churches to aid families, values erode, communities suffer, neighborhoods deteriorate, towns become less than what they should be.

As you read *Ministering to Twenty-First Century Families,* I'm confident you'll be challenged anew, as I was, to promote families through local-church ministries. This broadly experienced author is passionate about families, and it shows in his research and writing. He's not afraid to take on controversial topics like divorce, remarriage, adoption, abuse, and discipline. He writes with wisdom and wit, drawing from his relevant world of knowledge and reality. I commend this volume to your personal, church, or school library.

Families and churches alike can be thankful Dennis Rainey took the time to spell out exactly the direction family ministry should take as we move rapidly through the twenty-first century.

—CHARLES R. SWINDOLL
*General Editor*

# INTRODUCTION

For nearly twenty-five years my wife, Barbara, and I have been deeply committed to a church we helped start—Fellowship Bible Church, in Little Rock, Arkansas. In this family-oriented church we've served in a number of capacities as lay leaders.

I believe in the local church. But many local churches are facing challenges, including the serious needs of families. That's why this book addresses ways to help build godly marriages and families in the local church.

Being the pastor of a local church is one of the more difficult and challenging jobs a person could ever undertake. The average layperson cannot fathom the expectations pastors face from members of their congregation. From childcare to elderly care. From a hospital room, where a baby has just been born, to another hospital room, where a young mother of four is dying. The spiritual and emotional weight of leading and loving a flock of believers is an awesome burden. Pastors are busy—and burdened. They face discouragement as they see the messes some people have made of their marriages and their families.

I have three objectives in this book. The first is to encourage church leaders in their own homes. The ministry exacts a price from marriages and families, and it is my prayer that pastors will be stimulated to love and to do good deeds in their most important relationships—those at home.

Second, I pray that church leaders will be better equipped to build distinctively Christian marriages and families and strengthen the church at the same time. If there has ever been a time for the church to step forward on behalf of families, it is today.

Third, I hope this book stimulates dialogue and debate about how local churches can become marriage-and-family equipping centers.

After the last chapter I have included an Idea Inventory for your use. As you finish each chapter, consider recording in the Idea Inventory the *one memorable idea* from that chapter that made the strongest impression on you. When you complete the book, you will have a concise listing of material that is most relevant to your ministry situation. From there you can decide how and when to implement new approaches.

This book is *not* recommending that you reinvent your church. Much of what I propose in this book can be accomplished by judicious "tweaking" of existing programs and plans.

I pray that we will see a family reformation sweep across our nation, one home at a time. Perhaps as never before, local churches are needed to help restore our families.

# CHAPTER

## 1

## The Family Dunkirk

On May 24, 1940, about four hundred thousand Allied troops were trapped on the coast of France, near the port of Dunkirk. With little in their way, Hitler's tanks were advancing and were only ten miles away. There was no possibility of escape by land. The situation was bleak. In a matter of hours, thousands of British and French troops would die or end up as prisoners of war. A rescue was desperately needed—but by whom and how?[1]

In America I believe we are experiencing the "Dunkirk" of the family. There seems to be no route of escape from a culture that is destroying our families. Who will come to the rescue? I believe the answer lies in the local church—but more on that later.

Carl Zimmerman, a Harvard University sociologist, once studied the rise and fall of every major empire in world history. More specifically he traced what happened to the family in each of these empires. He concluded that families go through three phases, the last occurring just before each major empire fell apart. In his book *Family and Civilization*, he listed these characteristics of families in their final phase:

- Marriage lost its sacredness, and alternative forms of marriage were advocated.
- Feminist movements flourished.

- Parenting became more difficult.
- Adultery was celebrated, not punished.
- Sexual perversions abounded, including bestiality, but especially incest and homosexuality.[2]

America is certainly one of the great "empires" of history. Do Zimmerman's observations on the family send a shiver down your back as they do mine? Does your concern become more urgent when you realize that his book was published in 1947—more than half a century ago? He did not write his prophetic words—which now ring so true—with the benefit of reading today's newspaper, watching recent movies, or viewing a week's worth of prime-time television.

As you look at some facts about homes in America, ponder this question: Can our nation continue to survive if its most basic unit of society, the family, continues to unravel?

- In 1960 fewer than half a million unmarried couples lived together in the United States. But in 1998 four million unmarried couples were living together.[3]
- Families headed by single fathers are now the fastest-growing kind of family.[4]
- A researcher reported that 94 percent of the sex shown on TV is among people who are not married to each other.[5]
- In 1998 a U.S. Census Bureau study found that a majority of first-born children are born out of wedlock.[6]
- "As an adult stage in the life course, marriage is shrinking. Americans are living longer, marrying later, exiting marriage more quickly, and choosing to live together before marriage, after marriage, in-between marriages, and as an alternative to marriage."[7]
- "It has been estimated that after ten years only about 25 percent of first marriages are successful, that is, both still intact and reportedly happy; this represents a substantial decline from earlier decades."[8]
- Over one million divorces occur each year in the United States.[9]
- The presence of a stepparent in a family is the best predictor of child-abuse risk yet discovered.[10]
- In 1996, 1.3 million abortions were carried out in America.[11]
- From 1980 to 1992 the rate of suicide among young adolescents

(ages ten to fourteen) increased 120 percent and increased most dramatically among young black males (300 percent) and young white females (233 percent). About one-third of all adolescents in America say they have contemplated suicide.[12]

- In an Internet survey conducted in 2000, 51 percent of those registering an opinion answered yes to this question: "Should your place of worship bless same-sex commitment ceremonies?"[13]

What will become of America if these trends continue? Can our nation survive without traditional families?

In 1940 the leaders of the British government prepared for the worst. General Sir Edmund Ironside, Chief of the Imperial General Staff, wrote in his diary on May 25, "We shall have lost practically all our trained soldiers by the next few days—unless a miracle appears to help us."[14] In fact the leaders were surprised by one of the most unexpected and dramatic provisions of ingenuity and resources in history—a story I'll finish at the end of this chapter.

How will God answer our prayers for "the family Dunkirk"? How are we to rescue all the families we love, while also leading, nurturing, and protecting our own? Time will tell. But I am confident that the needs of the family in America and throughout the world are much on God's heart. God has long made known His commitment to the family. The Bible begins and ends with a marriage and is filled with stories and principles that reveal the importance of the family in accomplishing His aims.

What can we do to begin the rescue of the American family from its near-fatal "Dunkirk"?

## DARE TO DREAM?

Social-science research overwhelmingly shows that when a child is raised in a stable home environment by a mother and father who love, nurture, and teach the child the basics of life—honesty, care for others, and responsibility, to name just a few—that child usually grows up to be a mature adult who can then form his or her own marriage and family and repeat the process.[15]

In our sophisticated age, such a basic idea may sound grossly simple and naive, but that is God's design for humanity—and it works. I can't think of any contemporary social problem that ultimately will not be conquered if we will simply follow God's wise and eternal instructions for marriage and the family, and carry out our responsibility to help prepare the next generation to raise their families.

Imagine what would happen if every Christian couple determined to keep their marriage vows unbroken. Imagine Christian homes where husbands and wives understand and accept their complementing roles in serving and loving each other. Think of churches where the pastoral staff did not exhaust themselves caring for those wounded in domestic battles. Picture the glory of God radiating into dark neighborhoods from healthy families that look beyond their own needs to the needs of others.

Millions of Americans are asking, "How can I have a lasting marriage and a strong family?" The desire for successful families crosses all generations. A recent study showed that young people listed as their generation's number-one problem "an increase in divorce and single-parent families." These young adults between the ages of eighteen and thirty placed "having a strong family" as their most important goal, even above money and career.[16]

FamilyLife, the ministry I direct, has conducted a number of surveys of adults in local churches. We have found that of the top ten personal needs for which respondents say they want help from the church, six involve marriage and family issues. The hunger for help is there.[17]

Two conclusions are clear: First, the family represents the greatest unmet need in Western civilization. Second, because of the breakdown of many families, our culture is giving the church a strategic and profound opportunity for ministry.

## A STRATEGY: EIGHT "BIG IDEAS"

Even though I have been involved in a parachurch family ministry since the 1970s, I firmly believe that the real action in rescuing American families must take place in local churches. No doubt parachurch organizations can play a critical support role, but the family is an institution that requires the daily, hands-on attention that can be provided by the church.

A national ministry can beam a radio program into cars and homes, but it can't bring over a meal when a pregnant mom is ordered to bed by her doctor.

Books, audiotapes, and videos can provide outstanding insight on raising kids. But what can take the place of an older father counseling a younger man on how to comfort a middle-school daughter who wasn't chosen as cheerleader and thinks her life is over?

A weekend seminar can instruct a couple on how to resolve a conflict. But who can hold a couple accountable to help mend the heart and rebuild the wall broken by the most recent argument?

The rebuilding of the family will require cooperation and pooling of resources in the local church. No church should think it must create and sustain all the support that is needed by contemporary families. A major goal of this book is to show how family resources are distributed broadly throughout the church—in national organizations and denominations, as well as churches.

There is no single, best way for the church to do family ministry. As the Scriptures and our own experience frequently demonstrate, God accomplishes His objectives in infinitely creative ways.

In our ministry's research with pastors and leaders in a variety of churches throughout the United States, we have observed that many leaders are uncertain about what family ministry should be and should attempt to accomplish.

Confusion about the family does not stop at the church door. Just think about the impact of one issue—divorce. Even twenty years ago divorce was not common among Christians. Now we have to deal not only with the direct effects of divorce on adults and children, but we also face a host of related issues—single parents, theological questions related to remarriage, child custody and support problems, adjustments to stepparents—on and on. My pastor, Robert Lewis, once said a startling thing at a church-budget meeting: "Nothing we deal with in our church takes as much time as people contemplating divorce, those going through a divorce, or those recovering from divorce. In fact, divorce issues now take more time from our staff, more effort and expense, than *all the other issues in the church combined!*"

In this book I present eight suggestions on how to carry out an effective family ministry. I call them the "Eight Big Ideas of Family Ministry" in the church. These are the subjects of chapters 2 through 9. If those who work with Christian families concentrated on these major ideas, I believe we would see a spiritual revolution in families. A family reformation would occur. Families for generations to come would be rescued.

In developing this plan to clarify and focus family ministry in our chaotic contemporary environment, here are the benefits I hope you will receive from this book.

### My Best "Nuggets" from a Quarter Century of Family Ministry

God has allowed me to be involved in serving families for over twenty-five years. That's a lot of time to learn from mistakes! And I have been blessed to travel widely and meet scores of passionate and effective people studying and serving the family. Their good ideas and successes, too, will be found in these pages.

### Encouragement for Your Marriage and Family Life

Pastors and other church leaders and their spouses and kids face unique snares. My first "big idea" relates to what I think needs to be one of the pastor's top ministry priorities—his own marriage and family.

### The Best Family Ministry Resources

I don't attempt to offer exhaustive lists of resources, but I do share what I think are the best materials available for major categories of family ministry.

### Connections to Others in Family Ministry

The Internet provides a powerful opportunity for all of us to communicate and share ideas and resources. I list every helpful Web site I'm aware of today. My desire is that this book will help spur a far-reaching exchange of ideas as readers share their ideas with others via the Internet.

*A Family Ministry Paradigm*

Over the past half-dozen years I have had a growing conviction that we need to target certain stages in the development of a family. FamilyLife has developed what we call the Family Life Cycle. It helps clarify important issues that might otherwise be ignored as families pass through predictable stages. This paradigm is explained in detail in chapters 10 through 16.

*Insight on Unique Family Issues*

Parts three and four concentrate on subjects like adoption, singles, single parents, stepfamilies, divorce, and church discipline. Every effective ministry must help support and restore families that have been damaged as well as help build intact families.

## THE DUNKIRK MIRACLE

In May 1940 as the military situation in France deteriorated, even the normally bullish Winston Churchill thought England's naval resources could rescue no more than 30,000 of the retreating soldiers. The leaders of the armed forces were a bit more optimistic, thinking they might save 45,000 men with the 129 ferries, coasters, and other small craft at their disposal. What they did not realize was that British civilians were not going to see their bleeding, exhausted sons lost without a fight. Walter Lord wrote of the common citizens, "They were working at desks all over southern England, and it was their unannounced, unpublicized intention to confound the gloomy predictions of the warriors and statesmen."[18]

Informally, by word of mouth and without any public announcement, a vast armada of nonmilitary public and private vessels was assembled to bring the British boys home. Just six days after the beginning of the crisis near Dunkirk, an observer on a British destroyer saw on the horizon "a mass of dots that filled the sea" as he approached Dover. These dots were boats. "Here and there were respectable steamers, like the Portsmouth-Isle of Wight car ferry, but mostly they were little ships of every conceivable type—fishing smacks . . . drifters . . . excursion boats . . . glittering white yachts . . . mud-splattered hoppers . . . open motor launches . . . tugs towing ship's lifeboats . . . Thames sailing barges with their distinctive brown sails . . . cabin cruisers, their bright work gleaming . . . dredges, trawlers, and rust-streaked scows . . . the Admiral Superintendent's barge from Portsmouth with its fancy tassels and rope-work."[19] This ragtag navy was out to save the day, rescuing many thousands of British—and later—French troops.

For the rescuers this was not some kind of lark. The small boats faced the constant danger of capsizing, and German artillery, airplanes, and boats tried to sink as many of them as possible. Many volunteers labored to exhaustion, such as the two civilians who spent seventeen hours without a break rowing troops from the beach at Dunkirk to waiting rescue boats.[20]

Soon others at home added enthusiastic support. When the troops stumbled from the boats on England's shores, civilians rushed forward with cocoa and sandwiches. One man bought up all the socks and underwear in his town and handed them to grateful soldiers. As trains moved the troops from the coast to restaging areas across England, crowds gathered at station platforms to cheer and give the men cigarettes and chocolate. Banners made from bedsheets displayed messages like "Well Done," and children stood at railway crossings waving flags.[21]

The evening of June 4, 1940, two weeks after the beginning of the crisis and with the evacuation completed, Churchill went to a packed House of Commons and called this dramatic action a "miracle of deliverance." To the assembly's cheers he spoke the memorable words, "We shall fight on the beaches, we shall fight on the landing grounds, we shall fight in the fields and in the streets."[22]

In the end the rescue fleet numbered 861 "ships" that evacuated over 338,000 troops.

Can you see a similar picture as we face the Dunkirk of the family? Saving our families calls for an all-out effort by our churches.

Lay church leaders must be recruited to participate in rescuing our families. Without lay help, full-time church leaders will perish from exhaustion. A long-lasting family ministry will not occur in a church building or counselor's office. It will happen as husbands and wives, dads and moms, grandpas and grandmas first take responsibility for their own homes, then willingly give of their time, resources, and experience to help others obtain the family health so desperately desired and needed.

One fact about the evacuation from the coast of France, however, does not match the "family Dunkirk." We can't expect to rescue the family quickly. How long has it taken us to reach this point? How long will it take to reverse the family's slide? Only God knows, but we must prepare for a fierce struggle that may last through our generation and well into the next.

# PART

# 1

## THE BIG IDEAS OF FAMILY MINISTRY

# CHAPTER

## 2

## Big Idea 1: Minister to the "First Family" First

For the past five years our FamilyLife ministry has spent a lot of time listening to pastors—holding focus groups and meeting with individuals. I'll never forget attending a day-long focus group of more than twenty pastors. For hours we discussed family issues and what the church needs to do to strengthen families. At the end of the day I asked, "What is your greatest need when it comes to strengthening families in your church?"

I was unprepared for the response these church leaders gave. Nearly in unison they said, "My marriage and family." Ministry was extracting an incredible toll on these men's families.

We concluded that the number-one way our ministry could assist these pastors was to help them in their *own* families.

Ben Freudenburg, a pastor, revealed a portion of the problem when my co-host Bob Lepine and I interviewed him on our radio program "FamilyLife Today." He said, "We have become ministers because we have this great passion to care for and love people to Christ. We'll just do whatever it takes, and sometimes we get misguided and put so much energy into the work of the church that we don't realize what we are doing to our own families and to our own lives and children."[1]

The weight pastors carry is one of the more difficult assignments in all of life. Just the work schedule alone can create tensions at home.

Archibald Hart of the Fuller Institute of Church Growth reports that 90 percent of pastors work more than forty-six hours per week, and many work sixty hours. Nine out of ten feel inadequately trained to handle the demands of the ministry.[2] Another survey found that 80 percent of the clergy feel the church has negatively impacted their families, and 33 percent say the ministry is an outright hazard to their families.[3]

Pastors are no different from many men in that they too often struggle with providing leadership in the home. One pastor told me that it is easier for him to lead his church spiritually than it is to lead his wife and family. That's understandable but not excusable. When a pastor helps a person in the church, the results can be instantly gratifying. And if the pastor has a "bent" toward work, it's not long before the narcotic I call "ministry addiction" hooks its victim.

But ultimately the state of a pastor's marriage and family is a matter of integrity. The psalmist Asaph wrote of David, "So he shepherded them according to the integrity of his heart" (Ps. 78:72). Are those of us in the ministry leading lives that others can emulate?

When Paul spoke of his ministry, he emphasized both the sharing of the gospel and the example of his own life (1 Thess. 2:1–12). He backed his communicating of the gospel by his exemplary life. Probably nothing reveals more about a man's character than how he relates to his wife and children. I am continually challenged by the pointed remarks on personal integrity David made in Psalm 101. First, he said, "I will walk within my house in the integrity of my heart" (101:2). Then he commented on the kind of person who would influence him: "He who walks in a blameless way is the one who will minister to me" (101:6). This is what we all seek—to live clean, honest lives that will inspire and encourage others to do likewise.

This chapter gives ideas on how to improve your marriage and family. But I really have only one major point: *Your relationship with your spouse and children is the most important message on the family your church will ever hear you preach.*

Many pastors and their families are weary of feeling that they have to be "perfect examples" of a Christian family. But that's not what your church needs. In fact, we should reject this stereotype of what constitutes a godly marriage and family. You won't have a perfect family, and you shouldn't try to project to others that you have a perfect family.

You don't have to be perfect to be a model. In fact, people need to know how you apply the Christian life to the struggles in your marriage and family. I've learned that many times God wants to use my failures to show others how to get back on track. Many times our most profound ministry comes from our weakness.

H. B. London, a pastor for thirty-one years who now directs the ministry to pastors and their families at Focus on the Family, said in an interview for this book that the most strategic thing a senior pastor can do to encourage strong marriages and families in the church is to "model a strong marriage. Model attentiveness. Model intimacy. Model loving parenthood. That's the first thing. *Remember that your marriage and your family are more important than your ministry.*"[4]

Your people need to see what a Christ-honoring, growing marriage looks like. Let them see that you and your wife are full of sacrificial love and forgiveness, that you seek to obey God, to be honest about failures and successes, and to glorify the Lord through a love-filled marriage and family.

Instead of seeing a wife and the children—and the duties of husband and father—as a burden or even as a hindrance to your ministry, view your wife and children as gifts from God. A strong, refreshing relationship with your spouse and fruitful relationships with your children will strengthen your public ministry. Every one of us needs the love, affection, and support that come uniquely from a marriage partner. Because of the demands of your ministry, you may need this even more. If your marriage is full of joy and encouragement, then you will be refreshed and energized and able to minister more effectively to others. But if your marriage has strain and contention, it will drain you emotionally, physically, and spiritually.

At times a need in the church will consume your time and energy. But if this is the rule rather than the exception, eventually the debts you owe to the home front will come due, and the price may be more than you can pay.

In every church some people don't understand this, and some might even try to make life miserable for the man who insists that he must take time and energy to tend to the needs of his own wife and children.

### AN INTERVIEW WITH
### H. B. LONDON

*In preparation for this book we interviewed H. B. London, the "pastor's pastor" with Focus on the Family. Having spent years in the pastorate, H. B. has learned much that can help pastors and their wives and children. Except for questions printed in italics, all comments are direct quotations from Pastor London.*

I say this all the time—the pastor's role is to make sure when he candidates and expresses himself, he takes the pressure off his family by saying, "This is what you can expect of my family. Our kids are this old. They're going to be involved in Little League and things like that."

Most pastors are people pleasers. And because we are, we will often shortchange our family in order to help somebody else's family.

What I've found [in church] is that you can never give enough. There's never a limit to what people will let you give. So if you have twenty hours, they will take twenty hours.

The expectation level [of church members] is still very high when they need their pastor. The reality is that many churches think they have made great strides in reducing the time pressures and other pressures on the pastor, but I'm not sure they really have. It's never going to be idyllic. . . . But if you start with a premise, then you will be able to build on that premise. If you start with no parameters whatever, then the church and people in the church will set those parameters for you.

Remember that it's God's church. He loves the church and the people more than we ever could.

The one who suffers . . . is the pastor's spouse . . . because she doesn't have an outlet. The male pastor can lose himself in work, in his assignment, and find fulfillment in being with a bunch of men and doing "pastor things." So often the pastor's wife feels beleaguered because she's working—50 to 70 percent of them work at least part-time—and she has responsibilities for the children and the house.

So we find a lot of bitterness, and even anger, that comes through.

*Is there a particular trap in which pastors' wives fall?*

There are three traps. One is seeing the church as your enemy or as your competition. The other is finding yourself in competition with your spouse in ministry, where you are both looking for the same accolades from the people in church. The third [trap] is forgetting [that] you are first and foremost a wife and mother, and then a layperson.

*If you could give advice to spouses of pastors, what would you say?*

Be yourself. You cannot allow a congregation or a group of people's expectations to make of you somebody you're not. And if you use your best gifts most often, you'll be happier and more fulfilled, and you and your spouse will contribute better to one another's lives. If you try to be something you're not, if you try to fill a round hole when you're a square peg, then you will always feel frustrated.

Pastors are pretty elusive and not always real honest about the way things are. Or honest with themselves. . . . We get so many calls [at Focus on the Family] with violence and anger, conflict beyond what most church members would have.

Some clergy families we deal with [are in] a crisis without recourse. Other couples can go see their pastor when there's a marital problem, or they can go see the family pastor, or we'll recommend a counselor for them to go to. But because of the limited income, because of the stigma attached to a clergyman going for help, [they] often don't. So [they] live marriages that are that in name only. They're hollow.

Stand firm. Don't abandon the sheep at home in favor of the sheep at church.

One Christian leader was seldom home, and when he was with his family he was totally exhausted. Ultimately his love affair with the ministry cost him his marriage, his family, and even his ministry. His adult daughter later said of him, "Daddy believed that he and God had a 'deal.' He [daddy] would take care of God's sheep in the ministry and in return God would take care of Daddy's sheep at home. Unfortunately, he found out too late that the 'deal' was Daddy's and not God's."

## MINISTER FIRST TO YOUR SPOUSE

I can think of no other profession where the demands of the man's job can enter the home with such ease, frequency, and intensity. If a pastor is successful in ministering to the needs of his people, then the demand for meeting still others' needs will increase. If husband and wife fail to understand and regulate this, their marriage may become a casualty.

Lorna Dobson, a pastor's wife, wrote, "Since ministry couples are not exempt from Satan's fiery darts, they need to protect, tend, and fortify their marriages against stress, and even be prepared for a veritable earthquake."[5]

H. B. London says, "The thing we hear most from pastors' wives is they just don't have enough time together [with their husbands], and many times the church has become a mistress to the pastor. But he would not admit that, for it takes so much time and effort to keep the mistress happy."[6]

There's no room in any marriage for a mistress. And although the husband is primarily responsible for not letting church-related activities make his wife jealous, it's important, too, that the wife be an advocate for her husband and that she stand against his developing an overloaded schedule. Pastors should encourage their wives to hold them accountable, giving them freedom to say, "Honey, I love you enough not to let you keep doing all of this. You're making it too hard on yourself and your family."

At a conference I asked pastors' wives what advice they would give young pastors and their wives about marriage. Following are some of their answers.[7]

"Don't take yourselves too seriously!"

"Make dating a priority—see if you can have a date without discussing the church. Tell your husband if he's home by (a reasonable hour), you'll make it worth his while."

"I would advise them to take care of themselves as a couple first and foremost. They should remind themselves that as they counsel others, particularly the unmarried, they must focus on their oneness in Christ."

"Talk. Be sure that all of your activities are not church-related (have a life 'outside' the church). Laugh about things instead of getting defensive."

"Be who you are and not what others expect you to be."

"Pray about developing healthy boundaries for the two of you—what God would have you do to protect yourselves from being 'eaten up' by others. You want so much to help everyone, but without healthy boundaries , the two of you will suffer."

"For the man, find an older man to keep you accountable for the hours and energy you spend at the cost of your family. For the woman, purpose to make your husband as 'successful' as you can. Free him up, in terms of time, energy, or whatever, to do what God has called him to do."

"Have a family day once a week. Read and learn together."

"Each week set aside time, if possible, for at least three or four hours to spend together discussing what is important, what is going on that week, and concerns, as well as doing something fun weekly. Pray together daily."

Here are some additional ideas on how pastors can keep their marriages healthy.

- *Make time for romance*. Save some of your creativity, emotional energy, and time to add nice touches to your relationship. A two-night getaway alone once—or twice—a year will recharge your marriage and also refuel your passion for each other and for your ministry. Barbara and I have found that three nights away from the children two or three times a year are helpful. Going to a bed-and-breakfast or a friend's cabin can provide a needed spiritual and romantic oasis.
- *Have date nights*. For years Barbara and I have observed a date night each week. Much of the time we keep it simple—just an inexpensive dinner over which we catch up, compare schedules, make plans. The focused communication is invaluable.
- *Share everything.* Make your ministry a true partnership. Your wife doesn't need to know the details about every couple counseled, each tension with a staff member, every budget meeting. But she needs to know your heart, your dreams, your struggles. Also share openly any temptations—and urge your wife to warn you of potential problems

you may not be aware of. Lorna Dobson wrote, "Having talked to pastors' wives who have lived through having other women vie for their husbands' attention, we have agreed that we should not cast aside our uneasy feelings, but gently urge our husbands to observe and deal with the problem. One older ministry wife told me that 'red flags' seen by the wife should be considered a gift of intuition and should be taken seriously by the couple."[8]

- *Embrace suffering together.* Suffering is common to all. However, there are hardships that are especially difficult for those in ministry. Without the proper perspective, suffering can lead to discouragement and anger and hinder the accomplishing of your task. A pastor and his wife must "bear one another's burdens."

- *Pray together daily.* Not many pastors pray with their wives each day. If you are looking for a practical way to lead your wife spiritually, there is nothing with greater benefits than this spiritual discipline.

## RAISE CHILDREN, NOT PREACHER'S KIDS

Your legacy through your children is more important than the legacy of your ministry through your church.

Would you agree that as the shepherding goes at home, so it will go in the church? The two endeavors are more closely connected than most of us would care to admit. Again, our parenting won't be perfect, and we all make mistakes. But if we approach our responsibility as parents with integrity, there will be fruit in our broader ministry as well. Perhaps the "secret" is to view our children as our privileged responsibility and assignment from God. This is the quality one young man, himself now a pastor, saw in his relationship with his father, who was a pastor.

My dad could teach spiritual principles from the most ordinary circumstances. When Dad walked out the door, I was invited. When he played golf with his preacher friends, I rode in the golf cart. . . . I rode in a pickup with him and his buddy Red Moore when they went quail hunting. As Red lit up a Camel, I told him, in a serious voice, "Jesus doesn't like it when you smoke." Red laughed with that smoker's hack. Dad just grinned. . . . The beauty of Dad's method of bringing me into his world was that he did not have to alter his schedule, just his focus. There was never "family time" on his calendar. If he was doing something where I could be with him, I was.... The other day my dad commented, "I regret not being more consistent in my family devotions when you were growing up." I reminded him that our family altar was often a boat, a field, or a golf cart.[9]

Another child of a pastor has more painful memories. At her father's funeral she watched and listened as mourner after mourner described all the wonderful deeds done by this shepherd for his sheep. When at last the crowd departed, she asked, "Who was that man they spoke of?" All the man's children agreed that others had known the heart of their father better than they did. In sadness the daughter of this wonderful servant of God wrote of her father, "To Dad every request from a [church] member constituted a command performance. Family plans were canceled without question. Protests were pointless. Even the youngest child could recite Dad's response: 'Don't you understand? God called me, to serve these people. My work is to do the Lord's work. How can I refuse? They need me.' And he would be gone."[10]

Sadly, this pastor-dad must have perceived his family as something quite distinct from his ministry.

Also be alert to your children's spiritual needs. As parents we must be aggressive in protecting our children from evil. Satan crouches outside every door, and he would love to mess with your family. Here are some thoughts on how pastors and other church leaders can minister to their children.

- *Cultivate a focused relationship with each child.* Because a pastor must share so much of his time with nonfamily members, it's important that your children know that you will devote special time and attention to each one.
- *Explain to your kids what you do and why.* Your children need to know how important your ministry is—and appropriately, occasionally to observe you (in addition to Sunday) engaged in that ministry. Helping people relate to God is a high calling. Share your passion, enthusiasm, and sense of urgency with family members. They have a desire and a right to be proud of what you do.

- *Save some pastoral care for your own sheep.* Your children need their pastor too. I gave up leading Bible studies for businessmen for about a decade because I didn't want to be always rushing off to help others know God while failing to introduce my own children to Him. One of my fondest memories is that of meeting before school with two of my teenagers for a donut and a study in Proverbs. After your wife, your children are your most important disciples.

## REDEEMING THE TIME

I've been in ministry since 1970, and I know what it means to be stretched and challenged. But I cannot fully appreciate or understand the seven-day, twenty-four-hours-a-day tension that surrounds a pastor's schedule. The word "boundaries" hardly seems adequate to describe how a busy pastor must shape, guard, and patrol his schedule—if he is to remain effective at home.

Pastor Ben Freudenburg knows all about the schedule scenario. He became so ministry driven that his wife, Jennifer, had to confront him. He went to see a friend to seek advice. Here's how Ben reported on that conversation.

"He knew I wasn't spending time caring about Jennifer as I should have been. So he asked me to open my calendar. 'Ben,' he said, 'what is the most important thing to you in your life?'

"'Of course, Jennifer and my two girls.'

"'Well, let me see your calendar.'

"I opened my calendar and he looked at it and said, 'If those are the two most important things in your life, how come I don't see them anywhere scheduled in?'"

Ouch! Many of us would have felt similar embarrassment in Ben's situation. Usually it isn't bad motives—most of us want to spend time with our spouse and children. We simply have difficulty coming up with that little word no. But it can be a pastor's best friend!

I appreciate what a pastor, Daniel Langford, wrote about how he says no.

First, I use my calendar as a way of saying no: "I'm sorry, but that date conflicts with another appointment."

Second, I appeal to higher authority: "There are legal restrictions on that type of counseling." "I must consult with my wife."

Third, I decline by using personal boundaries as a reason for saying no rather than a personal rejection of the requester: "Thank you for that offer, but I need time for rest." "That was kind of you to ask, but what you want me to do does not fit my personal goals at this time."

Fourth, another choice is to have someone else say no for you. Generally my wife acts as this kind of buffer; while in a larger church a secretary would assist in guarding the minister's time and priorities.

Fifth, despite the controversy generated by this technique, I sometimes use an answering machine to screen phone calls.[11]

The telephone is one of the great boundary invaders in the home. A good answering machine and a beeper will help. In addition, devices like caller ID, a cell phone (perhaps with very limited dissemination of the number), and e-mail can limit interruptions and facilitate communication. These mechanisms can help protect your privacy at home.

When emergencies arise, we need to respond. Some things you will not be able to predict and decide on how to handle ahead of time. That's okay; God will provide the guidance required in those situations. Your wife and family need to understand that your calling and work involve responding to people's emergencies, often at the most inopportune moments. But you must have strong enough boundaries to know what is and is not an emergency.

If you have not established your criteria and limits before the telephone call comes, you will almost inevitably say yes and head out the door. Let's face it—some in the ministry are rescuers. It finally dawned on me one day that I was getting calls all hours of the day and night from people who had just spent the last twenty years of their lives disobeying God. What they wanted me to do was drop everything and be available to "fix" their long-standing problem by talking on the phone or meeting with them right away. I had to realize that if Barbara and I didn't establish boundaries, then other people "loved me and had a wonderful plan for my life"!

Take a day off each week—without guilt. Having one day a week for rest and refreshment is God's idea. Most of the time, ministry can wait twenty-four hours. H. B. London says, "I'm not sure a pastor of any kind of growing church can experience normalcy, especially if they don't take their days off. We live in a world where the light is always on. We fight the tyranny of the unfinished."[12]

## A SPECIAL WORD TO ELDERS, DEACONS, AND OTHERS WHO CARE ABOUT THEIR PASTORS

I believe an elder or deacon board and the congregation must assume responsibility for the health of their shepherds, especially their shepherds' marriages and families. Research shows that more than 90 percent of couples in pastoral ministry feel pressure to be an ideal role model. "Salaries are inadequate, retirement benefits insufficient, and in most cases clergy are lonely with few friends, thus receiving very little affirmation and encouragement."[13] A survey of pastors reported that 19 percent of pastors admitted to having an affair or "inappropriate sexual contact with someone other than their spouse," and 55 percent said they had no close friend or family member with whom to discuss sexual temptations.[14]

In your pastor's annual review, evaluate not only his job performance but also find out how he is doing in his walk with God and in his relationships with his wife and his children. Require him to go on vacations, to take days off, to get away with his wife for a few days once or twice a year—at the church's expense.

Over the past few years more than five thousand pastors and their wives have attended our FamilyLife Marriage Conferences. Nearly all of these have been financed by churches and laypersons who understand the pressure of ministry and who love their pastoral staff enough to make arrangements for them to attend. Attending a marriage seminar or receiving some counseling ought to be a part of every pastor's job description, no matter how well the congregation thinks he is doing in his marriage.

H. B. London proposes this idea: "I think every church needs what I call a Pastoral Concern Committee—made up of three to four people, their main role being to pray for and see to the care and feeding of the local pastor, his family, and staff members. This committee is responsible to the elders and deacons, and maybe one member of the committee is an elder or deacon, but it needs to be something that's not intimidating to the senior pastor."[15]

It is less expensive to minister to your pastor's marriage than to replace him. We are losing more men out the back door of the ministry than we have coming in the front door. We're losing them to marriages that are disintegrating. Don't let that happen in your church! Help your pastor experience his own family reformation.

## GUARD YOUR HEART

Modeling a healthy, God-honoring marriage and family can be one of the most significant contributions you make to your church, to say nothing of the pleasing results in your own home and life.

Too many pastors are losing the battle at home. Is there anything you need to repent of in your life and family? Selfishness? Arrogance? Disrespect for your spouse? Ignoring your children? Anger at a child who is difficult to love? Failure to pray with your wife? Not reading Scripture to your children? Are you involved in an emotional affair? Are you attaching yourself to someone in an Internet chat room?

A surprisingly high number of pastors struggle with pornography. Are you hooked? Repent and get help. Claim cleansing and forgiveness. (A number of organizations offer assistance and counseling on this issue, including Harry Schaumberg's Stone Gate Resources. Phone: 1-303-688-5680. Internet: www.stonegateresources.com.)

As you walk in integrity in your own home and honor God through your marriage and your relationships with your children, your home will be a visual sermon the sheep in your flock will welcome and never forget.

*Free Alaska Vacation for Pastors*

You read that right!

The Christian owners of Alaska Vacation Packages, Sid and Kathy Cook, have been led by the Lord to offer a free vacation package on a limited, space-available, as-needed basis at their Wolverine Lake facility near Palmer, Alaska. The goal of this is to help individuals in full-time local-church Christian ministry in need of refreshment, especially those needing to be restored physically, emotionally, and spiritually.

The offer includes a fully furnished one-, two-, or three-bedroom cottage and boat and motor. You must pay your way to Alaska, take care of your food, and obtain a rental car (at Alaska Vacation Package's wholesale rate; in some cases a free loaner car may be available). If you are interested, particularly in fishing and hunting, this could be the place for you.

I have not taken advantage of this opportunity myself but have spent a good amount of time visiting with the Cooks. Check it out! It may be available for only a limited time.

For information call Alaska Vacation Packages at 1-888-745-8872
or 1-907-745-8872.
Fax: 907-745-8873.
E-mail: info@alaskavactionpackages.com.
Internet: www.AlaskaVacationPackages.com.

# CHAPTER

## 3

## Big Idea 2: Reclaim the Covenant

After having done CNN and the Superstation, winning the America's Cup in 1977 and the '95 World Series with the Atlanta Braves, I feel that I can do just about anything. Except have a successful marriage.

—TED TURNER, multibillionaire and
Time Warner vice chairman

It is time for the Christian community to say no to divorce and yes to marriage—yes to a marriage covenant that lasts for a lifetime.

At some of my speaking engagements in recent years in which most of the people in the audiences are Christians, I have asked, "How many of you have ever seen a marriage covenant?" Usually one person in about three hundred will raise a hand. Then I ask, "How many of you have seen a prenuptial agreement?" As many as one in four raise their hands.

This sums up a problem we face. Reverence for the sacred, lifelong commitment of marriage has been replaced in our popular consciousness by a cynical pragmatism that assumes many marriages are doomed to fail. We have "dumbed down" marriage so that as a commitment between people it's about one notch above a car loan. In fact in most states it is easier to end a marriage than to get out of a car loan.

But ironically, in spite of the cultural pessimism about marriage, people long for a married love that lasts. And this is exactly what the church has to offer—a plan from the very Creator of marriage on how to make love endure "as long as we both shall live."

Although staying committed in marriage has become difficult for so many people, affection for the institution of marriage remains intense. A Louis Harris survey conducted in the late 1990s among American college students found that 96 percent of them either wanted to marry or were already married, and 97 percent agreed with the statement, "Having close family relationships is a key to happiness."[1]

Even though many children growing up since the 1980s have seen their own families torn up by divorce, a USA Today 1998 survey of Americans between the ages of eighteen and thirty-four found that their "highest priority in life" was a "close-knit family." This was mentioned by 83 percent of the respondents. This was *an increase of 15 percentage points from a similar survey done with the same age-group in 1989!*[2] There is hope!

The problem is that the vision of a lifelong, satisfying marriage doesn't hold up for many hopeful couples. How can the Christian community keep this vision alive? I think a significant part of the answer rests with the restoration of a high view of the marriage commitment.

It is time for churches to step forward and become guardians, protectors, and enforcers of the marriage covenant. But that is not enough. We must also speak the truth about divorce. God spoke clearly when He said in Malachi 2:16, "I hate divorce." Divorce breaks the sacred promise between two people and God Himself, and it also interferes with the propagation of godly offspring (2:15).

Quite perceptively the novelist Pat Conroy said of his own marriage breakup, "Each divorce is the death of a small civilization."[3] Pollster George Gallup has noted, "If divorce were a physical disease, we would declare a national emergency."

Divorce has become a disease of the national soul. Divorce has resulted in a role reversal of the most tragic proportions, as author and social commentator Barbara Dafoe Whitehead observes. "Traditionally, one major impediment to divorce was the presence of children in the family. According to well-established popular belief, dependent children had a stake in their parents' marriage and suffered hardship as a result of the dissolution of the marriage. Because children were vulnerable and dependent, parents had a moral obligation to place their children's interests in the marital partnership above their own individual satisfactions. This notion was swiftly abandoned after the 1960s. Influential voices in the society . . . claimed that the happiness of individual parents, rather than an intact marriage, was the key determinant of children's family well-being."[4]

This generation is the most "divorced" generation of young people in the history of our nation. It's time we told the truth about divorce. Divorce is bad for a person. It's bad for a child. Bad for a family. Bad for a church. And bad for a nation.

It's time for radical action. It's time for the church to stop allowing the bully of divorce to wreck Christian marriages at a higher percentage rate than those of nonbelievers![5] (For more on the subject of divorce see chapter 21.)

## WHAT IS A MARRIAGE COVENANT?

In 1997, just days before the wedding of our oldest child, Ashley, I was thinking about what else Barbara and I might do to ensure that our child and her husband-to-be would enjoy a lasting marriage. The Lord brought to my mind the biblical concept of a covenant.

I knew, of course, that marriage is often referred to as a covenant, but I realized that even this term is not mentioned much in modern ceremonies. I found it fascinating that the most sacred bond that two people ever make is seldom put in writing and displayed proudly in homes as a reminder of what was promised. I came up with an idea for Ashley and Michael's wedding, but before I share the end of that story, let's review the meaning and history of a covenant and why it is such a key component of marriage.

The Bible speaks frequently of a covenant, because God chose it as His means of demonstrating unshakable promises. So it should be no shock that God connected covenant with marriage.

The Hebrew word for *covenant* comes from a verb that means "to cut." This is exactly what God instructed Abraham to do as he prepared the sacrifices for the event that would seal the covenant between God and Abraham, and in which God guaranteed that the patriarch would have a son, a vast number of descendants, and a land for them to possess (Gen. 15). When Abraham had cut the animals in half, to signify the sealing of "the promise," the Lord passed between the pieces in the form of a "smoking oven and a flaming torch" (15:17). It was a solemn event that brought "terror and great darkness" to Abraham (15:12). This is the historical background of the covenant idea. It represents a serious occasion in which the parties seal their promises in the midst of a "cutting" that involves blood.

The original marriage covenant was achieved when God "married" Adam and Eve, and the importance to God that a man and woman maintain fidelity for life is a recurring theme throughout the Old Testament. But the first actual use of the term "marriage covenant" in the Bible does not occur until Malachi: "Yet you say, 'For what reason?' Because the LORD has been a witness between you and the wife of your youth, against whom you have dealt treacherously, though she is your companion and your wife by covenant" (Mal. 2:14).

Jesus reinforced the importance of the marriage covenant when He said, "Have you not read, that He who created them from the beginning made them male and female, and said, 'For this reason a man shall leave his father and mother and be joined to his wife; and the two shall become one flesh?'" Then Jesus added, "So they are no longer two, but one flesh. What therefore God has joined together, let no man separate" (Matt. 19:4–6).

When the Pharisees pointed out to Jesus that even Moses had allowed for the covenant-breaking activity of divorce (Deut. 22:13–21; 24:1–4), Jesus corrected them by saying, "Because of your hardness of heart Moses permitted you to divorce your wives; but from the beginning it has not been this way. And I say to you, whoever divorces his wife, except for immorality, and marries another woman commits adultery" (Matt. 19:8–9). Jesus here made clear that "from the beginning" it was God's intention that one man and one wife would be united as one flesh for life.

Marriage at the beginning of the church age probably followed Jewish customs and included the betrothal, followed later by a formal agreement, and finally the marriage ceremony.[6] A high view of marriage was evident early in church history. Tertullian wrote this in about A.D. 200: "How beautiful, then, the marriage of two Christians, two who are one in hope, one in desire, one in the way of life they follow, one in the religion they practice. They are as brother and sister, both servants of the same Master. Nothing divides them, either in flesh or in spirit. They are, in very truth, 'two in one flesh'; and where there is but one flesh there is also but one spirit. They pray together, they worship together, they fast together; instructing one another, encouraging one another, strengthening one another. Side by side they visit

God's church and partake of God's Banquet; side by side they face difficulties and persecution, share their consolations."[7]

Although the concept of covenant was long implied in the Christian marriage ceremony, it wasn't until the fourteenth century in northern France and England that the typical wedding ceremony included marriage vows (more accurately "vow" because it was recited only by the husband).[8] This example of such an early vow clearly reveals covenant concepts: "I take you as my wife, and I espouse you; and I commit to you the fidelity of my body, in so far as I bear for you fidelity and loyalty of my body and my possessions; and I will keep you in health and sickness and in any condition which it pleases our Lord that you should have, nor for the worse or for better will I change towards you until the end."[9]

The full expression and breadth of the marriage covenant, however, did not occur until the time of the Reformation. John Witte explains the expansive view of the Reformers.

> The *Calvinist tradition*, established in mid-sixteenth century Geneva, set out a *covenantal model* of marriage. This model confirmed many of the Lutheran theological and legal reforms, but cast them in a new ensemble. Marriage, Calvin and his followers taught, was not a sacramental institution of the church, but a covenantal association of the entire community. A variety of parties participated in the formation of this covenant. The marital parties themselves swore their betrothals and espousals before each other and God—rendering all marriages triparty agreements, with God as third-party witness, participant, and judge. The couple's parents, as God's lieutenants for children, gave their consent to the union. Two witnesses, as God's priests to their peers, served as witnesses to the marriage. The minister, holding God's spiritual power of the Word, blessed the couple and admonished them in their spiritual duties. The magistrate, holding God's temporal power of the sword, registered the couple and protected them in their person and property. Each of these parties was considered essential to the legitimacy of the marriage, for they each represented a different dimension of God's involvement in the covenant. To omit any such party was, in effect, to omit God from the marriage covenant.[10]

From this high view of marriage, which was embraced by the entire Christian and secular community, we have slowly descended to our contemporary position in which the marriage promise—often even in the church—is at best a sanctified "contract." As many couples exchange vows, often aided by the safety nets of prenuptial agreements, they are thinking, "We will do our best to make this work—as long as we feel love. But if we can't, oh, well, it wasn't meant to be, and we can try again with someone else."

The precipitous decline in a covenant emphasis in the marriage ceremony probably began gradually after World War II as respect for authority and tradition in Western culture eroded. For example, Kenneth Stevenson, citing a guide used by the Congregationalist Church, wrote in *Nuptial Blessing*, "It is not until the 1959 *Book of Services and Prayers* that a slightly new style of language begins to appear; the exhortation describes marriage as 'a sacred relationship,' which probably meant more to couples than the '*covenant*' imagery we have seen before."[11]

Many Christians have stood by silently as respect for the marriage covenant has eroded. Now the only document most modern couples sign is the marriage license, the legal instrument of the state. What does that signify? We also have driver's licenses, fishing and hunting licenses, automobile licenses, and professional licenses. All these expire and are renewable. Unfortunately, for too many people, the wedding license fits in that category—a commitment that one can either renew or revoke.

But let's not fault the state for failing to do what is beyond its role. The protector of the marriage covenant must be the church.

So as Barbara and I were thinking of our daughter Ashley's wedding, we came up with an idea to refocus attention on the marriage covenant. We decided to have a calligrapher inscribe Ashley and Michael's vows on a sheet of pure cotton paper, suitable for framing.

As part of the wedding ceremony, Ashley and Michael said their vows to one another. Then they turned and signed their marriage covenant. Space had been left at the bottom for witnesses to sign too, so in the ceremony the pastor invited people to sign the marriage covenant in the reception. He told them this would indicate their promise to pray for Michael and Ashley and to hold them accountable for keeping their vows.

Later during the reception I stood by their marriage covenant as more than one hundred people signed it. A comment that totally caught me off guard was, "Wow, they're really serious about this, aren't they!" On further reflection, I have determined that this comment reflects the casual and cavalier attitude that the Christian community has about the most sacred pledge two people ever make to each other. This also anchors my conviction that by signing a formal, written covenant we can begin to recapture lost ground.

## THE COVENANT MARRIAGE MOVEMENT

At a meeting on May 11, 1999, in Dallas, Texas, a group of twenty-four Christian denominations and organizations representing a combined constituency of approximately thirty-one million people announced the launch of the Covenant Marriage Movement. The purpose of this coalition, which includes organizations as diverse as the American Association of Christian Counselors, the Assemblies of God denomination, Moody Bible Institute, Focus on the Family, PromiseKeepers, Marriage Savers, FamilyLife, and others,[12] is to strengthen marriage in America by challenging millions of married couples to sign a Covenant Marriage statement. I believe that an emphasis like this may help reduce the plague of divorce in our society.

On the societal side, a number of state legislatures continue to debate so-called Covenant Marriage bills, but only two have actually passed laws. Louisiana led the way in 1997, with Arizona following in 1998. Some states are providing incentives, such as a reduced fee for the marriage license, to those who undergo premarital counseling. All this is good and needs to be encouraged. Oklahoma, which is considered part of the Bible belt but which has one of the highest divorce rates in the country, is making a special effort to build up marriages. Governor Frank Keating has pledged to work toward reducing the state's divorce rate by one-third in ten years.[13]

Perhaps the most significant statement in favor of covenant marriages was made by the Southern Baptists, who at their annual convention in 1998 ratified a change in their faith-and-message confessional statement.

In part the new article reads, "God has ordained the family as the foundational institution of human society. It is composed of persons related to one another by marriage, blood, or adoption. Marriage is the uniting of one man and one woman in covenant commitment for a lifetime. It is God's unique gift to reveal the union between Christ and His church, and to provide for the man and the woman in marriage the framework for intimate companionship, the channel for sexual expression according to biblical standards, and the means for procreation of the human race."[14]

In March 2000 the National Association of Evangelicals (NAE) adopted a resolution urging cooperation among all denominations to create community marriage policies and engage in other actions with a goal to slash America's divorce rate in half by the year 2010. The NAE also expressed support "in principle" for covenant marriage laws like those in Louisiana and Arizona.[15]

Together we Christians can become known in society as the keepers and protectors of the marriage covenant. In doing so the church can make a statement to the world that there is an answer to the tragedy of divorce.

## ELEVATING THE MARRIAGE COVENANT IN THE LOCAL CHURCH

How can church leaders elevate the deep meaning of marriage, as opposed to just adding another ceremony or piece of paper that has grand sentiment but doesn't change how we view the world or influence our behavior? Here are seven ideas to consider.

### Keep Your Own Covenant

As emphasized in chapter 2, pastors and other church leaders must vigorously work at keeping their own marriage vows. Every leader must realize that many others are watching to see if his ways match his words. Keeping one's vows doesn't mean simply avoiding getting a divorce. It means caring for and cherishing your spouse. It means doing what you have promised.

## Teach the Sacredness of Marriage to Your Children

As your children grow up and marry, etch on their souls the sacredness of their marriage vows and their covenant. Instruction and exhortation concerning marriage needs to begin early. Don't wait until your child starts dating or is engaged.

## Preach the Fear of God

The number-one reason we have lost the sacredness of the marriage covenant is that we have lost the fear of God. If we do not fear Him or our accountability to Him, then what is there to cause us to keep our vows? Fearing God is a preventive action. "By the fear of the LORD one keeps away from evil" (Prov. 16:6). We need to emphasize the character of God and that He is to be feared.

## Call Others to Fulfill Their Marriage Covenants

Abraham Lincoln said, "To sin by silence when one should protest makes cowards of men." We should strongly encourage couples to sign a marriage covenant and to have it witnessed at their wedding. I also suggest that churches schedule an annual marriage-covenant Sunday service in which couples face each other to repeat their vows and are given the opportunity to sign a marriage covenant if they have not done so before. Ideally this should be done throughout America and the world on the same Sunday each year.[16]

## Join with Other Churches to Elevate the Marriage Covenant

Churches in communities throughout America are uniting, especially through the efforts of the Marriage Savers organization (see www.marriagesavers.org on the Internet). At a minimum, no couple should be allowed to get married in a church facility or receive the wedding services of a pastor if they are unwilling to go through the church's required marriage preparation course. The same denial of opportunities and services should apply to any couple with a prenuptial agreement.

*Wedding Vows*

Traditionally church denominations have exerted fairly tight control over the wording of marriage vows. This is still the case in many churches, but the independent spirit of the age has resulted in more couples writing their own vows. Set firm boundaries on what may be included in wedding vows in your church. For certain, never allow the incredibly sentimental and dangerous phrase in a wedding vow, "as long as we both shall *love*." Why not consider making the signing and witnessing of marriage covenants a standard part of each wedding ceremony?

*Practice Loving Church Discipline in Response
to Covenant Abuse or Breaking*

We will never be able to restore respect for the marriage covenant if we refuse to discipline those who threaten to become covenant breakers (divorce with no biblical grounds) or who habitually are breaking their vows through adultery, abuse, or abandonment. Should the church do nothing while people break up what God has joined together? We need to lovingly admonish those who are committing such acts. (For more on this subject, see chapter 22.)

### HIT A SPIKE!

Peachtree Christian Church, in Atlanta, Georgia, has hosted an annual "Wedding Bells" ceremony on the second Sunday of each January to honor marriage. Each year all the married couples stand during the service and recite and renew their vows. Rev. Robert Burns started the tradition in 1931 after preaching the funeral of a man who committed suicide because of marital problems. Peachtree's current pastor, Jim Collins, said, "The idea is that as we begin a new year, we identify our priorities and make resolutions. For those who are married, we make one of the priorities recommitment to each other and renewal of their vows. The service is a reminder of the church's collective responsibility to recognize and support marriage as a covenant instituted by God."[17] Thousands have participated in this service. What a statement on marriage to make to multiple generations!

Currently there are approximately three hundred thousand churches in America. What if just 10 percent of them decided to host a similar annual service calling people back to the priority of their marriage and family? I believe that in less than a decade we would see the divorce rate slashed in half.

The nation is desperate for the church to take the lead in restoring the grandeur of marriage. Our society is looking for help to save our families. In volleyball terms it's as if the culture is giving the church a set for a spike. The church has been given a stepladder, and the ball hangs suspended about six inches above the net. The question is, Do we have the courage to spike it?

I pray that we do. The future of the family depends on it.

# CHAPTER

## 4

# Big Idea 3: Remarket the Designer's Design

In a culture where "experts" sell their theories on what makes a great marriage, who will define human sexuality and the basic design of the male-female relationship?

This chapter looks at the war raging over the definition of manhood and womanhood in the family. I will offer recommendations on how we can achieve victory in the arenas that truly mean the most—in our own homes and churches.

In 1999 I traveled to a number of major American cities to host an event called "I Still Do," a one-day celebration of marriage that calls husbands and wives to keep their marriage covenants and to embrace God's design for their marriages. On two occasions I've been in San Francisco when the city held its annual Gay Pride Parade. There and in other major cities I've watched local TV stations report on small gatherings of homosexual couples saying their "marriage vows," hugging, and kissing. But how much coverage has been given to the gatherings of thousands of heterosexual couples honoring their vows? *None!* That's a telling summary of where we are in our society. News reports often feature the world's "politically correct" design for men and women and ignore God's design.

The contrast between God's design and the world's distortion of the sexes is still relatively clear today. But how clear will the contrast be a decade from now? An attitude of tolerance is sweeping the Christian community further downstream into a muddy, confused state in reference to male and female identity in marriage and family. We are in an ideological battle over the fundamental definitions of male and female sexuality, especially as it relates to the roles of husband and wife.

Nowhere was this more vividly evident than when the Southern Baptist Convention made its recent statement related to their stance on the family. The core beliefs of the SBC, called the "Baptist Faith and Message," had not been modified since 1964. So it was a momentous occasion in 1998 when for the first time in their history the SBC crafted a doctrinal statement related to marriage and family. With an unprecedented 99 percent of the convention delegates voting their approval, the Southern Baptists clearly affirmed their convictions from Scripture about the smallest unit of our society. The Creator's design for marriage was unashamedly embraced. Here is the text of that statement.

### Baptist Faith and Message, Article XVIII, The Family

God has ordained the family as the foundational institution of human society. It is composed of persons related to one another by marriage, blood, or adoption.

Marriage is the uniting of one man and one woman in covenant commitment for a lifetime. It is God's unique gift to reveal the union between Christ and His church, and to provide for the man and the woman in marriage the framework for intimate companionship, the channel for sexual expression according to biblical standards, and the means for procreation of the human race.

The husband and wife are of equal worth before God, since both are created in God's image. The marriage relationship models the way God relates to His people. A husband is to love his wife as Christ loved the church. He has the God-given responsibility to provide for, to protect, and to lead his family. A wife is to submit herself graciously to the servant leadership of her husband even as the church willingly submits to the headship of Christ. She, being in the image of God as is her husband and thus equal to him, has the

God-given responsibility to respect her husband and to serve as his helper in managing the household and nurturing the next generation.

Children, from the moment of conception, are a blessing and heritage from the Lord. Parents are to demonstrate to their children God's pattern for marriage. Parents are to teach their children spiritual and moral values and to lead them, through consistent lifestyle, example, and loving discipline, to make choices based on biblical truth. Children are to honor and obey their parents.[1]

The result? A media firestorm erupted! Instead of using its influence and creating a national debate and dialogue about divorce and how it is destroying our national soul, the media went ballistic over three words in the article that address a wife's role in marriage. Media personnel said, in essence, How dare the Baptists call on a wife to "submit herself graciously" to the servant leadership of her husband?

Never mind that schools are filled with kids from broken homes. Never mind that men abuse women and children in the home. Never mind that the family is being totally redefined by so-called experts who theorize that in order to save our families people have to be more inclusive of all kinds of alternate "lifestyles" and structures!

I marveled at those who reported on this "alarmist group," as though members of the world's largest Protestant denomination were a cult from Waco. But what astonished me even more was that other Christian leaders did not publicly stand with the Southern Baptists.

The silence of other Christians was so deafening and the media coverage so patently unfair that I decided to write leaders to see if we could gather names of leaders who would stand with their Baptist brethren. The response was overwhelming. More than 180 prominent Christians signed a statement that said, "We Stand with You." Leaders from a wide assortment of denominations, parachurch organizations, colleges, universities, and seminaries heartily agreed with the SBC Family Statement. In fact so many said yes to the statement that FamilyLife paid for a full-page advertisement in *USA Today* in public support of the Southern Baptists. Those leaders are listed here so that you can see how many have courageously embraced the biblical definition of marriage and family.

# WE STAND WITH YOU!

*We are pastors and lay leaders, civic and business leaders, husbands, wives, fathers, and mothers representing a variety of denominations. We believe in and strongly affirm this statement on the family.*

| | | |
|---|---|---|
| Dr. Joe Aldrich | President Emeritus, Multnomah Bible College | Portland, OR |
| Kerby and Susanne Anderson | President, Probe Ministries | Richardson, TX |
| Dr. Hudson and Miriam Amerding | Former President, Wheaton College | Quarryville, PA |
| Dr. Steve Arterburn | CEO, New Life Clinics | Laguna Beach, CA |
| Jack and Kay Arthur | President, and Vice President, Precept Ministries | Chattanooga, TN |
| Gary and Carol Bauer | Former President, Family Research Council | Washington, DC |
| Scott and Theresa Beck | Former CEO, Boston Market | Boulder City, CO |
| Joel and Carol Esther Belz | Publisher, *World* magazine | Asheville, NC |
| Gary and Donna Bishop | President, Missionary Aviation Fellowship | Redlands, CA |
| Ronald and Judith Blue | President, Ronald Blue & Co. | Atlanta, GA |
| Reinhard Bonnke | CEO, Christ for All Nations, Germany | Frankfurt, Germany |
| Dr. Bill and Vonette Bright | President, Campus Crusade for Christ International | Orlando, FL |
| Dr. Frank Brock | President, Covenant College | Lookout Mountain, GA |
| Harold and Grace Brown | Professor, Trinity Evangelical Divinity School | Deerfield, IL |
| Bob Buckel | Editor and Publisher, *Azle* (TX) *News* | Azle, Texas |
| Larry and Judy Burkett | President, Christian Financial Concepts | Atlanta, GA |
| Dr. Bryan and Kathleen Chapell | President, Covenant Theological Seminary | St. Louis, MO |

| | | |
|---|---|---|
| Dr. Ron and Barbara Cline | President, HCBJ World Radio | Quito, Ecuador |
| Dr. James and Debra Cogdill | Vice President, Midwestern Baptist Theological Seminary | Kansas City, MO |
| Dr. Robert and Marietta Coleman | Director, Billy Graham School of Evangelism | Wheaton, IL |
| Chuck and Patty Colson | CEO, Prison Fellowship | Reston, VA |
| Adolph and B.J. Coors IV | National speaker | Grand Lake, CO |
| Dr. J.B. and Bette Crouse | President, OMS International | Greenville, TN |
| James and Carol Cymbala | Pastor, Brooklyn Tabernacle | New York City, NY |
| Nancy Leigh DeMoss | Director of Women's Ministries, Life Action Ministries | Niles, MI |
| Dr. Lane and Ebeth Dennis | President, Crossway Books | Chicago, IL |
| Dr. Dennis and Karen Dirks | Dean, Talbot School of Theology | La Mirada, CA |
| Dr. James and Shirley Dobson | President, Focus on the Family | Colorado Springs, CO |
| Dr. Tony and Lois Evans | Pastor, Oak Cliff Bible Fellowship | Dallas, TX |
| Steve and Mary Farrar | President, Point Man Ministries | Dallas, TX |
| David and Teresa Ferguson | President, Intimate Life Ministries | Austin, TX |
| Dr. Norman and Barbara Geisler | Provost, Southern Evangelical Seminary | Charlotte, NC |

| | | |
|---|---|---|
| Dr. Gene and Elaine Getz | Founder, Fellowship Bible Churches | Richardson, TX |
| Franklin Graham | President, Samaritan's Purse | Boone, NC |
| Bill and Rhonni Greig III | President, Gospel Light Publications | Ventura, CA |
| Bill and Doris Greig, Jr. | CEO, Gospel Light Publications | Ventura, CA |
| Lars and Elisabeth Elliot Gren | Author and speaker | Magnolia, MA |
| Dr. Wayne and Margaret Grudem | President, Council on Biblical Manhood and Womanhood | Libertyville, IL |
| Brandt and Mary Gustavson | President, National Religious Broadcasters | Manassas, VA |
| Dr. Jack Hayford | Pastor, The Church on the Way | Van Nuys, CA |
| Daniel Heimbach | Professor, Southwestern Baptist Theological Seminary | Ft. Worth, TX |
| Dr. Howard and Jeanne Hendricks | Distinguished Professor, Dallas Theological Seminary | Dallas, TX |
| Dr. E.V. Hill | Pastor, Mount Zion Baptist Church | Los Angeles, CA |
| Don and Barbara Hodel | President, The Christian Coalition; former U.S. Secretary of the Interior | Washington, DC |
| David and Phyllis Howard | President, Latin American Mission | Miami, FL |
| Mike and Janet Huckabee | Governor and First Lady of Arkansas | Little Rock, AR |
| Todd and Debbie Hunter | National Director, Association of Vineyard Churches | Anaheim, CA |
| Bishop T. D. Jakes | President, T. D. Jakes Ministries | Dallas, TX |

| | | |
|---|---|---|
| Charles and Kay James Sr. | Dean, Robertson School of Government, Regent University | Virginia Beach, VA |
| Charles and Victoria Jarvis | Executive Vice President, Focus on the Family | Colorado Springs, CO |
| Dr. John and Helena Kelly | President, Antioch Churches and Ministries | Redlands, CA |
| Dr. D. James Kennedy | Pastor, Coral Ridge Presbyterian Church | Fort Lauderdale, FL |
| Dr. Jerry and Patricia Kirk | President, National Coalition for the Protection of Children and Families | Cincinnati, OH |
| Tim and Beverly LaHaye | Author, and President, Concerned Women of America | Washington, DC |
| Dr. Robert and Sherard Lewis | Pastor, Fellowship Bible Church | Little Rock, AR |
| Dr. Daniel Lockwood | President, Multnomah Bible College | Portland, OR |
| H. B. and Beverly London Jr. | Vice President, Ministry Outreach, Focus on the Family | Colorado Springs, CO |
| Dr. Crawford and Karen Loritts | International speaker and author, Campus Crusade for Christ | Union City, GA |
| Anne Graham Lotz | President, Angel Ministries | Raleigh, NC |
| Dr. Erwin and Rebecca Lutzer | Pastor, Moody Bible Church | Chicago, IL |
| C. J. and Carolyn Mahaney | Senior Pastor, Covenant Life Church | Gaithersburg, MD |
| Dr. John and Margaret Maxwell | Founder, Injoy | Atlanta, GA |

| | | |
|---|---|---|
| Bill and Lyndi McCartney | CEO, PromiseKeepers | Denver, CO |
| Mike McCoy | Co-CEO, McCoy Corporation | San Marcos, TX |
| Josh and Dottie McDowell | Director, Josh McDowell Ministries | Dallas, TX |
| George McKinney | Bishop-Pastor, St. Stephens Church of God in Christ | Denver, CO |
| Dr. Johnny and Jeanne Miller | Pastor, Calvary Church | Lancaster, PA |
| Norman and Anne Miller | CEO, Interstate Battery Corporation | Dallas, TX |
| Sam and Peggy Moore | CEO, Thomas Nelson Publishers | Nashville, TN |
| Dr. Tommy and Teresa Nelson | Pastor, Denton Bible Church | Denton, TX |
| Dr. Marvin and Susan Olasky | Professor, University of Texas, and editor, *World* magazine | Austin, TX |
| Dr. Stephen Olford | CEO, Encounter Ministries | Memphis, TN |
| Dr. Gary and Carrie Oliver | Executive Director, Marriage and Family Studies, John Brown University | Siloam Springs, AR |
| Dr. Raymond and Anne Ortlund | CEO, Renewal Ministries | Anaheim, CA |
| Greg and Kathleen Parsons | Executive Director, U.S. Center for World Missions | Pasadena, CA |
| Dr. John and Noel Piper | Senior Pastor, Bethlehem Baptist Church | Minneapolis, MN |
| Bishop Phillip Porter | Pastor, All National Pentecostal Center | Denver, CO |
| Tom and Brenda Preston | Director, Executive Ministries International | Greenville, SC |

| | | |
|---|---|---|
| Dennis and Barbara Rainey | Executive Director, FamilyLife | Little Rock, AR |
| James and Betty Robison | President, Life Outreach International | Fort Worth, TX |
| Kyle and Mary Lynne Rote, Jr. | CEO, Athletic Resource Management | Memphis, TN |
| Al and Margaret Sanders | Chairman of the Board, Ambassador Advertising Agency | Fullerton, CA |
| Phyllis Schlafly | President, Eagle Forum | Alton, IL |
| Kennedy and Mary Smartt | Moderator, Presbyterian Church in America | Atlanta, GA |
| Larry and Melanie Stockstill | Pastor, Bethany World Prayer Center | Baker, LA |
| Dr. Joseph and Marti Stowell | President, Moody Bible Institute | Chicago, IL |
| Dr. Elmer and Ruth Towns | Dean, School of Religion, Liberty University | Richmond, VA |
| Dr. Thomas and Shirley Trask | General Superintendent, Assemblies of God | Springfield, MO |
| Dr. John and Cindy Trent | President, Encouraging Words | Scottsdale, AZ |
| Bishop and Mrs. Kenneth Ulmer | Pastor, Central Missionary Baptist Church | Denver, CO |
| Glenn and Susan Wagner | Pastor, Calvary Church | Charlotte, NC |
| Rick Warren | Pastor, Saddleback Valley Community Church | Mission Viejo, CA |
| Rev. Raleigh and Paulette Washington | Vice President of Reconciliation, PromiseKeeprs | Denver, CO |

| Jack and Esther Wease | Director, Evangelical Methodist World Missions | Indianapolis, IN |
|---|---|---|
| Dr. Stu and Linda Weber | Senior Pastor, Good Shepherd Community Church | Boring, OR |
| Dr. Terry and Mary White | President, The Navigators | Colorado Springs, CO |
| Dr. Bruce and Darlene Wilkinson | President, Walk Thru the Bible | Atlanta, GA |
| Douglas and Nancy Wilson | Editor, *Credenda/Agenda* | Moscow, ID |
| Dr. Norman and Joyce Wright | President, Christian Marriage Enrichment | Long Beach, CA |
| John and Susan Yates III | Rector, The Falls Church (Episcopal) | Falls Church, VA |

These are all leaders of major ministries in America—all taking a stand with the SBC's family statement.

Then a year later Campus Crusade for Christ, in a step unprecedented in its fifty-year history, adopted its own statement on marriage and family. It read as follows.

The husband and wife are of equal worth before God, since both are created in God's image. The marriage relationship models the way God relates to His people. A husband is to love his wife as Christ loved the church. He has the God-given responsibility to provide for, to protect, and to lead his family. A wife is to submit herself graciously to the servant leadership of her husband even as the church willingly submits to the headship of Christ. She, being in the image of God as is her husband and thus equal to him, has the God-given responsibility to respect her husband and to serve as his helper in managing the household and nurturing the next generation.

In a marriage lived according to these truths, the love between husband and wife will show itself in listening to each other's viewpoints, valuing each other's gifts, wisdom, and desires, honoring one another in public and in private, and always seeking to bring benefit, not harm, to one another. [2]

What would motivate the largest Protestant denomination and one of the largest parachurch ministries to define where they stand on marriage and family? And what would cause so many Christian leaders from various backgrounds and denominations to stand together in support of a family statement? Two reasons: First, these proclamations are biblically based and represent what Christians have believed and embraced since the founding of the church. Second, the family crisis in America is forcing us to define where we stand in an increasingly pluralistic and tolerant culture.

God has made His design for marriage unmistakably clear. We can no longer afford to be silent. The world is winning the day in the ideological battle for marriage and the family. One campaign that the church cannot afford to lose is the one over the roles and responsibilities of men and women in marriage.

## HOW DID WE GET IN THIS MESS?

Marriage is not just another lifestyle choice; it's a spiritual endeavor and a relational design emanating from the creative brilliance of God. We need to honor and glorify the Designer of marriage by extolling how He designed it to work.

Mike Mason wrote, "Throughout the Bible marriage is employed as the most sublime metaphor for the relationship between man and God. . . . A good Christian marriage, indeed, is more than a religious metaphor; it is a first, tangible, visible, and most glorious fruit of the Kingdom of God. A wedding was not only the occasion for the first miracle of Jesus; it was, after Creation itself, God's own first miracle: 'He brought the woman to the man' (Genesis 2:22)."[3]

What has happened to the beautiful creation of marriage?

In many marriages the husband has one idea of what a marriage should be like, and the wife has another. And neither one totally reflects the biblical instructions. What would happen if a couple built a house using two *different* sets of blueprints drawn by two *different* architects and built by two *different* builders? It would be a mess of conflicting designs, a physical "structure" that would look weird and hardly resemble a home. With couples using this approach in marriage, is it any wonder that we have so many family messes today?

Pastor John Piper writes, "Confusion over the meaning of sexual personhood today is epidemic. The consequence of this confusion is not a free and happy harmony among gender-free persons relating on the basis of abstract competencies. The consequence rather is more divorce, more homosexuality, more sexual abuse, more promiscuity, more social awkwardness, and more emotional distress and suicide that come with the loss of God-given identity."[4]

In America the institution of marriage began to erode during the 1960s and 1970s. Several cultural and historical factors were prevalent: the birth-control pill; no-fault divorce; radical feminism; the Vietnam War; a general questioning of authority; rising numbers of women in the workforce; declining moral standards in pervasive media; stereotyped or inadequate portrayals of marriage in television programming. The baby-boomer generation was growing up critiquing everything, which included questioning the true state of happiness of their parents' marriages. The "traditional family" was under fire.

I want to make three observations.

First, the Christian community needs to realize what is at stake in the battle over biblical roles in the family. Genesis 1:27 states, "In the image of God He created him; male and female He created them." Ultimately the glory and image of God is at stake in a man and woman embracing God's design for their sexuality. When the divinely designed roles and responsibilities are distorted, men and women cannot glorify God as He intended.

Within the body of Christ this is a question of the authority of Scripture and how Scripture is interpreted. It is a biblical issue, not a politically correct issue. And in our culture the glory of God is being undermined by the distortion and perversion of the sexes. Imagine where our culture is headed with our children growing up in a society where they are encouraged to wonder if they are heterosexual or homosexual. A failure to stand clearly for God's design for men and women in the family will take us one step closer to a culture fully like that of Sodom and Gomorrah.

Second, for the last thirty years feminism has assaulted a number of biblical values that support marriage and family, not the least of which is that the husband is the leader of his wife at home.

The SBC Family Statement represents a serious setback for those who embrace egalitarian theology. Not only did this statement express the convictions of the overwhelming majority of biblical scholars and leaders, but it also marginalized a scant number of those who have been bending to the cultural winds of feminism. For too long a couple of denominations (who have already caved in to liberal theology), a handful of churches, and a few parachurch organizations have made it sound as though *they* were speaking for the majority of evangelicals. In reality the overwhelming majority of evangelical leaders *and their constituencies* hold the convictions expressed in the SBC Family Statement.

Third, we need to realize that many couples who are getting married in our churches do not have a clear biblical understanding of God's design for husbands and wives. Many are oblivious to the way feminism has impacted them. *They are already conformed to the world.* Leaders must realize that a generation of young people are marrying without the foundation of solid Christian families and that no longer can we assume that they understand how a man and woman are to relate to each other as husband and wife.

When biblical roles are unclear or not taught, men tend to become lazy and passive, even abusive. When men don't feel responsible, they are tempted to sit back and let their wives take over. This leads to a lack of respect and anger in women. Someone must take charge, so women assume leadership of their families. That gives the men even greater reason to be passive, but it also makes them angry. And so the cycle escalates. And when men don't learn to lead and serve their wives and family well at home, the church suffers. According to 1 Timothy 3:4–5 a prerequisite for a man to be a leader in the church is his effective leadership in his home.

## THE DESIGN

God's design for marriage includes the following eight concepts.

*A man and woman reflect the image of God and are to complement each other (Gen. 1:27–28).* Marriage is the most stunning, majestic relationship—the husband and wife show to the world the very image of the eternal God. One of the best places to get a living snapshot of His image is to look at a godly marriage. And the two sexes need each other. The image of the rugged, self-sufficient individualist is an American concept, not a biblical one. As Paul stated, "However, in the Lord, neither is woman independent of man, nor is man independent of woman" (1 Cor. 11:11).

*One woman and one man are to be married for life (Matt. 19:4–9; 1 Cor. 7:39).* Marriage is a covenant relationship between a man and a woman that is not to be broken except for sexual infidelity or death. There is not a hint in Scripture that two men living together or two women living together constitute a "marriage."

*Men and women are equal in value (Gen. 1:27; Gal. 3:28).* Unfortunately Bible-honoring Christians are getting blamed for advocating and perpetuating the idea of male superiority. Those who hold this view need to review the life and teachings of Jesus Christ. In His culture He opened the way for women to have their rightful place in God's order. Elisabeth Elliot Gren writes, "Both male and female are created in His image. They bear the divine stamp. They are equally called to obedience and responsibility, but there are differences in the responsibilities. Both Adam and Eve sinned and are equally guilty. Therefore both are equally the objects of God's grace."[5]

*A husband and wife are to multiply a godly legacy (Gen. 1:28).* As much as marriage is designed to meet the needs of a man and woman, married couples can also have the joy of having children and raising them to honor Christ. Children are a blessing and will enrich a marriage. Christian children are to be prepared with a sense of mission and direction to live for and serve the Lord.

*A husband and wife have been given divinely prescribed roles in marriage (Eph. 5:22–33; 1 Pet. 3:1, 7).* One major reason marriages fragment and fall apart is confusion about the roles of husbands and wives. Many marriages are adrift with no leader or direction. Every marriage falls into some kind of pattern. Who will make the final decision if there's a tossup on an issue? How will wives have any expectation that someone is protecting her, providing for her, and being a loving leader in the relationship?

I appreciate what Robert Lewis says about roles for men and women in marriage. "I use the term 'core roles,' because it means the most important part of the role. I think what the Scriptures lay forth is a core role that can't be violated—regardless of your capacities or personality. There are a lot of things you can do around a core role and it's good to use creativity. Different people with different gifts and different personalities will do all kinds of different things around their core role."[6]

*The husband is the head of the wife (1 Cor. 11:3; Eph. 5:23).* This is an offensive idea to many people, especially when respect for authority of any kind has withered. But we need to return to what the Scriptures teach. Bob Lepine wrote,

> The objections to the traditional understanding of headship are directed more at the abuses of the biblical idea than they are rooted in New Testament scholarship. The idea that God would ordain any hierarchical structure to male/female relationships is repugnant to the critics, seeming to imply a limited role and limited value to women in the home and in the church. In the same way, the concept of female submission seems demeaning and degrading to the worth of a woman. Certainly, biblical passages have been misunderstood and misapplied by some in a way that has devalued a woman's role in the home and in the church. But those abuses do not constitute grounds for attempting to reinvent a meaning for difficult biblical passages. Our goal should be to better understand the way in which Christ serves as head of his church, or in which God is the head of Christ, in order to know how a man should be the head of a woman.[7]

*A husband is to be a sacrificial, servant leader in the marriage (1 Cor. 11:3; Eph. 5:25–29).* God's design is for the husband to be a loving, sacrificial servant who gives himself to his wife as Christ did for the church. And how did Christ love the church? Start with self-denial. He went to the cross on her behalf. And He served others.

*A wife is to be a supportive helper in marriage (Gen. 2:18; 1 Cor. 11:8–9; Eph. 5:23).* A wife is to carry out three roles. First, she is to be a helper, to come alongside and support her husband, to believe in him and cheer him on in all he does. Unfortunately for many contemporary women the word *helper* means a slave. But this is not what it means in the Bible.

Dorothy Patterson has said, "In fact God has chosen to use this word to describe himself, for when you call on God to be your helper, you do not ask him to divest himself of his deity and to come squeaking under the door just to be there to shake and tremble with you. You want him to come with all the angels of heaven, all the power he has and come to your assistance. . . . It is a very wonderful privilege we have that God would use this term, that he uses to describe himself, to describe that role and that function."[8]

Second, the wife is to be submissive to her husband. The Greek word translated *submit* literally means "to place or arrange under the authority of another." It is a voluntary subordination. It does not mean a wife should say nothing. A wife should share her ideas and thoughts and give guidance in various situations. But when a final decision needs to be made, the wife is to follow her husband where moral or ethical absolutes are not involved.

Third, when children are involved, a wife has a third calling—to make mothering a priority. She is to be a home "maker." Motherhood is an all-important part of the role of women in families today. But it is not receiving the honor that Scripture clearly places on it. That needs to change, beginning in the Christian community.

That's a quick sketch of God's divine design for marriage. Yet in our sin-saturated world many distortions and abuses are defacing the beauty of what God created in the Garden of Eden. But this *is* the design, and we are foolish if we think anyone can improve on it.

John Piper writes, "In the home when a husband leads like Christ and a wife responds like the bride of Christ, there is a harmony and mutuality that is more beautiful and more satisfying than any pattern of marriage created by man. Biblical headship for the husband is the divine calling to take primary responsibility for Christlike, servant-leadership protection and provision in the home. Biblical submission for the wife is the divine calling to honor and affirm her husband's leadership and help carry it through according to her gifts."[9]

## RECLAIMING THE DESIGN

Church leaders need to "remarket" the Designer's design for marriage—and to do so courageously, creatively, and passionately. Too often we have allowed the discussion on marriage to descend to the world's level, which tends to center around meeting individual needs rather than seeing the majesty of what God can create and accomplish when the two become one! We must boldly proclaim the truth—that a "good" marriage is priceless—but it must be pursued in God's way to achieve results. Larry Crabb writes, "The central truth that serves as the platform for Christian marriage—and for all Christian relationships—is that in Christ we are at every moment eternally loved and genuinely significant."[10]

What can church leaders do? Here are seven ideas.

1. Clarify your convictions on what the Bible presents as the divine design for the roles and responsibilities of husband and wife. Craft a statement of belief similar to the SBC statement or something like the Family Manifesto (see Appendix A) that puts in writing what you believe about these core issues related to marriage and family. Your people need the benefit of a clear statement of the beliefs of your church.

2. Ask your leadership team to be accountable to live out in private what you teach publicly. There is no greater apologetic for the family than a godly couple practicing what they preach.

3. In your preaching, feature an expository series on marriage and family issues at least once a year. The Bible needs to be taught verse by verse so that congregations gain confidence in the relevance and authority of Scripture.

4. Encourage young married adults in your church to have a Bible study called "Building Teamwork in Marriage" (see page 122).

5. Challenge men's groups to read and study Bob Lepine's book, *The Christian Husband* (Ann Arbor, Mich.: Servant, 1999). We must call men out of their passivity. They need to be shown how they are to

love and lead their wives. Then they need to be shown how to deny themselves, serve, and give spiritual leadership to their families.

6. Challenge women's groups to read and study Susan Hunt's book, *God's Distinctive Calling for Women* (Wheaton, Ill.: Crossway, 1998) or Elizabeth Elliot's, *Let Me Be a Woman* (Wheaton, Ill.: Tyndale, 1976). Wives need to be encouraged to distinguish between biblical truth and the feminist-inspired rhetoric coming from our culture.

7. Equip and challenge parents to instruct their sons and daughters in the biblical blueprints of marriage and family. In your church's youth and college/career groups, why not teach a class on God's design for the family—including a straightforward discussion of the roles and responsibilities of husband and wife? (Fellowship Bible Church, Little Rock, Arkansas, has such a class for youth called "Rocking the Roles." Contact the church at 501-224-7171 or www.fbclr.com for further information.)

Reestablishing love and respect for God's design in marriage is one of the most strategic things we can do. The future of the church and society hangs in the balance. If the Christian community is not willing to step up and be "salt and light" on issues of male and female responsibilities in marriage and the family, then who will?

The road most traveled is the downward slope of silence or compromise with the culture that leads to more confusion on issues of sexual identity, homosexuality, and perversion. The road least traveled is courageous leadership and clear teaching that encourages married couples to embrace the Creator's design.

Wayne Grudem has warned, "We are at a turning point in history, and we may not realize it. It [the meaning of manhood and womanhood] touches all of life. And there are massive spiritual forces at work."[11]

We have the answer that experts are seeking when it comes to marriage and how men and women are to relate to each other—the Designer's design.

# CHAPTER

## 5

## Big Idea 4: Make Your Church a Marriage- and Family-Equipping Center

**W**e're in a family crisis! Countless young people who are marrying and starting families have no idea how to build a godly home. Who should take the lead in addressing the needs of families? The local church!

Families are of supreme importance to God; He created them. Stories of marriages and families are a silver thread all the way through the Scriptures. Marriage and family are central to what God is doing on this planet.

Many young adults are crying out for help. They are asking, "How can we make our marriage and our family succeed?" Many of them grew up in broken homes with parents who were divorced. They want help. They *need* help.

When families fall apart, the church's goal of raising mature followers of Jesus is made more difficult. The church ends up assuming part of the role of a healthy family, and portions of the church's ministry suffer. Weak families are a drain. Strong families, however, can become an incubator for growing leaders who can serve in the local church.

Researcher George Barna reported in 1998 that among born-again parents, more than eight out of ten want their local church to become more involved in helping them be better parents.[1] Research conducted by FamilyLife has revealed the same desire. Our Family-Needs Survey, conducted with more than twenty thousand adults in American churches, has revealed three parenting areas where church members particularly want help from their churches.

- Helping a child grow spiritually
- Establishing and teaching Christian values in the home
- Developing a child's character and morality[2]

Our research revealed that about one-third of the parents expressed lack of confidence in parenting skills. What a need—and what an opportunity!

When a pastor stands up to deliver his Sunday morning sermon, he should remember that the vast majority of individuals listening to him arrived and will leave church in the context of family. In what environment will individuals be most likely to make that "twelve-inch transfer" of content from head to heart? Minutes after they leave church, with whom will they be in the car? Why would we not aim the majority of our resources at this target? If we want to help people grow in Christ, we need to help them apply truth where they live—at home.

Although a strong emphasis should be placed on families—whether intact, single-parent, or step—we must not forget the many single adults in our churches. The unique needs of singles must be addressed; and churches need their skills, gifts, resources, and leadership. Singles must play a huge role in a family reformation; God's unique call for them to participate in His work is clearly spelled out in Scripture (1 Cor. 7:25–35). They must be fully equipped for life and service, and for establishing godly relationships.

But my point remains: The future generation of the church begins with a family—a mother and father loving each other and nurturing godly children.

## THREE KINDS OF CHURCHES

Our churches must become local centers for marriage and family equipping because *the family represents the largest unmet felt need in all of Western civilization*. What need in America even begins to approach the depth of despair found in numerous marriages and families? What other need in America causes so many people to wake up early in the morning wondering how they will make it through the day?

When the Samaritan woman met Jesus at the well, she thought her real need was water. But Jesus built on that need and explained that there was a thirst in her life that would not be satisfied by the liquid from that well. He told her of living water, and He met her greatest need. Her life was changed by her encounter with Jesus, so much so that she brought her entire village to meet Him.

Marital and family needs are the thirst in modern Americans that will bring them looking for "water" at a local church. And after receiving a cup of water for their families, they will listen when we tell them the good news—and they will run to get their friends.

In our FamilyLife weekend marriage conferences we see this scene repeatedly. A couple struggling in their marriage comes seeking help, experience a dramatic change, reconnect with Christ (or meet Him for the first time), and then go back to their churches and enthusiastically start ministering to others.

But are churches ready to seize this great opportunity? Three brief exhibits from my personal experience temper my enthusiasm.

*Exhibit A:* I met with a leader of a major denomination in America, a man who has been in ministry for nearly fifty years. I asked him to list the top ten churches in his denomination that were family-oriented churches—churches that were strengthening marriages and families. I will never forget how he leaned back on his chair, wrinkled his forehead, then leaned forward and said, "I can't think of any."

*Exhibit B:* At FamilyLife we occasionally conduct focus groups with pastors. One of the first things we ask them to do is to define their family ministry. Their answers have been disheartening. They think of family ministry as everything from children's ministry to youth work. Unfortunately many church leaders do not know what family ministry should look like in the church.

*Exhibit C:* In audiences all over the nation I've asked people what religious group in America is leading the charge to help the family? What name do you suppose is mentioned most often? The Mormons! Why should a cult be considered the most family-friendly group?

We need churches that realize that the greatest unmet need in Western civilization is the family. We need churches that are aggressively addressing the physical, emotional, and spiritual needs of families. We need churches that see themselves as marriage- and family-equipping centers.

## OPENING A MARRIAGE-AND FAMILY-EQUIPPING CENTER

If we are to see a true reforming of families, we must abandon some old practices and embrace some new tactics and innovative strategies. Be warned—taking a new path is never easy, and change is unlikely to occur without the passion and energy of the leaders. In the local church this usually means that the senior pastor must "buy into" the ideas and then lead or facilitate the charge with other leaders, staff, and ultimately all the laity.

The first step in making your church a marriage-and-family equipping center is to realign your vision and philosophy of ministry. We must be intentional about helping marriages and families become distinctively Christian. The church exists for many reasons. Near the top of the list is "equipping of the saints for the work of service" (Eph. 4:12). That "service" occurs most naturally, frequently, and powerfully in the around-the-clock relationships of the family—first, husband-wife and then, parent-child. Obviously the church has been commissioned to do much more, but it must not fail to address family needs.

George Barna discusses this need for churches to have an intentional family emphasis. "The churches that have the most effective ministries to families are the ones that help families become efficient, independent problem-solvers. These churches do not have a huge range of family programs and classes. Instead, they focus upon helping parents and children become self-sufficient by recognizing the warning signs of approaching crises. These churches invest time and energy in helping those family members develop problem-solving skills and to be committed to resolving those problems in a biblical manner."[3]

Families need wisdom. Wisdom, as Proverbs makes clear, is skill in everyday living. It is living life with a godly perspective instead of a worldly one. And churches need to have a vision for helping families function with godly wisdom.

Second, clearly articulate some basic definitions. Every church needs to define what it means by "family ministry." It also needs to state its position on topics such as premarital sex, cohabitation, divorce, remarriage, and so forth. Begin by embracing this definition of marriage: Marriage is the sacred union of a man and a woman in a legally binding, lifelong, covenantal relationship.

Third, know the *real* needs of the families in *your* church. Although counseling with families in trouble reveals a great deal, what about all the marriages and families that never receive pastoral counseling? What are their deeply felt but usually unspoken needs?

A word of caution is in order. Don't pull families apart by always taking the kids off in their own direction and the parents elsewhere. Many churches don't focus enough on helping families grow spiritually together, perhaps because this can be awkward and threatening for parents. Of course, children do need to be with their peers. But churches need to find innovative ways to bring families together.

Pastor Ben Freudenburg made the following comment: "I think people in the church are asking desperately for help . . . and when they find churches that are doing [family ministry], they tend to move to those churches."[4]

For assistance and ideas contact the National Association of Family Ministries, led by John Irwin (5300 France Ave., South Edina, MN 55410). I urge you not to miss out on a fantastic opportunity to help people and share the gospel. Become known in your area as the church that cares for and equips families![5]

# CHAPTER

## 6

## Big Idea 5: Create a Church-wide Web

The day before Mother's Day I was on my way to see my eighty-seven-year-old mother. As I was driving into my hometown, which used to be a quiet little burg tucked away in the hills of southwest Missouri, I noticed a literal "sign" of the times. As I drove by my home church, I saw a sign proudly declaring it was a "new millennium" church:

First Baptist Church
Services 9:30 & 11:00
www.ozarkfirstbaptist.org

How times have changed! Like many churches today, this one too has created a Web site on the Internet.

I believe the Internet may help foster a family reformation much as the printing press aided the Protestant Reformation. Walt Wilson wrote, "There are watershed events that shape human history. . . . Today we live during one of those life-altering historic events that is being orchestrated by God. This is the Internet moment in human history. From now on, nothing will be the same."[1] The Internet is changing the way we gain information, connect to each other, buy and sell goods and services, and even the way we look at life.

The public's acceptance of the Internet has been rapid compared to other innovations. For example, it took fifty-five years for the automobile to reach saturation use. The telephone took thirty-five years. Even television took twenty-six years. But the Internet has required only seven years to become a normal part of daily life in America.[2] More than two out of three Americans have access to the Internet. Of these, 54.6 percent use e-mail. In 1998 the U.S. Postal Service delivered 101 billion pieces of mail. But that same year an estimated four trillion e-mails were transmitted![3] And yet only a few years ago we didn't even know the meaning of the term *e-mail*.

The average Internet user now spends 7.1 hours a week online, a time commitment to media that trails only the time given to television and radio and exceeds the time people spend reading newspapers and magazines. Computers now outsell television sets in the United States and Japan.[4]

According to Barna Research, 25 million people per month use the Internet for religious purposes. And by 2010 between 10 and 20 percent of the population will rely primarily or exclusively on the Internet for their religious input.[5] Currently the Christian Internet community consists of tens of thousands of church Web sites, hundreds of organization sites, and a few large "destination sites," such as Crosswalk and OnePlace. Unfortunately awareness and usage of these Christian Web sites remain low.

The "fellowship-community" dimension of the Internet is what should catch the attention of local churches. The Internet is a great leveler of persons. Age, sex, race, education, physical appearance, and other qualities that tend to separate people really don't matter much in cyberspace. Although the Internet is in some ways highly impersonal, many people are gravitating to it as a way of connecting with others. No doubt the anonymity does make it easier for people to ease into relationships. Here people can be honest about their interests and can find likeminded people without the time commitment and risks associated with seeking others in more traditional ways. The popularity of this facet of the Internet is revealed by the fact that community usage represents about 50 percent of the time people spend online.[6] Much as the telephone has done in the past, the Internet offers people a new way of "relating" to one another.

As new media have evolved, the Christian community has done better with some new technologies than others in disseminating truth. Print media have been used with great success. But the church's use of television, for example, is not as encouraging. A problem with television has always been the high cost of production and airtime. But this is not a drawback with the Internet. Almost any local church, without a huge investment of resources, can enhance communication with its members and nonmembers.

The opportunity is fantastic, and many churches are seizing it. But only the surface—in numbers and creativity—is being scratched. Most Christian Internet sites are now centered on the needs and activities of the sponsoring church or organization. That's not bad, but this approach does not maximize the opportunity of the Internet to play a huge role in evangelism and discipleship. Churches need to clarify their target audiences and become member-focused rather than organization-focused.

The Internet allows us to minister to any type of family, anywhere, anytime. In addition to information and services we can deliver, we can also creatively network families in need with mentors who can provide hands-on assistance and encouragement.

## THE DARK SIDE OF THE INTERNET

As with other media the Internet can be a tool for evil too. *USA Today* reported late in 1999 that the Internet has about three thousand witch, Wiccan, and pagan Web sites.[7] Wren Walker, codeveloper of a Web site called "Witchvox," said, "We see ourselves as a clearinghouse for information.... We get e-mails all the time from people thanking us for providing a sense of security and community."[8]

The Internet has become a huge new delivery system for pornography, a growing 56-billion-dollar-a-year business.[9] One study found that for every "hit" on the Internet for the word "marriage," there were ten searches for the word "sex."[10]

In addition to "overt evil," four other downsides of the net are evident. First, no matter how "virtual" communication may become, nothing can take the place of face-to-face relationships. We can use the Internet to connect with people we may otherwise never have met, but any serious friendship or ongoing fellowship ultimately requires getting together in person. This is true regardless of a person's age.

A second problem is time. The Internet is a marvelous tool, but it is an add-on innovation. Most people were overcommitted before the Internet showed up. In some ways it saves time, but excessive surfing and chatting means that other important activities of life may be neglected. Just as television replaced relationships in the family, so the Internet competes for relational connectedness. The Internet may be "limitless," but time isn't. We must remember in our Information Age that time is the new "currency" in which we all deal. Paying attention to how we treat this "new capital" is critical individually, relationally, maritally, financially, and ministerially. Time is too precious to waste (Eph. 5:15–17; James 4:13–14).

Third, the Internet has a huge amount of garbage. Witchcraft and pornography are just the beginning. Since the Internet is "free," this means every type of foul idea, vulgarity, and twisted perspective can be found on the net. The usual filters or barriers to information (e.g., limited access, cost, unavailability) do not exist for most people. That's why many parents install screening software on home computers, especially those used by children.

Fourth, another downside is the risk of illicit or even dangerous relationships. Because of the anonymity of the Internet, individuals drop inhibitions and quickly share intimacies with a stranger—not nearly so likely in a face-to-to-face relationship. Many adults are being sucked into adulterous affairs via the Internet. Many times these liaisons stop at emotional unfaithfulness, but they can lead to physical adultery and even divorce. Also some child molesters are using the Internet to entice children, thereby easily invading otherwise secure homes. Another problem with the Internet is the ease of making unwise purchases on credit.

We need to understand the negatives, give warnings, and erect appropriate safeguards. But let's not cower in the face of evil; let's overcome it with good.

## CATCHING THE WEB

Here's a sampling of possible Internet uses by a local church—in both general ministry and in specific assistance to families.

- Communicate with church members, giving reminders of upcoming events, emergency prayer needs, daily insights from pastors
- Recruit, train, and empower laypeople for special outreaches
- Post question-and-answer bulletin boards around family needs and issues
- Build community in your church
- Attract young people to the church
- Set up Web links to family-friendly sites and services
- Locate ministry resources for staff and lay volunteers

Here are some simple initial steps by which a church can join the electronic revelation.

1. Get on the Internet, use it, and explore it. The more you see how the Internet works and how other churches and Christian organizations are involved, the clearer idea you will have of how the Internet might work for you. These are some of the many Web sites operated by churches or organizations that provide quality information and Internet ideas for your ministry:

   www.brooklyntabernacle.org

   www.cbmw.org

   www.crosswalk.com

   www.family.org

   www.familylife.com

   www.fbclr.com

   www.gospel.com

   www.gospelcom.net

   www.oneplace.com

   www.pastors.com

   www.promisekeepers.org

   www.saddleback.com

   www.sbc.net

   www.sermonsearch.com

   www.willownet.com

2. Encourage your staff to become Internet savvy. The more brains the better. Others will see Internet applications that you may not see.

3. Identify and know your target audience. This should be an early step in every endeavor; the Internet is no different. If your target audience is older, you may not need as sophisticated an approach as if you are trying to attract GenX users.

4. Identify a layman to lead your Internet initiative. Possibly a person in your church already knows much about the Internet. If so, ask him or her to set up a Web application appropriate to your congregation.

5. Create an Internet plan and launch it. The Internet is all about flexibility and change. Once you have a good plan, don't wait. Do the best you can, and constantly be assessing how you need to change Internet efforts. If you have a Web site, be prepared to "freshen its face" every few months. You will need adequate funding. An investment in the Internet is not like buying carpeting or new pew Bibles—items that can last a long time. To have an impact in this arena you will need to stay on the cutting edge.

Churches *need* to be on the Internet. Otherwise this great communications medium will increasingly be used for the wrong purposes. We cannot afford to miss the Internet the way the church missed mainstream television. Use it both to create community among your families and to communicate content.

To do this you will need to invest some significant financial resources, perhaps between 5 and 10 percent of your annual budget. That may seem like a large amount, but just think of the short- and long-range opportunities. Churches that avoid this commitment risk being marginalized into irrelevancy. Be aggressive in using this tool God has entrusted to us!

## PORNOGRAPHY AND THE INTERNET

One of the downsides of the Internet is the easy access it gives people to pornography. For too many people this is almost their exclusive reason for using the Internet. And God alone knows the damage done daily to millions of individuals who are dabbling with this evil in the privacy of their own homes.

Although precise statistics are not readily available, since the Christian community often mirrors the broader culture in behavior, it's likely that pornography is a much larger problem among men—and growing numbers of women—in the church than we realize.

As a leader it is important that you first protect your own heart and stay clear of pornography. Do not dabble, do not do "research," don't look at pornographic Web sites for any reason. You would not take swigs of rat poison to learn its taste. Treat pornography the same way. If provocative-looking e-mail messages show up in your "mailbox," delete them immediately without opening any attachments.

If you supervise other staff members, take the lead in making sure that pornography-screening software is installed on all computers. This may seem like an extreme measure with adults in ministry, but again, don't underestimate the insidious nature of pornography. Think of protective software in the same way you would a good fire alarm and sprinkling system—it's prudent protection against a threat.

Use your position in the church to ensure that in particular those in charge of men's ministry regularly address the issue of Internet pornography. Point out the dangers, and explain God's remedies through repentance and forgiveness (1 John 1:9).

Use of pornography should not be held up as a "greater sin," but like all sin, it needs to be confessed and dealt with. Some individuals may need special help in breaking the bonds of addiction to pornography. Be ready with an action plan for such cases. Know where to find professional Christian counseling in your area for pornography addiction.

Several studies reveal that pornography is particularly a problem for pastors. If you are caught in this web, I urge you to seek help. (If none is available locally, call a national ministry like Focus on the Family or

FamilyLife for prayer support and assistance.) Your marriage, your family, your family, your ministry, perhaps even your life could destruct if you do not receive freedom from this sin. Find someone to confess to, and, if possible, ask that person to hold you accountable.

Your spouse will need to know, but first you may need to confess to a trusted friend who can guide you in taking steps with your wife, other pastors on staff, the church board, and/or even the congregation. You will experience embarrassment, and there may be a price to pay for your courage. But God will smile. Do the right thing for your good and His glory.

# CHAPTER

## 7

## Big Idea 6: Maximize Mentors

James Patterson and Peter Kim report a startling statistic in their book *The Day America Told the Truth*: Over half of the adult population of America is so concerned about the erosion of our moral and physical environment that they would volunteer up to three weeks a year to "fix America."[1] That's 130 million Americans waiting for the call!

If Americans will volunteer to improve the environment, surely lay volunteers in our churches can be enlisted to help preserve our families. We might call this volunteer army the "Family Reformation Army."

I once observed a group discussing the needs of Christian families in the church. Many of these men and women agreed that they wanted help from a person who had already gone through the stretch of river they were currently navigating. They wanted a mature, honest, trustworthy guide who was willing to share both successes and failures and to give the Bible's perspective on critical issues. They were asking not for perfect mentors but for Christians who have not quit, who, in spite of failure, continue to fulfill their most basic commitments at home.

Obviously, getting an army of family workers is a huge task. Implementation of this will be challenging but rewarding. Far too many Christians are comfortable with their status in the "peace-time reserves" in the church. But we must give them the challenge. The average church has too many people resources not involved in ministry. Let's challenge mature couples to become mentors of newly marrieds. Let's challenge adult Christians who may be "rusting out" in the church to take on a spiritual assignment that will engage them in spiritual battle on behalf of the next generation of families.

Pastor Lon Garber says this about such a mentoring ministry: "I believe it is the single-most effective leadership development or personal development tool available for personal, relational leadership and ministry development. We are making a concerted effort to employ it throughout the ministries of the church. But it takes time."[2]

As is often the case, the mentors will be as blessed—if not more so— than the couples receiving their mentoring. One mentor couple we interviewed said, "We have been married twenty-nine years. Being mentors has forced us to deal with and correct some poor habits that otherwise we would have let go unchecked. It has made our relationship so much better."[3]

With so many people today coming from broken and dysfunctional families, many young couples do not know how to have a meaningful Christian marriage nor how to handle basics like conflict, money management, and child rearing. One person being mentored described his need this way: "My parents and my wife's parents divorced when we were young, and we want a mentor relationship with a godly couple so we can see how a marriage can survive and even thrive."[4]

In previous years this kind of mentoring occurred more naturally. Families did not move from one city to another as often as they do today. Usually a newly married couple lived nearby—or even in the same home with—one set of parents. At a minimum the couple probably lived in the same community as a large number of relatives—grandparents, parents, aunts, uncles, cousins—in addition to nonfamily members who may have known them for years. This environment created stress and problems, too, but certainly a significant amount of advice was shared informally and passed on as a young husband and wife interacted with people they knew well.

This system of nurture and accountability no longer exists because people move away from home and then keep moving. Susan Hunt, director of women's ministries for the Presbyterian Church in America, comments, "So many families isolate today. They barricade. They try to go the journey alone. And that is not God's way. We are to circle the wagons. We are to join hands with one another and declare our interdependence."[5]

Couples end up fending for themselves in communities and churches where no one knows them well. Such isolation is not a good thing, because often no one is there to give any kind of context to the challenges every marriage and family face in different life stages. I believe a mentor strategy in the local church could solve this problem and become an extremely satisfying ministry opportunity for many people.

Let's say your own son or daughter marries and moves to another city. Would it not be a great comfort to know that in their new church a marriage mentor would be assigned to walk beside them in their early years of marriage? At the same time, you or others in your church could offer the same service to a young couple that just moved in from a distant city. I believe there are thousands of couples in our churches, perhaps many of them entering the empty-nest stage of life, who would gladly volunteer a few hours each month for this kind of mentoring.

Ideally a mentoring couple would begin visiting a young couple during their engagement and then meet with them in the early years of their marriage. Other mentors could provide assistance with the next stages in the Family Life Cycle.

The premarried/newlywed mentoring approach is already successfully implemented at Frazer Memorial United Methodist Church in Montgomery, Alabama. In 1996 that church instituted a policy on premarital counseling for engaged couples that involved mentor couples. Family minister John Schmidt tells the story about their mentoring program, which has ministered to more than four hundred married couples.

We want to pass the ministry on to volunteers, to lay people, as often as possible. . . . We created a pool of thirty mentoring couples who had been married ten years or more with strong marriages. . . . The net result of all this has been fantastic. Our mentoring couples love it and have been personally enriched. They defend it to the teeth, and have found their own marriages strengthened in the process. . . . It gives them a chance to really fulfill the biblical duty of the older men teaching the younger men and the older women teaching the younger women. . . .

The mentoring approach . . . also allowed us to guarantee a maximum of flexibility. We have two engaged couples who will go through the curriculum with one mentoring couple. The schedule only has to accommodate three couples. . . .

[Also] it took the relational pressure off of our pastoral staff. . . . By decentralizing the instruction, the phone calls are decentralized too. The pastoral staff gets involved only if there are serious problems. People will go back to their mentoring couples for years and years.[6]

Mentoring is also a very effective evangelistic strategy to reach couples. An exciting by-product of the training at Frazer Memorial Church is that the mentors have had the opportunity to lead a number of individuals to Christ.

Pastor Schmidt reports that mentoring couples are required to be in touch with the mentored couples at six and twelve months after the wedding. However, in reality the couples have more frequent contact.

The pastoral staff has benefited because through the shifting of this ministry to others there is more time for other ministry responsibilities. But the greatest benefit may be in knowing that couples have received a superb premarital preparation. As Schmidt says, "It's a scary thing when you are the clergy and are pronouncing God's blessing [on a couple in a wedding]. You don't want to give your sanction to a bad marriage."[7]

If churches would seize the opportunity to assign mentor couples to engaged couples in the months before their marriage and in the first two years thereafter, the divorce rate among Christians could be significantly reduced. This is because the instruction done before marriage can help guide the couple in areas such as finances, sex, conflict, and others. As newlyweds their hearts may not be hardened, and so good habits can be established and concepts reinforced early on.

A side benefit of this approach, but one that should loom large in the back of every pastor's mind, is that any couple that provides mentoring will grow as quickly or more so than the couple they are mentoring. They will desire to grow spiritually and stay sharp as they seek to guide their couples through the nitty-gritty issues of life.

## BECOMING A MENTORING CHURCH

In many churches getting people to "enlist" as mentors takes prayer, planning, patience, training, perseverance, and time. In smaller churches a concept like mentoring may seem impractical. Perhaps a formal mentoring program is not necessary, for it may already be occurring informally among people who know each other well. But even in a small congregation, initiation of mentoring need not be complicated.

At a smaller church Pastor Mickey Thorpe, of Canoga Park, California, took a direct approach: "I preached on Titus 2. Then I asked the people under the age of fifty to stand if they would like to be mentored by an older man, woman, or couple. Almost all of them stood up. We then developed a form for the 'younger' to fill out, and one for the 'older' to fill out. Then, through phone calls we brought them together."[8]

This is not surprising, because everyone admits that families are in trouble. Unfortunately most believers don't know what to do about it. So they need to be challenged and given some direction. And this can start in the pulpit, by pastors explaining how simple this strategy is and what the benefits are.

Following enlistment there needs to be recruitment and training.

I had the opportunity to team-teach a series of sessions to a large group of men on the stages of a man's life. The men eagerly soaked up this topic. To help these men visualize the path toward manhood, we built a set of portable steps as a symbol of what men go through in life as they "step up to maturity." The five steps were labeled "Boyhood," "Adolescence," "Manhood," "Mentor," and "Patriarch."

In one session I asked Dr. Carl Wenger, a retired surgeon, to stand on the top step and address the men. Nearly five hundred men moved to the edge of their seats as they listened to this white-haired spiritual leader who had been married for fifty-eight years. This older man helped mentor hundreds of younger men as he spoke.

Susan Hunt, who for years has been a pastor's wife, became burdened some years ago for a mentoring ministry with women. Since then she has written a number of books, including *Spiritual Mothering*, which explains how women can serve the church and families through obeying the Titus 2:3–4 mandate for older women to mentor younger women.

In a seminar entitled "Older Women Mentoring Younger Women," Mrs. Hunt said, "Today we have a generation of young women who are longing for spiritual mothers with a heightened intensity, because most of them have not been mothered or they have been mothered destructively. In many ways my generation has abandoned this calling."[9]

She states that a Titus 2 ministry is "not just about formal Bible instruction. It is not just about a program. It is about a way of life. It is about a lifestyle. . . . It is to permeate church life. It is an essential element of who we are as the body of Christ. A spiritual mothering ministry should include both a relational and an educational component ministry or it will lack integrity."[10]

As you move toward becoming a mentoring church, set some reachable three-year goals. For example, you might want to consider establishing an initial goal of recruiting four mentoring couples for every three hundred people in your church.

First, recruit one couple to mentor engaged couples. If you have only one couple interested in mentoring, this is the place to begin. Targeting the first five years of marriage is strategic, because the divorce rate peaks in the first four years of marriage.

Second, consider designating a crisis mentor couple—a husband and wife who have a heart for couples in trouble. If the mentoring couple has experienced a crisis in their own marriage, they can readily relate to couples whose marriages are in trouble.

Third, appoint two couples as parenting mentors—one for parents of preschool and elementary children and another for parents of adolescents.

As the mentoring idea catches on and more volunteers are available, recruit mentors with particular qualifications to help others with similar backgrounds, such as a blended couple mentoring blended families, a divorced and remarried couple mentoring divorcées or couples facing a divorce.

Over the years I have challenged many lay couples to step forward as mentors. But many feel they are not qualified. They say they have nothing to share with younger adults. Some perhaps are haunted by their own mistakes, not realizing that those mistakes will be their most valuable tools in teaching a younger couple.

People must be shown that everyone struggles with marriage and family issues. The central truth taught by a family mentor is that the "core curriculum" in marriage and family life is experience, including both successes and failures. What God teaches from both mistakes and successes provides the "content" for those who want to follow in the mentor's steps. Mentors need to be taught and assured that their failures and weaknesses will provide some of their best resources for teaching marriage and family "life" messages to their protégés.

It is important that you carefully select and train your mentors. If the mentors lack understanding and adequate spiritual maturity, vision, and confidence, the mentoring may be less than satisfactory and the entire effort may not succeed.

I think mentors should be married at least five years. Also they need to be able to teach and minister to others. This doesn't mean that they must have the ability to teach a larger group in a more formal setting. But it does mean they must be able to communicate basic content to another person in an edifying manner that produces life change.

Potential mentors could be trained on a Friday evening and Saturday morning or in several evenings. In these sessions help the mentor-couples to know clearly what they should seek to accomplish in the twelve or twenty-four months they may mentor another couple.

Help mentors understand the difference between personal preferences and biblical principles in marriage and in parenting techniques. Some mentors may overstep biblical convictions and begin to think their personal preferences are the biblical directives. "Make sure mentors know they are not counselors. They need to understand and know the line that separates counseling from giving advice," says Wayne Younger of Family Guidance in Pittsburgh.[11] Wayne has found that setting up lay couples to become "counselors" without proper training can be counterproductive.

In tailoring such a mentoring effort, do not underemphasize either the instructional or the relational elements. In developing her "spiritual mothering" concepts Susan Hunt found that "there must be both educational and a relational components to our ministry. If they are just educational, they will be academic. And if they are just relational, they will be anemic."[12]

If you establish this approach, when you introduce those first four couples you will never be short of people wanting to be mentored. The problem won't be finding the people who want to be mentored. The problem will be in enlisting enough of the right people to invest themselves in mentoring the younger couples.

Start your mentoring program on a small scale. Quality, not quantity, will provide the base for a program that will grow in the future.

Mentoring husbands and wives and moms and dads can bring healing and hope to a generation wounded by divorce, dysfunctional family backgrounds, and an evil culture.

## SAMPLE JOB DESCRIPTION FOR A MENTORING COUPLE

*Position title:*   Mentoring Couple for "Preparing for Marriage" Course

*Supervisor:*   "Preparing for Marriage" Coordinator

*Function:*   To lead two or three engaged couples through the "Preparing for Marriage" course and help them evaluate their relationship.

**Regular duties:**

1. Lead two or three couples in the eight-session "Preparing for Marriage" course at least once a year
2. Assist with one "Preparing for Marriage" Saturday workshop each year
3. Build an open relationship with the assigned engaged couples
4. Evaluate the relationship of each engaged couple and openly discuss problem areas as well as strengths with them
5. Report serious problems to the "Preparing for Marriage" coordinator

**Occasional duties:**

1. Have a fellowship dinner with the assigned couples (optional)
2. Conduct a six-month and one-year follow-up session with each couple after their marriage

**Qualifications:**

- Church member

- Married five to ten years

- Willing to share openly about personal struggles and problems in marriage

- Burden for preparing young couples for marriage

*\*Thanks to John Schmidt, pastor at Frazer Memorial United Methodist Church, Montgomery, Alabama, for permission to reprint this job description.*

# CHAPTER

## 8

## Big Idea 7: Empower Parents as Faith Trainers

Today we take our children to gymnastics classes to learn gymnastics. We send them to summer camps for tennis, volleyball, baseball, basketball, soccer, and other sports. When our daughters tried out for cheerleading, Barbara and I found that we had to send them to an instructor if they were to have any chance of making the squad. We've become a culture of "specialists." And when it comes to teaching our children about God and how to relate to Him, I'm afraid we've slipped into the same mind-set.

Too many parents today seem to have this attitude about educating their children in spiritual things. "Would you please teach them the Christian faith? Isn't that what the church is supposed to do?"

If there is to be a family reformation in America, parents must assume their place as the faith trainers and instructors of their children.

Every leader of a church needs to ask, Who bears the primary responsibility for faith formation in the lives of our children? Does that rest principally at church, to be supported at home? Or does the responsibility of spiritual equipping of children rest first and foremost at home, to be supported by the church? Most pastors would *say* that faith formation and instruction need to be the primary responsibility of the parents, with the church assisting the process. But are their churches doing anything to *equip parents* to help their children grow spiritually? One way to measure this is to look back over your church calendar and programs for the past couple of years and total up the number of hours children have received instruction from the church in Sunday school, children's church, retreats, and youth groups. Now total the number of hours you've instructed *parents* in how to develop the spiritual lives of their children.

Over the past three decades churches have made great strides in preparing couples for marriage. Churches have increasingly addressed this need through an assortment of classes, mentoring, and conferences. Now equipping parents in their responsibility of spiritually rearing and training the next generation is one of the greatest opportunities for growth and outreach in the church today. It is the new frontier of present-day churches. Our research from the Family Needs Survey shows that of the top ten issues where Christian adults want help from the church, three pertain to parenting issues. They are spiritual growth of the children, teaching values in the home, and developing character and morality in children.[1]

George Barna wrote, "The only way in which the Church will thrive in the future is if families lead the process of directing and furthering their own spiritual growth. . . . Let me again emphasize this notion: *The future of the Church in America depends largely upon the spiritual commitment of families.*"[2]

Parents were God's first choice to train children in His ways. Why? Because *faith formation begins at home*, for both children and adults. God designed it that way. Family is the place where faith is forged, where life and truth collide. Family is where we apply what we're learning in the Christian life.

Charles Swindoll said it well: "Whatever else may be said about the home, it is the bottom line of life, the anvil upon which attitudes and convictions are hammered out. It is the place where life's bills come due, [it is] the single most influential force in our earthly existence. No price tag can adequately reflect its values. No gauge can measure its ultimate influence . . . for good or ill. It is at home, among family members, that we come to terms with circumstances. It is here life makes up its mind."[3]

In a strong Christian family mom and dad would not think of entrusting the core activity of their parenting responsibility to someone else.

They should look to the church for assistance and support, but parents are responsible to be their children's spiritual trainers and nurturers. A good home cannot be equaled as a place for a child to learn about and experience God.

Yet today far too many Christian families have abdicated to the church their spiritual responsibility to train their children. They reason, "The church can do a better job. The paid, seminary-trained professionals run a better program. They are younger and thus more relevant to the needs of our children. Let them do it."

In Deuteronomy God revealed His reasons for commanding parents to be fruitful and multiply—to produce godly children. "Hear, O Israel! The LORD is our God, the LORD is one! You shall love the LORD your God with all your heart and with all your soul and with all your might. These words, which I am commanding you today, shall be on your heart. You shall teach them diligently to your sons and shall talk of them when you sit in your house and when you walk by the way and when you lie down and when you rise up" (Deut. 6:4–7).

Psalm 78:5–8 further affirms the role of parents in training their children. "For He established a testimony in Jacob, and appointed a law in Israel, which He commanded our fathers that they should teach them to their children, that the generation to come might know, even the children yet to be born, that they may arise and tell them to their children, that they should put their confidence in God, and not forget the works of God, but keep His commandments, and not be like their fathers, a stubborn and rebellious generation, a generation that did not prepare its heart, and whose spirit was not faithful to God."

But many Christian parents feel inadequate for this task. A complaint I often hear, from men in particular, is this: "I can operate confidently and achieve superb results on the job. But when I come home, I feel incompetent, awkward, ineffective." One businessman confessed to me, "I can lead several hundred employees in achieving their goals. And I can make a sizable profit in the marketplace. But to sit down at the dinner table and lead my wife and three children spiritually scares me to death!"

What has happened in the ministry of the church to allow such a situation to evolve? How did the false gods of career, materialism, entertainment, leisure, and other things rise up to compete with and even squeeze out the goals and plans of Almighty God?

## THE CURRENT PARADIGM

Although we often *say* we believe that parents are to train their children in the things of God, in reality many of the educational efforts in our churches seem to ignore or go around parents as the rightful faith trainers.

George Barna observed, "The typical church tries to help a family by identifying its problems and then solving those problems for the family. Those churches think they are doing a great service. However, our research clearly shows that such an approach is often counterproductive. Solving a family's problems for them creates a dependency upon the church."[4]

Although many in our culture send the message that parents are not competent to raise and train their children in our sophisticated society, this is not God's idea. We must empower parents to pass on a legacy of spiritual life and vitality.

At this point some church leaders may be thinking, "We are already exhausted from bandaging up wounded families in our flock. Now you want us to shift how we think about educating children too?" In fact, I do, because the only hope for relief for our families and for church leaders is to get this responsibility back where it belongs—*in the home.*

One pastor told me, "You finally wake up and find out that you can't do it alone. You can't be the counselor, the activity director, the faith former of every kid in your congregation. You wonder, *Why am I doing this by myself? Why am I not being successful? If God is with me, how come it's not working?* It may be because we are finally realizing that the plan we are using is the wrong plan."

If we do not refocus our ministries and equip parents to be "family ministers," where is our hope of ever moving from a defensive posture to an offensive one on family problems? What is at stake here is not merely the health of families for generations to come; it's the health of the church as well. If we don't strengthen families, the church will be weak because its most basic social unit is weak. And another thing at stake is the spiritual and emotional well-being and health of the church staff and their marriages. No wonder there are so many in the ministry who have such needs in their own marriages and families; they are not only loving their spouses and raising their own children, but they are seeking to help scores of other spouses, children, and extended family members as well. No wonder church leaders go home so tired every evening!

I know there are objections to what I'm proposing. The most compelling objection is, "Where are the parents who can adequately train their children? Many of them are a spiritual mess themselves." My answer is twofold. First, God is known for making mountains of faith out of "messes." Second, if we don't go all the way upstream to the headwaters of the family and address the source, then we will forever be playing defense with today's dysfunctional families. The church must give more of its energy to a preventive ministry, assertively training couples and families in anticipation of their needs.

## SHIFTING THE RESPONSIBILITY
## FOR FAITH TRAINING

Here are several ideas on how such a change can come about. (On this topic I highly recommend the book *The Family Friendly Church*, by Ben Freudenburg and Rick Lawrence.)[5]

Church leaders, starting with pastors, must accept, endorse, and apply the idea of making parents the faith trainers of their children. *If the senior pastor in particular is not leading the charge on this topic, the church will probably never totally accept this approach.*

Beyond the staff and other leaders, you need at least a small band of laypeople who believe in this concept and will support it passionately throughout the church. The more people you have in the congregation whose lives have been transformed by this message, the more success you will see.

I would suggest that this issue be a part of the purpose statement of the church: "We believe that faith formation and character development are the primary responsibilities of every parent, and it is the church's role to support this in every family."

*Evaluate your current situation.* You may be further along than you think. Take a look at present programs and activities and assess how well they are supporting parents as the primary agents in developing faith and teaching character development in the family.

*Don't forget that parents won't do too well at faith training if their own faith and Christian walk are weak.* We can never expect to see godly families if the parents are not progressing toward maturity in their relationship with Christ. A person who understands and lives out a life dominated by obedience and loyalty to God and the Bible's teaching will find it difficult *not* to be a growing and responsible parent. There will be problems and potholes along the way, of course, but ardent disciples of the Lord will be learning how to relate to others in the most positive ways possible.

*Offer parents extensive equipping for their role as faith trainers.* We should never assume (especially in our depraved culture) that any parent feels competent or confident enough of his or her knowledge and ability to train a child in the ways of God. So acquire materials and provide ongoing training opportunities for parents. Also consider some type of gentle accountability-encouragement process through small groups.

*Challenge parents in their faith training clearly, passionately, and frequently.* Many parents don't seem interested in taking the lead in teaching their children spiritual truths. Therefore you need to be persistent in encouraging parents in this area.

*As you plan church events and programs, especially those that directly involve children,* think, "Parents are the faith trainers." Always ask, "How can we directly involve the parents?" For several years I taught a sixth-grade Sunday school class of about seventy students. Each Sunday I had about a dozen parents present for support and assistance. And two or three times each year we invited all the parents to come and sit in on the class. Also we frequently gave the kids projects to take home, "homework" that required parental involvement.

Or you might plan a mission trip involving parents and teenagers. My wife and I sent our children on a mission trip and we have also gone with them on a mission trip. When you go together, you bond by sharing a "spiritual bunker."

*Curtail any of the church's programs and activities that may be interfering*

*with parental faith training. Many parents who do attempt to be the faith train-
ers of their children are concerned that the church is competing with family time.*

As a parent I sometimes feel I'm in a battle for the spiritual welfare
of my family. Are we going to be a family, or are we going to be this
disassembled unit scattered throughout the entire community with only
an occasional opportunity to connect relationally, emotionally, and spiritually? Sometimes Barbara and I have actually kept our children home
from a church youth activity on a weeknight because our children *need
a family*.

I believe the church that empowers and equips parents to function as
God intended will be meeting a felt need in helping parents develop godly
homes.

## PREPARE FOR THE LONG HAUL

Like turning an aircraft carrier in the ocean, this will take time. You are
engaged in a massive paradigm shift, even if it is back to something that's
biblical.

Ben Freudenburg, based on his own family-ministry experience, offers wise counsel. "I don't want churches to get discouraged, because this
isn't like an instant change. It is a long-term commitment to the home as
the primary agency for faith formation. So one thing I would really encourage churches to remember is that it doesn't happen overnight.... It's
so culturally different; don't let that be a hurdle that stops you from going
on. Or when people begin to attack your ideas . . . don't let that discourage you. You know pioneers get arrows."[6]

Richard Baxter, well-known seventeenth-century Puritan pastor, once
took a new church and preached for three years without seeing much
happen in his congregation. Finally he cried out, "O God, You must do
something with these people or I'll die!"

According to Howard Hendricks, "Baxter said, 'It was as if God spoke to
me audibly, "Baxter, you are working in the wrong place. You're expecting
revival to come through the church. Try the home." '" Richard Baxter went
out and called on home after home. He spent entire evenings in homes

helping parents set up family worship times with their children. He moved from one home to another. Finally, the Spirit of God started to light fires all over until they swept through the congregation and made it the great church that it became—and made Baxter a man of godly distinction."[7]

I think God wants to bless every church in similar ways as we give back to godly parents the responsibility for the faith training of their children.

# CHAPTER

## 9

## Big Idea 8: Follow the Life Cycle for Effective Family Ministry

Much like the inevitable seasons of nature, our lives on earth advance in a predictable pattern. This basic truth is the foundation for a simple but effective paradigm of ministry to individuals and families that I call the Family Life Cycle (FLC).

Some years ago at FamilyLife I sat and listened as we had a research firm ask Christian adults what they needed to be successful in their homes. Two responses were heard repeatedly: First, the participants wanted marriage and parenting mentors in their local church. Second, the respondents wanted to be better equipped and trained for the major phases through which their families would go.

Their reactions encouraged our ministry team to begin thinking about the many predictable steps individuals and families take in the natural processes of growth and aging. Our discussions resulted in a seven-stage life cycle that most individuals in a typical family will experience. In the next seven chapters each stage is discussed in detail. The illustration at the beginning of each of these chapters highlights the stage being discussed.

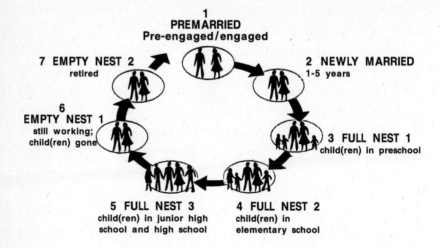

*1. Premarried: Pre-engaged or Engaged Stage (prior to marriage).* Typically this period involves a single person in the late teens on into the twenties. This is the dating or courtship phase. Important premarital instruction and training occurs.

*2. Newly Married: Years 1–5 of Marriage.* This is a critical transitional phase for every marriage and family. Statistically more marriages fail in this period than in any other. The relational habits and disciplines that have been formed will significantly influence the quality of one's marriage later in life.

*3. Full Nest 1: Child(ren) in Preschool.* This life cycle stage begins with the first child and lasts until he or she is about five years old. The new parents must acquire parenting skills that will determine the tone of family relationships for the remainder of their existence. And if a husband and wife are not careful, they may drift apart.

*4. Full Nest 2: Child(ren) in Elementary School.* This is a relatively placid period for the family, when children are between the ages of six and twelve. A primary parenting task is to prepare children for the coming challenges of puberty and adolescence. The wise couple continues to refresh their intimacy and clarifies values that may be tested by children during the upcoming teenage years.

5. *Full Nest 3: Child(ren) in Junior High School and High School.* Much of the family's attention during this stage revolves around the increasing activity and independence of teenage children. Parenting responsibilities gradually move from controller to coach. The family spends less time together at home. Schedules are hectic. Parents will find it increasingly difficult to have time alone because children stay up later and have needs that are often time-consuming and demanding.

6. *Empty Nest 1: Child(ren) Gone, with One or Both Parents Still Employed.* This can be a challenging time for a marriage as the couple now shifts attention back to each other. Parenting is not complete as the children are often still dependent financially and emotionally. Usually one or more children marry during this time, and parents must release them to "leave and cleave" to their own spouse. The first grandchild may arrive in this stage.

7. *Empty Nest 2: Parents Retired.* The focus now shifts to grandchildren, and grandparents have the opportunity to help shape yet another generation to love and follow Christ. The children will assume a greater role in caring for aging parents. The marriage covenant terminates with the death of the family's patriarch or matriarch.

The Family Life Cycle concept is like a map that can guide us from one "destination" to another in nurturing healthy individuals and families. It is a way of visualizing ministry to families in local churches with a "big-picture" perspective. Any church—large or small, denominational or independent, congregational governed or elder governed—can design its family ministry using the navigational aids provided by the FLC model.

The FLC gives church leaders both a long-term and short-term strategy for family ministry. The basic idea of the FLC is long-term. Then as detailed plans are developed for each life stage, a short-term "here's-how-we-will-do-this" plan emerges.

Almost all the issues encountered in each of these phases will be similar for every family. And of course, with several children, a family may be experiencing more than one phase at any given time. (We have arbitrarily chosen the age of the oldest child as the way of determining a family's current stage in the FLC. Empty Nest 1 is an exception because all children must "leave" for this phase in the FLC to occur.)

## INITIATING A FAMILY LIFE CYCLE EMPHASIS

If you want to move toward a life cycle approach, before you do anything else—including the important task of recruiting lay help—you will need to understand your church's demographics. You or someone who knows your church membership should assign all families by life cycle stage. With this in mind you can designate appropriate resources to the dominant groupings. Initially you won't need a detailed plan for every FLC stage. Start where your group needs help most. (You may want to conduct a Family Needs Survey to gain a precise view of demographics and needs. See the end of this chapter for further information.)

Once you have identified the life cycle concentrations that need the most attention, you can begin creating plans to address needs. The following chapters discuss how to do this in greater detail, but in a nutshell you must consider your goals for both children and parents in each life cycle stage and then decide how to implement your strategy through large groups, small groups, Sunday school classes, family units, and mentoring teams.

This takes some thought and planning, but the process should bring considerable clarity and purpose to your ministry efforts. For example, if your church has a large number of younger families, then a larger portion of your teaching and mentoring should emphasize the basics of good parenting, how to grow as a parent, and so forth. You may choose to provide resources for and training to parents for family worship at home that will support the biblical education the younger children are receiving as part of the Sunday school curriculum. Mentors will give more attention to marriage and parenting issues that tend to dominate during this life cycle stage.

Pastor Jeong Nam Lee, pastor of the Lynchburg Baptist Church, Forest, Virginia, says that in his church he introduces the mentoring system to new couples when they begin attending. "They really enjoy this program with their mentors who are mature couples."[1]

As already suggested, a significant key to a fully effective FLC approach is a committed cadre of lay volunteers. Marriages and families cannot thrive on just good preaching and classroom instruction—as valuable as both are. People are hungry to interact with real people who are walking with God and who can show them the way through the maze of life.

Jerry Daley, a pastor in Chapel Hill, North Carolina, comments, "There is a difference between teaching and training. People don't need someone telling them they ought to do something. They need somebody to walk along beside them and do it with them."[2]

In many churches a number of people are not involved in any kind of ministry, and they need to be challenged. "Empty nesters" especially have so much to offer younger generations. Many young couples are hooked on materialism and, as a result, they are losing their marriages and families to financial debt. Many of them have not had the benefit of mature adults warning them, pointing the way, and clearly articulating biblical values in contrast with worldly values.

Many churches need to encourage laypeople to use their gifts, talents, and energy for the Lord. Obviously not all are qualified to do so, but many could rise to the challenge of a mentoring ministry. Think for a moment of the number of laypeople in your church who have been through Bible Study Fellowship, Kay Arthur's Precept Ministries, or other excellent Bible study training. Or what about those who listen and learn regularly from radio programs such as "Back to the Bible," "Grace to You," "Insight for Living," or "Renewing Your Mind"?

In recruiting helpers begin with prayer, just as Jesus did before He selected His disciples.

The start-up need not be complicated. Tom Clark, a pastor in Lincoln Park, New Jersey, tells how mentoring started in his congregation. "One couple had the vision, acquired training materials, recruited potential mentoring couples, took them through the training, then linked them with mentoree couples."[3] Initially this may seem like more work for you as a leader, but if the right people step forward this can eventually lighten your load in some areas of marriage and family ministry.

You may experience some resistance—as is true with almost anything new. The following are objections often voiced when couples are challenged to become mentors.

- "We have not done well as a married couple and therefore we have nothing to share." However, their failures may provide some of the greatest lessons to pass on to succeeding generations.
- "We don't feel equipped." If this is true, then teach (or find someone

to teach) a class of several sessions in which you give them the confidence they need to step into this ministry.

- "We don't have time." True, some people are overcommitted already, but others may need to spend some time in prayer, grappling with their priorities. Retirement may mean a person steps out of his job; but it doesn't mean that his life is now completely his own, to do with it as he pleases.

Obstacles like these can be overcome without your having to be the solution at every turn.

Perhaps the best time to plant the idea of becoming a mentor is at the beginning of the FLC process; encourage couples then to plan to become mentors by the time they are in Full Nest 3. If these parents are deeply involved in the final training of their own teenagers, they are perfect candidates to consider training other parents, now that they are just a few years away from having an empty nest.

If you don't have enough mentors at the beginning, at least provide mentor-type situations. Perhaps schedule a "mentor panel," in which mature couples in your congregation can answer questions asked by others.

Keep the Family Life Cycle always in front of your congregation. It should be explained frequently in the pulpit, in Sunday school, and throughout the life of your church. The better the concept is understood by individuals, the more they will gain from the teaching and activities meant to support the growth and development of families.

## ORGANIZATION OF CHAPTERS 10–16

Each of the following seven chapters explains one of the stages in the Family Life Cycle and offers practical suggestions that may spur further ideas of your own. Each of the chapters includes these elements: Goals and strategies for married couples, goals and strategies for parents, goals and strategies for children, ideas for mentors, a family life cycle checklist, and resources.

## THE FAMILY-NEEDS SURVEY

*Marriage Issues: Percentage of Christian Adults Who Said They Want Help*

| | |
|---|---|
| Developing and maintaining good communication | 41% |
| Understanding your spouse's needs/expectations | 38% |
| Building a strong marriage | 34% |
| Rekindling and maintaining romance | 31% |
| Understanding biblical roles and responsibilities for a husband/wife | 25% |
| Developing and maintaining sexual intimacy in marriage | 20% |
| Understanding different personality types | 18% |
| Relating to in-laws | 10% |
| Dating and preparing for marriage | 9% |
| Living in an interfaith marriage | 5% |

*Source: The Family -Needs Survey, FamilyLife, Overall breakdowns, Parenting Issues, National Database, March 2000, 8.*

*Parenting Issues: Percentage of Christian Adults Who Said They Want Help*

| | |
|---|---|
| Helping a child grow spiritually | 41% |
| Establishing and teaching Christian values in the home | 34% |
| Developing a child's character, identity, and morality | 32% |
| Developing and improving family communication | 32% |
| Developing and sharpening parenting skills | 29% |
| Disciplining a child | 22% |
| Releasing and moving a child toward adult independence | 21% |

*Source: The Family -Needs Survey, FamilyLife, Overall breakdowns, Parenting Issues, National Database, March 2000, 9.*

## RESOURCES

*For Pastors or Mentors*

FamilyLife, "The Family-Needs Survey." For information on obtaining this research tool for the local church, call FamilyLife at 1-800-FL-TODAY (1-800-358-6329) and ask for the Church Strategy division.

Freudenburg, Ben, with Rick Lawrence. *The Family Friendly Church.* Loveland, Colo.: Vital Ministry Group, 1998. An innovative look at making a local church ministry family focused. Contains extensive practical information and numerous anecdotes.

Rainey, Dennis. *One Home at a Time.* Wheaton, Ill.: Tyndale House Publishers, 1999. Explains the four foundations of a "family reformation." Includes an introduction to the Family Life Cycle and discusses ideas for restoring family vitality.

# PART

# 2

## THE FAMILY LIFE CYCLE

# CHAPTER

## 10

### Preparing for a Lasting Marriage
### Family Life Cycle 1—Premarried

This *first stage of the Family Life Cycle, although it actually begins at birth, intensifies in the later teenage years and reaches its crescendo during the engagement period before marriage.*

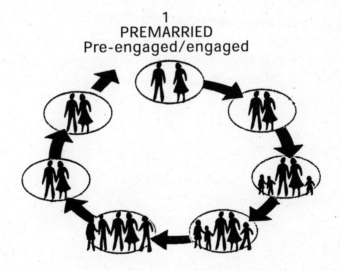

1
PREMARRIED
Pre-engaged/engaged

The premarried life cycle stage, more so than any of the other stages, requires both a long-term and a short-term approach in a church's ministry to families. The short-term involves the necessary and intense premarital preparation for the bride and groom during their engagement. But perhaps even more important is the long-term instruction on marriage that begins at home when parents give birth to a child.

Parents need to be helped in preparing their children for marriage and for establishing godly homes of their own. Couples beginning the family phase of their marriage need to be aware that for the rest of their lives they will be showing their sons and daughters a living picture of Christian marriage.

In many marriages the right attitudes and behaviors are not modeled. As a result churches need to be both proactive and reactive in this area. Proactively they need to encourage parents to teach the meaning of covenant marriage, and reactively, churches need to fill in the blanks if children are not getting adequate marriage instruction at home. The church's marriage and family ministry should occur regularly in Sunday school and youth groups all the way through the college-age years and with singles. It should permeate every stage of church ministry to every age.

And churches that have Christian schools should include in the junior high and high school curriculum the biblical basics of healthy, biblical, God-honoring marital and family relationships. A course on "Christian Marriage and Family" should be required in every Christian school across the nation, and Christian colleges and universities should develop similar courses as part of their core curricula.

## GOALS AND STRATEGIES FOR MARRIED COUPLES

Much of the emphasis for adults during FLC 1 will be on getting them ready for a strong marriage.

### Premarital Preparation

A pastor and his staff and/or elder board need to determine the basic requirements expected of all engaged couples who want to get married in the church.

For example, if the couple does not attend the required number of sessions with the pastor or a mentor couple, they should not be allowed to marry.

As part of premarital counseling, I suggest informing a couple that for the first two years of their marriage, at regular intervals—three months, six months, twelve months, and two years—the pastor or a mentoring couple will conduct a brief, friendly "marital checkup" with them. If this is communicated to the couple before the wedding, they will seldom balk at it later. The knowledge that someone will be checking up on them will help strengthen their marriage. Jeong Nam Lee says that in his church he or a mentor meets with each newlywed couple within three months after their marriage.[1]

Consider initiating or cooperating with a community marriage policy (see chapter 3 for more details). Be a leader in your community in setting minimum standards for what couples must do to be married in your church. The link between such a policy and decreasing community divorce rates is well established.[2]

In addition I suggest you never marry a couple who want to sign a prenuptial agreement (unless the agreement is to enter into a marriage covenant with a binding arbitration clause that gives the church sole jurisdiction to resolve any and all marriage and family disputes that might arise in the couple's marriage and family). At FamilyLife we have created such a covenant. We are calling it the Marriage Covenant with Binding Arbitration Clause (MCBAC). We are beginning to partner with ministries and churches around the country to seek a broad, grass-roots implementation of such a prenuptial agreement in churches.

We at FamilyLife are convinced that a community marriage policy and the MCBAC are strategic keys to reversing the devastation of divorce in the church. How else will we be able to reduce the shameful statistic reported by George Barna late in 1999 that born-again Christians were slightly more likely to divorce than non-Christians?[3]

### Topics for Premarital Counseling

What should a church include in its premarriage counseling and preparation package? A number of issues can be covered by a pastor alone or in

## QUESTIONS FOR AN ENGAGED COUPLE

Tom Elliff, pastor of a large church in Oklahoma, uses a list of criteria to evaluate the advisability of marrying any couple. We recorded these during a radio interview, so Pastor Elliff is quoted verbatim:

1. Both individuals must know Christ and be walking in a dynamic relationship with Him. (This also means they will be in church together following their marriage.)
2. Both individuals must be scripturally free to marry.
3. Both must have parental blessing and encouragement in this relationship and the timing of the marriage. (We have a meeting with the parents. . . . Twice I've refused to marry the children of deacons in our church because one of the four parents had reservations. The wisdom of that decision was vindicated in both instances.)
4. The groom must be vocationally focused. I do not perform a marriage if the wife must work outside the home. (I am challenged most on this point before marriage. . . . but [I am] thanked most for it afterwards. The evidence is overwhelming in support of this position.)
5. The couple must be bringing out the best in each other. [There must be] no moral or ethical compromise.[6]

Many readers may not agree with Tom's standard. I cannot embrace it fully myself. However, the reason I've included it here and featured Tom on our "FamilyLife Today" radio program is that I believe Christian leaders need to rethink the counsel they are giving young couples as they start their marriages. With the divorce rate soaring among Christians, I believe it's time we call on young couples to make value-based decisions in favor of their marriage and family, not against it. I fear that many times we get so caught up in critiquing another leader's "position" that we miss the point.

conjunction with mentors. A team of men and women at FamilyLife along with a number of churches spent five years developing and field-testing a curriculum for a couple getting married. They found that at least the following topics need to be covered:

- The meaning of marriage—this is God's idea (biblical foundations)
- God's plan for marriage—receive your mate, leave your parents, cleave to your mate (biblical foundations)
- Expectations in marriage
- Intimacy/communication—listening, expression, resolving conflicts
- Roles and responsibilities in marriage
- Money
- Intimacy/sex

For more of these ideas see David Boehi, Brent Nelson, Jeff Schulte, and Lloyd Shadrack, *Preparing for Marriage* (Ventura, Calif.: Gospel Light, 1997).

### The Marriage Covenant and Wedding Vows

It is the church's responsibility to be the guardian and protector of the marriage covenant before and after a couple's wedding. One of the best ways for a bride and groom to honor their commitment to each other is through their signing a written agreement at the marriage ceremony. When their vows are put in writing and signed, they can be displayed in the new couple's home as a reminder of what was promised. (Appendix B includes two sample marriage covenants. Also a printed covenant document is available from FamilyLife. Call 1-800-358-6329 or visit www.familylife.com for details.)

Each church should have minimum requirements for what wording should be included in wedding vows. A mushy love poem should not be substituted for traditional covenant promises used in the church for centuries. A couple should be fully aware of and committed to what each one is promising to the other.

## GOALS AND STRATEGIES FOR PARENTS

Family-centered, church-supported ministries are emerging in churches all across the country. Pastors are realizing the need to help parents teach youth about responsible relationships, moral purity, and how marriage and family work. A little encouragement from pastors can go a long way in helping parents assume their role of shaping their children's perspective on relationships, marriage, and family.

In FLC 1, long before a couple receives formal premarital instruction in the church, parents need to begin equipping their children—through some formal teaching but mainly by modeling—with the following life skills, which will someday bear great fruit in a marriage.

- Relational skills, including how to resolve conflicts
- The process of determining God's will for choosing a life partner
- What to look for in a spouse—character qualities, spiritual prerequisites, emotional balance, and others
- How to handle money
- The fact that marriage is intended by God to be a lifetime commitment

Although this is just a partial list, children who are taught in areas like these will be better prepared for a meaningful marriage.

## GOALS AND STRATEGIES FOR CHILDREN

The best age at which to begin formal instruction in the church on relationships and marriage is eleven or twelve. How much truth you can drive into the heart of a young person differs according to the person's level of maturity, but teaching moral purity, commitment, boundaries in relationships, and how the sexes are to relate should begin in the sixth grade.

My eleven years of teaching a sixth-grade Sunday school class taught me one unforgettable lesson: We are not adequately challenging preteen and early teens with biblical teaching and standards related to their moral, spiritual, and relational responsibilities.

As children move into their high school years, the instruction needs to be more specific. It should include issues like marriage commitment, conflict resolution, how the sexes relate, why men and women think differently, biblical roles of husbands and wives, and others. They should also receive instruction on dads' and moms' responsibilities for the spiritual nurturing of their children.

Children must be told why marriage must be for life and why God hates divorce. They need to understand biblical concepts about marriage, including the fact that marriage is a covenant. And they also need to see their church leaders living out godly marriages.

To help facilitate instruction on marriage and family:

- Include special relationship-marriage-family emphases in your Sunday school curriculum—starting in the elementary age-groups.
- Consider giving your youth ministry a double focus—one on youth and the other on the parents so that dads and moms feel responsible to teach their teens about these issues. One of the benefits of such an emphasis is that the parent-couples who are walking with the Lord can minister not only to young people from dedicated homes but also to youth whose parents are absent, divorced, estranged, dysfunctional, or otherwise ineffective.
- In junior high and high school Sunday school and youth functions, give marriage-related instruction. (See chapters 13 and 14 for more on this topic.)

## IDEAS FOR MENTORS

A mentoring relationship is best established before marriage when the engaged couple's eagerness to learn is at its peak. A husband and wife are never as motivated to cooperate with the "powers that be" as they are before their wedding.

Lon Garber, a pastor in Longwood, Florida, notes, "At our church we have a premarried class that lasts twelve weeks (thirty class hours, with sixty homework hours) that is required for any couple wanting to be married by one of our pastors. During that course each couple has a mentor couple that has been married for at least ten years and has a healthy growing relationship. This program is directed by two lay couples. Often these mentor relationships continue after the course is finished."[4]

One of the more important goals for these mentors is to establish a good, open relationship with the couple. This will prepare the way later for giving assistance when tensions and questions surface. Mentors assisting with this stage of the Family Life Cycle need to be available to track with a couple for the first twenty-four months of their marriage.

Mentors need to be involved in establishing biblical marital expectations up front with the couple they are mentoring. Mentors should frequently be asking, "Have you thought about . . . ?" Such questions will help the young couple anticipate many bumps in the road.

Here are some sample questions.

- How will you handle family finances?
- Do either or both of you know how to establish and live by a budget?
- How many children do you want to have?
- When do you want to start a family?
- What expectations do each of you have regarding sex in marriage?
- What does the wife want most from marriage?
- What does the husband want most from marriage?
- What does God want most from the husband in marriage?
- What does God want most from the wife in marriage?
- What will you do when you have your first disagreement?
- When do you need to ask for forgiveness?
- Why do you need to ask for forgiveness?
- How do you ask for forgiveness?

*Starting Your Marriage Right,* written by my wife, Barbara, and me, discusses these and other topics of marriage in a way that makes it easy for mentors to talk about them with a couple. Application exercises are included in the book.

At Jacksonville Chapel, in Lincoln Park, New Jersey, lay leader Jack Parzek reports, "A very important goal of mentoring . . . is to prevent bad marriages from taking place, or delaying marriages in which the parties are not yet ready to be married. It is hoped that the mentoring of seriously dating and engaged couples will at times lead a couple to realize that they are getting married for the wrong reasons or are ill-prepared for it, and postpone or call off their plans. As hard as that may be, it is far better than the possible alternative of a later divorce."[5]

Prayer cannot be emphasized enough. With their vast reservoir of knowledge and experience, mentoring couples know what to pray for and how to pray (or at least they should). With hindsight they know what they wish they had known before they were married. Thus they can prayerfully plan how to discuss such issues with the couple they are mentoring. Regular prayer for the protégé couple is critical at every stage of FLC 1.

## THE FAMILY-NEEDS SURVEY

### Premarried

*The FamilyLife's Family-Needs Survey can bring clarity in determining the needs of couples. Here are the percentages of premarried respondents who said they want help from the church with the following needs.*

| | |
|---|---|
| Spiritual growth | 70% |
| Spiritual disciplines | 62% |
| Dating and marriage preparation | 52% |
| Managing my time | 42% |
| Having a ministry | 39% |
| Managing finances/money | 37% |
| Healthy living and eating habits | 36% |
| Establishing adult friendships | 33% |
| Good communication in marriage | 28% |
| Understanding different personalities | 27% |

*Source: The Family-Needs Survey, FamilyLife, Breakdowns by Family Life Cycle, National Database, March 2000, 89.*

## FAMILY LIFE CYCLE CHECKLIST

*Premarried*

**Key Ministry Objectives for Leaders**

*Topics/Issues:*
- ❑ God's plan for marriage
- ❑ High expectations for marriage
- ❑ Marriage covenant
- ❑ The Christian family
- ❑ Biblical roles for men and women
- ❑ Finances (expectations)
- ❑ Developing spiritual oneness
- ❑ Dealing with the past
- ❑ Communication
- ❑ Physical oneness

*Actions/Activities:*
- ❑ Promote community marriage policy
- ❑ Relationships and marriage preparation, beginning in middle school
- ❑ Marriage covenant instruction, beginning with young teens
- ❑ Premarital counseling with a mentor couple
- ❑ Covenant marriage ceremonies (possible marriage covenant renewal service)

*Mentor Focus:*
- ❑ Place engaged couples with mentors
- ❑ Define mentor and protégé expectations

## RESOURCES

*For Pastors or Mentors*

Boehi, David, Brent Nelson, Jeff Schulte, and Lloyd Shadrach. *Preparing for Marriage*. Ventura, Calif.: Gospel Light, 1997. Includes a dynamic program designed to help lay a good foundation for biblical marriage. Six romantic sessions and five projects can be done alone or under the guidance of a mentor.

Hergenberger, Gordon Paul. *Marriage as a Covenant*. Grand Rapids: Baker Book House, 1998. Argues convincingly for interpreting the covenant of Malachi 2:14 as a marriage covenant.

*For Individuals or Couples*

Allender, Dan, and Tremper Longman, III. *Intimate Allies*. Wheaton, Ill.: Tyndale House Publishers, 1995. Discusses God's design for marriage and offers solid counsel on leadership, submission, conflict, disappointments, and sexuality.

Elliot, Elisabeth. *Passion and Purity*. Grand Rapids: Fleming H. Revell Co., 1984. Wisdom on bringing one's love life under Christ's authority. Discusses singleness and marriage, virginity and chastity, and roles of men and women.

"FamilyLife Marriage Covenant." Printed, framable document. Little Rock: FamilyLife, 1999. Attractive full-size covenant for couple to sign, frame, and display. Available at 1-800-358-6329 or www.familylife.com.

Harris, Joshua. *I Kissed Dating Good-bye*. Sisters, Oreg.: Multnomah Press 1997. Offers an alternative to dating, and reveals how young adults can live a lifestyle of sincere love, purity, and purposeful singleness.

Holzman, John. *Dating with Integrity*. Nashville: Word Publishing, 1992. Following the Bible's plan so that God is glorified and the opposite sex is respected. For single adults of any age.

Mack, Wayne A., and Nathan A. Mack. *Preparing for Marriage God's Way.* Tulsa, Okla.: Hensley Publishing, 1995. Discusses roles in marriage, communication, finances, sex, and education of children.

Mason, Mike. *The Mystery of Marriage.* Sisters, Oreg.: Multnomah Publishers, 1985. Beautifully written classic that celebrates the wonder of marriage.

Rainey, Dennis. "Are You Ready? Becoming Mr. or Mrs. Right." Audiotape series. Little Rock: FamilyLife, 1998. Ten messages on God's purpose for marriage, mirroring God's image in marriage, complementing one another, and raising a godly family.

————. "Becoming One: God's Purpose for Marriage." Audiotape series. Little Rock: FamilyLife, 1996. How to match pieces of the pattern together to have the marriage that God intends.

————. "More Than a Wedding." Audiotape series. Little Rock: FamilyLife, 1997. Includes topics like "The Value of Premarital Counseling," "Goals for the Engagement Period," "Purpose for Getting Married," and "Meaning of Leave-Cleave."

### Sexual Intimacy

Cutrer, William, and Sandra Glahn. *Sexual Intimacy in Marriage.* Grand Rapids: Kregel Publications, 1998. Medically and spiritually competent answers to questions many couples would like to ask but don't.

Nelson, Tommy. "The Song of Solomon." Audiotape series. Dallas: Hudson Productions, 1995. God's ultimate guide to a romantic relationship with one's spouse.

Rainey, Dennis. "My Lover My Friend." Audiotape series. Little Rock: FamilyLife, 1997. A paragraph-by-paragraph look at the Song of Solomon. Includes eight cassettes and two project guides.

Wheat, Ed. *Before the Wedding Night.* Springdale, Ark.: Scriptural Counsel, 1982. Two cassettes with medical, emotional, and spiritual counsel to brides and grooms.

————, and Gaye Wheat. *Intended for Pleasure.* Grand Rapids: Fleming H. Revell, 1997. Standard reference on every aspect of sex in marriage from the biblical perspective.

# CHAPTER

## 11

### Honeymoon's Over
### Family Life Cycle 2—Newly Married

The second stage begins at the wedding and generally includes the first three to five years of marriage.

The newly married phase of the Family Life Cycle (FLC) is strategic in the life of a family and in the life of the church. The habits and disciplines formed in these early years will determine what the marriage will become. Patterns of communicating, dealing with conflict, and handling money are all hammered out during this critical period.

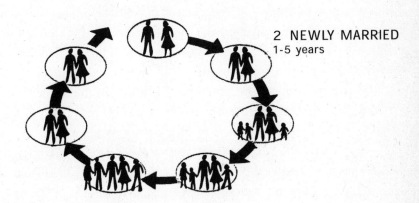

2 NEWLY MARRIED
1-5 years

A report released in 2000 from a long-term study of married couples documents the critical nature of the beginning stage of a marriage. Ted Huston, professor of human ecology and psychology at the University of Texas, stated, "The first two years are key—that's when the risk of divorce is particularly high. And the changes that take place during this time tell us a lot about where the marriage is headed."[1]

The beginning of a marriage represents one of the most teachable moments in couples' lives. Spiritually couples may never be as open as they are in marriage preparation and in the first years of their marriage. But if they don't find solutions, their hearts may harden. Choices these couples make can send them off in the wrong direction.

Newly married couples may need more attention than engaged couples. Why? Because the divorce rate starts high in year one, climbs through years two and three, and doesn't start to dip until year four.

Many churches do not have a specific plan for addressing the needs of these newly married couples. This is where the FLC and the expectations that flow from it can help. It can provide benchmarks and critical reminders for married couples during this phase of adjustment.

## GOALS AND STRATEGIES FOR MARRIED COUPLES

The focus during FLC 2 must be on the men. FamilyLife asked pastors what one problem in ministering to couples and families they would like to solve. Here's the reply of John Morrison of Fellowship Bible Church in Winchester, Virginia: "Giving men a clear foundation of (a) life as a disciple, (b) life as a man, (c) life as a husband, and (d) life as a dad through repeated instruction [and] example."[2]

Before a child enters the family and consumes so much energy and time, a newly married couple provides an opportunity for men to learn how to become spiritual leaders in their homes. When a husband and wife clash over unmet expectations, serious threats to the marriage can arise. Thus men need to be held accountable for growth in Christlike communication during this critical phase of marriage.

Men at this stage are prone to devote much of their time and attention to their jobs. All too often this results from the example set for them by their own fathers, which may be followed consciously or unconsciously. This may send the husband and wife in separate directions and can be a great threat.

Husbands need to understand what is involved spiritually in loving, leading, and serving an emerging family. Most men are not trained in family responsibilities and thus feel insecure in leading a family.

With women the role of a wife should be exalted and explained as a way of life. Talk about the value that wives have in the lives of their husbands. Most young wives will appreciate this focus and training. Like husbands, they need to be equipped in how to be a godly spouse.

## Needs of Newlyweds

Here are six areas where newlyweds need help.

1. *Their walk with God.* A young husband and wife first need to be grounded spiritually. Does each individual have a basic understanding of how to have a vibrant relationship with Christ? Do they know how to pray and study the Bible? Beyond their own personal relationship with God, do they pray together as a couple, and do they have some kind of joint devotional life? One of the most fascinating responses from the Family Needs surveys we have taken is that this issue is the number-one need being expressed by couples today—help in how to grow together spiritually.

2. *An outside relationship.* Newlyweds need ongoing contact with persons outside their marriage. This can help them realize that what they are experiencing in adjusting to married life is normal. Mentors and small-group relationships can help newlyweds realize that they are not the only ones in the world who are experiencing these struggles.

3. *Instruction.* Although it's a great start, sharing one's struggles with another person is not enough. A husband and wife can benefit from a mentor couple instructing them biblically in the right ways to do things.

4. *Accountability.* Someone in the life of every newly married person should be asking them some hard questions. Are you resolving your conflicts? Are you praying together? How are you handling your money? Topics like these need attention in a direct but concerned fashion. A mentoring couple can probably do this best, but even a small class of several couples led by an older couple could accomplish this.

5. *Communication skills.* This involves learning how differences in men and women create communication challenges, and how to resolve conflicts.

6. *Assistance with in-laws.* Often a new husband or wife or both face problems with their in-laws. In-laws may not be letting their "child" go, they may be hostile to their child's mate, or they may be manipulative or demanding.

## Implementation Strategies for Couples

Here are some thoughts on how to influence young couples during the newly married phase of the FLC.

- Once a year in a Sunday school class for young couples spend six weeks on a marital topic.
- Encourage couples to sign a "title deed" in which they give all their hopes, dreams, and assets to the Lord. My wife and I did this, and we put it with other valuable documents in a safety deposit box.
- Another benefit the church can offer new couples is a "marital health" checkup. As suggested earlier, this should occur three months, six months, twelve months, and two years after the wedding. The pastor who married the couple should inform the couple in premarital counseling that this is to be expected. If there are no mentors, then checkups should be done by the pastor or some other trusted, spiritually mature individual.

## Goals and Strategy for "Pre-Parents"

Churches need to emphasize the value of children—that children are a reward, a blessing, a legacy. For Christian parents, that ultimately means training children to fear God, obey Him, experience Him, walk with Him, and lead others to Him. This is the ultimate goal of parenting. And the parents need to lead Christ-honoring lives of purity and godliness that will set the example for the children born in their family.

Here are some practical tips for helping couples succeed in this phase of their lives.

- Before married couples have children, encourage them to maintain a daily walk of fellowship with Christ to keep the marriage strong.

- Talk about the importance of family values and develop a joint "mission statement" as a couple. Such a statement should include the character qualities and spiritual values they desire for their children. The mission statement should be written and prayed over regularly before the first child arrives.

Soon after we married, Barbara and I spent a couple of hours one spring afternoon, each of us writing out the values we wanted God to build into our children through us. I remember being so excited about my values and coming back and asking Barbara to share hers and being astounded that we had only one or two of the same values! We had to discuss and reach agreement—a great exercise that continues to influence our family to this day.

## IDEAS FOR MENTORS

Earlier in this chapter I cited some recent research on indicators in the early years of marriage that predict success or failure later on. Mentors need to know that this study found that "loss of initial levels of love and affection, rather than conflict, was the most salient predictor of distress and divorce. This loss sends a relationship into a downward spiral, leading to increased bickering and fighting, and to the collapse of the union. [According to researcher Ted Huston] 'This ought to change the way we think about the early roots of what goes wrong in a marriage. The dominant approach has been to work with couples to resolve conflict, but it should focus [instead] on preserving the positive feelings.' "[3]

These findings suggest that mentors need to try to pick up on the emotional mood of the new husband and wife and encourage them to guard their hearts against a critical spirit and negative speech toward their spouse.

- Encourage the young couple to schedule a date night each week. The couple need not go out and spend money. They can have a candlelight dinner at home. The focus should be on concentrated time alone with each other. If children have arrived and are past the stage where they can be taken out, then the mentor couple can offer to baby-sit once a month or even pay for a baby-sitter.

## THE FAMILY-NEEDS SURVEY

### *Newly Marrieds*

*These are the issues newly married respondents cited most often when asked on what issues they wanted help.*

| | |
|---|---|
| Spiritual growth | 76% |
| Spiritual disciplines | 69% |
| Building a strong marriage | 59% |
| Understanding your spouse's needs/expectations | 57% |
| Developing and maintaining good communication | 54% |
| Establishing adult friendships | 43% |
| Having a ministry | 41% |
| Biblical roles for husband/wife | 39% |
| Rekindling romance | 39% |
| Healthy living and eating habits | 37% |

*Source: The Family-Needs Survey, FamilyLife, Breakdowns by Family Life Cycle, National Database, March 2000, 89.*

- Mentoring couples should encourage their couples to attend marriage and/or parenting conferences or seminars, and should suggest helpful marriage and parenting resources.
- Encourage newly married couples to realize that they will face some surprises in their relationship. Perhaps a personality quirk will start to annoy, or something unpleasant from the spouse's past will be disclosed. Wise godly counsel from the mentoring couple can be helpful. But if the mentors feel inadequate in the situation—if there is severe depression or a deep emotional trauma—then they should

help the person find professional help. Mentors should also show their protégés how to use their failures, things they did wrong or things they wished they had done, as opportunities for growth.

- When the first child is on the way, mentors need to point out how a child in the family will change the marriage relationship. And after the child arrives, the mentors should review with the couple the issues of money, sex, and conflict.

- The mentor of the husband should ask tough questions (in love, of course) such as these: Are you loving your wife as Christ loved the church? Are you angry at her for any reason? Are there any sins she has committed against you that you haven't forgiven? Are you responding to her in anger or harshness? Have you hurt her in any way, either mentally, emotionally, or physically? How are you communicating with her? Are you taking time to talk with her, to listen to her (twice as much as you talk)? Have you yelled at her? How does she feel about your relationship? How do you feel about her?

- Mentors should also ask these questions of the young husband: How have your thoughts been lately? Have you been looking at anything on TV you shouldn't have been viewing? Have you seen movies that are unwholesome? How about the Internet or magazines? Mentors must never assume that their protégé is free from temptation.

- The mentor of the wife should ask tough questions as well: Have you been submitting to your husband as to the Lord? Are you loving him and respecting him? Are there any sins he has committed against you that you haven't forgiven? Is there any unresolved anger toward him? How is your sex life? Are you meeting his needs sexually? Is he angry at you right now for any reason? Is there any unresolved conflict in your marriage? How do you feel about your marriage? Has he done anything to hurt you? Has he yelled at you? Has he treated you in any way different from the way Christ would treat you? How is your communication with him?

- Help young marrieds understand the basics of conflict resolution. Peacemaker Ministries is an excellent resource of materials on conflict resolution.[4]

The Family Life Cycle 2 stage is a critical time for family ministry. As mentioned previously, the risk of divorce is greatest during this time period. This fact alone is sufficient to alert churches to focus attention on this stage of its couples' marriages.

## FAMILY LIFE CYCLE CHECKLIST

*Newly Married*

**Key Ministry Objectives for Leaders**

*Topics/Issues:*
- ❑ Spiritual leadership in the home
- ❑ Role of husband and father
- ❑ Role of wife and mother
- ❑ Value of children
- ❑ Marriage covenant
- ❑ Marriage and family expectations
- ❑ Spiritual values for the family
- ❑ Prayer as a couple
- ❑ Stewardship of finances and resources
- ❑ Career and family planning
- ❑ Communication and conflict resolution

*Actions/Activities:*
- ❑ Young married small group or Sunday school class
- ❑ Marital health checkups
- ❑ Preparenting instruction
- ❑ Marriage conference
- ❑ Resources on communication
- ❑ Marriage covenant renewal service

*Mentor Focus:*
- ❑ Discuss early marriage challenges (particularly communication and conflict resolution)
- ❑ Discuss issues related to having children

❑ Encourage accountability
❑ Emphasize openness and spiritual oneness
❑ Encourage attendance at a marriage conference
❑ Encourage financial accountability

## RESOURCES

*For Pastors and Mentors*

Piper, John, and Wayne Grudem, eds. *Recovering Biblical Manhood and Womanhood.* Wheaton, Ill.: Crossway Books, 1991. A reasoned, thorough response to feminist influences. All relevant Scripture passages on the topic are considered.

Rainey, Dennis, and Barbara Rainey. *Starting Your Marriage Right.* Nashville: Thomas Nelson Publishers, 2000. Covers a wide assortment of topics for newly married couples—communication, sex, money, in-laws, values, time pressures, expectations, and more.

*Small Groups*

HomeBuilders Couples Series. Loveland, Colo.: Group Publishing, 1999. Easy to lead, interactive series of studies on central marriage issues. Newly updated for the twenty-first century. Topics include:

Blue, Ron. "Mastering Money in Your Marriage." Put finances under God's control and manage money wisely.

Horner, Bob, and Jan Horner. "Resolving Conflict in Your Marriage." Learn to transform conflicts into opportunities to energize your marriage.

Lewis, Robert. "Building Teamwork in Your Marriage." Individual differences are gifts from God that help complement one's mate.

Rainey, Dennis. "Building Your Marriage." Discover and apply God's blueprints for a marriage lasting a lifetime.

_____. and Barbara Rainey. "Building Your Mate's Self-Esteem." Improve your marriage by learning how to encourage your mate.

Rosberg, Gary, and Barbara Rosberg. "Improving Communication in Your Marriage." Communicating clearly helps reduce and resolve conflict.

Sande, David. "Growing Together in Christ." An exciting relationship with Jesus leads to an exciting, growing marriage.

Coons, Drew, and Kit Coons. "HomeBuilders Leaders Guide." Instruction and tips for leading a small group effectively.

## For Individuals or Couples

Dobson, James C. *Love Must Be Tough: New Hope for Families in Crisis.* Nashville: Word Publishing, 1996. A most serious indicator of potential family breakup is disrespect. At the core of most marital conflicts lies a vicious kind of indifference that can sabotage a relationship.

Nelson, Tommy, and Dennis Rainey. *I Am My Beloved's.* Nashville: Thomas Nelson Publishers, 1998. Inspirational gift book based on the Song of Solomon. Celebrates God's plan for romance and intimacy in marriage.

## Roles in Marriage

Chappell, Bryan. *Each for the Other.* Grand Rapids: Baker Book House, 1998. Instructions on living sacrificially in marriage.

Lewis, Robert, and William Hendricks. *Rocking the Roles.* Colorado Springs: NavPress, 1999. Examines what the Bible says about male-female roles. Shows a perfect blend in marriage of structure and equality, balance and beauty.

## Communication

Chapman, Gary. *Five Love Languages.* Chicago: Northfield Publishing, 1996. Explains how people communicate love in different ways and the rewards in marriage of learning how to speak each other's language.

Rainey, Dennis, and Barbara Rainey. *Two Hearts Are Better Than One.* Nashville: J. Countryman, 1999. Gives a husband and a wife the opportunity to write and discuss answers to joint questions on memories, values, and goals.

Rosberg, Gary. *Dr. Rosberg's Do-It-Yourself Relationship Mender.* Wheaton, Ill.: Tyndale House Publishers, 1999. Tools from Scripture on how to enjoy forgiveness, heal hurts, improve communication, and increase intimacy.

## Walking with God

Kopp, David, and Heather Kopp. *Praying the Bible for Your Marriage.* Colorado Springs: WaterBrook Press, 1998. Helps overcome awkwardness of praying with a spouse. Bible-based prayers lead to deeper love relationship with God and spouse.

Rainey, Dennis, and Barbara Rainey. *Moments Together for Couples.* Ventura, Calif.: Regal Books, 1996. One-year devotional offers practical words for couples who want to keep their trust in the Lord and their commitment to each other a daily priority.

## Money

See the study guide "Mastering Money in Your Marriage," by Ron Blue, in the HomeBuilders Couples Series, listed earlier in this section under "Small Group" (p. 121). Talking about money in a small group is an excellent way to address the topic with young married couples.

Blue, Ron. *Taming the Money Monster.* Wheaton, Ill.: Tyndale House Publishers, 2000. Slipping into debt is easier than climbing out. Practical advice on how to get out of debt and stay out.

Burkett, Larry. *The Complete Financial Planning Guide for Young Couples.* Colorado Springs: ChariotVictor Publishing, 1990. Everything a couple should know and put into practice about dealing with their finances.

Crown Financial Ministries, P.O. Box 2377, Gainesville, GA 30503-2377. 1-800-722-1976 or www.cfcministry.org. An interdenominational ministry using an effective small-group study to help adults apply financial principles from God's Word. Designed for use in the local church.

## Developing Friendships, Mentoring

Otto, Donna. *Between Women of God.* Eugene, Oreg.: Harvest House Publishers, 1995. Keys to mentoring based on Titus 2. Includes insight on listening, availability, sharing perspective, and being a hero.

Rawlins, LeeAnn. *Loving for Life.* Sisters, Oreg.: Loyal Publishing, 1999. A mature woman trains younger women on womanhood.

Weber, Stu. *All the King's Men.* Sisters, Oreg.: Multnomah Publishers, 1998. Shatters the myth that strong men stand alone. Urges men to seek out brothers in Christ for direction and encouragement.

## For Men

Davis, Harold. *Talks My Father Never Had with Me.* Champaign, Ill.: KAJC Publishing, 1996. Solutions for young men, especially those who are African-American.

Lepine, Bob. *The Christian Husband.* Ann Arbor, Mich.: Vine Books, 1999. Helps men understand the meaning of being godly, the three roles of husbands, and how to love their wives.

Lewis, Robert. "Men's Fraternity. A Journey to Authentic Manhood." Audiotape series. Little Rock: Fellowship Bible Church Associates, 1997. Extensive, compelling look at major issues men face. Excellent discussion-starter for men's groups.

Loritts, Crawford. *Never Walk Away: Lessons on Integrity from a Father Who Lived It.* Chicago: Moody Press, 1997. Encourages men who did not grow up in a strong family to help turn the tide for God in coming generations.

Morley, Patrick. *Man in the Mirror.* Grand Rapids: Zondervan Publishing House, 2000. Invites men to take a probing look at their identities, relationships, finances, time, and temperament. How to seek and find godly manhood.

Schaumburg, Harry W. *False Intimacy.* Colorado Springs: NavPress, 1992. Offers hope to those suffering from sexual dysfunction. Explains causes of sexual addiction and how to recognize and pursue healing for sexually addictive behaviors.

Weber, Stu. *Tender Warrior.* Sisters, Oreg.: Multnomah Publishers, 1999. Provides the biblical blueprint for manhood. Explains how to balance roles of leader, protector, friend, and lover.

Welch, Bob. *A Father for All Seasons.* Eugene, Oreg.: Harvest House Publishers, 1998. Includes riveting, humorous stories on being a father.

Yates, John. *How a Man Prays for His Family.* Minneapolis: Bethany House Publishers, 1996. Tells how to pray effectively for one's wife and children.

*For Women*

Allender, Dan. *The Wounded Heart.* Colorado Springs: NavPress, 1990. A counselor discusses the process of healing from sexual abuse. For both victims and those who love them. Includes discussion ideas.

DeMoss, Nancy Leigh. "Biblical Portrait of Womanhood." Audiotape series. Buchanan, Mich.: Life Action Ministries, 1999. True liberation is based on accepting and following the standards of God's Word. Discusses God's design for women as responders and the wife's calling.

Heald, Cynthia. *Becoming a Woman of Excellence.* Colorado Springs: NavPress, 1986. The first of a series of Bible studies that examine spiritual issues from a woman's perspective.

_____. *Becoming a Woman of Freedom*. Colorado Springs: NavPress, 1992.

_____. *Becoming a Woman of Purpose*. Colorado Springs: NavPress, 1994.

_____. *Becoming a Woman of Prayer*. Colorado Springs: NavPress, 1996.

_____. *Becoming a Woman of Grace*. Colorado Springs: NavPress, 1998.

_____. *Becoming a Woman of Faith*. Colorado Springs: NavPress, 2000.

Hunt, Susan. *By Design: God's Distinctive Calling for Women*. Wheaton, Ill.: Crossway Books, 1994. Explains God's "helper design" for women and rallies the church to equip women to help a hurting world. Strongly affirms a woman's value.

Masse, Synda, and Joan Phillips. *Her Choice to Heal*. Colorado Springs: ChariotVictor Publishing, 1998. These abortion survivors and postabortion counselors examine the effects of abortion and reveal the path to emotional healing.

Omartian, Stormie. *Power of a Praying Wife*. Eugene, Oreg.: Harvest House Publishers, 1997. Shows a wife how to focus in prayer on every aspect of her husband's life.

Peace, Martha. *The Excellent Wife: A Biblical Perspective*. Bemidji, Minn.: Focus Publishing, 1997. Former feminist and marriage counselor carefully presents the case for the biblical model of marriage.

Rivers, Francine. *Atonement Child*. Wheaton, Ill.: Tyndale House Publishers, 1999. The story of a young woman struggling with issues related to an unwanted pregnancy.

Weber, Linda. *Woman of Splendor: The Four Facets of a Godly Woman*. Nashville: Broadman & Holman Publishers, 1999. Presents femininity as a four-faceted jewel—helpmate, nurturer, relater, and designer, which complement the king, warrior, mentor, and friend roles of a man.

# CHAPTER

## 12

## Sleepless in Suburbia
## Family Life Cycle 3—Full Nest 1

*F*amily Life Cycle 3 begins when children are born and lasts until they are *about age five.*

The primary goal in this stage of the Family Life Cycle is to help each young couple make the transition from twosome to threesome. Just as the newlywed stage is particularly critical to getting the marriage off to a strong beginning, so Full Nest 1 is crucial in establishing healthy parenting patterns.

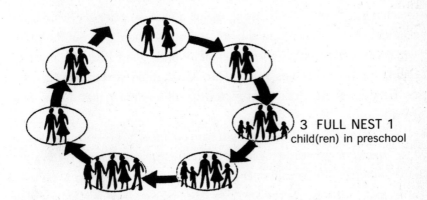

3 FULL NEST 1
child(ren) in preschool

Before continuing this section I want to comment briefly on childless couples. I am sympathetic to the pain that infertility can bring into a marriage. Churches should not forget to acknowledge couples and families that do not fit the "norm." Using the FLC approach, the main focus will always be on families with children, but with a little effort, churches can also focus on other types of families.[1]

Many young men and women who are starting their families are ill-prepared for parenting because of divorce or poor role models in the families in which they grew up. As a result many of these young men and women become parents with little or no idea of what their new job requires. A couple's oneness will be uniquely tested by the demands of raising children. If a couple is not "one" before they begin having children, they shouldn't expect a child to draw them closer together. The opposite is more likely—the weaknesses of the relationship will be revealed by the parenting process. Full Nest 1 is therefore a critical and opportune stage for effective ministry to these families.

## GOALS AND STRATEGIES FOR MARRIED COUPLES

Because of stresses that come from a child joining the family, many marriages do not prosper in this time period. After the first child arrives, the husband may feel like he has been abandoned. His wife, who is still recovering physically and emotionally from childbirth, is now a mother, so her attachment to her child is strong. Being a wife is no longer her central relational focus. This means she has less time to share with her husband, which can lead to jealousy and hurt on his part. These issues are normal, but with proper coaching and patience they can be worked out.

Here are some ideas on how to help solidify marriages during Full Nest 1.

- Create opportunities—even if for just a few hours—for couples to spend quality time together. Recruit experienced mothers in your congregation to volunteer an evening of baby care for couples with infants. Young mothers will be more relaxed leaving a baby with a more mature woman. Encourage these couples to use getaways as dates, a time for the couple to enjoy romance and communication.

- Encourage new parents to take part in small groups They need to relate to other couples facing the same issues.
- Establish men's groups that cover key issues, and arrange for a one-on-one accountability component. In these groups men can share helpful tips and suggestions on how to love their wives and children, how to provide self-sacrificial service to their family, and how to avoid common pitfalls during this stage of life. They can ask each other some of the tough questions mentioned in the mentor sections of both this and the previous chapter. Such groups also provide a context in which men can pray for each other.

## GOALS AND STRATEGIES FOR PARENTS

During FLC 3 the church has two responsibilities to these new parents. One is to commission them in their new role, that is, dedicating their babies but also heightening their awareness of their responsibility to raise their children to love the Lord and to obey His commands. Another church responsibility is to provide instruction on child rearing in a class and in informal mentoring.

*Four Goals of Parenting*

The Scriptures set forth four broad requirements or goals for Christian parenting.

1. *Identity.* Children need to learn throughout life that they are created in the image of God and have great value and worth as people. At the appropriate time children need to be invited to confess that they are sinners and need to receive Jesus Christ as their Savior. A rewarding life requires obedience to God.
2. *Relationships.* Children need to learn how to love others in the home. Parents need to train their children to love the Lord and others.
3. *Character formation.* This involves giving children boundaries, discipline, penalties, correction, forgiveness, and encouragement—all in an effort to help them develop Christlikeness.
4. *Spiritual mission.* Children need to be taught that they have a divine

calling and mission from heaven, a responsibility to share the gospel with others. And they need to be trained in how to present the plan of salvation to the unsaved.

All four of these purposes of parenting will become foundation stones not just for the child's life but ultimately for his or her own Christian marriage and family. In our surveys over the past fifteen years, families repeatedly said they want help in passing on Christian values to their children.

## Family Nights

One of the most important traditions we need to establish in homes today is Family Night. Focus on the Family has the finest material available. (See recommended resources at the end of this chapter.)

## Discipline

Second Timothy 3:16–17 gives an outline for a godly approach to discipline, four aspects that apply to disciplining children, regardless of their age. (1) Teaching. From the very beginning a child needs to learn right and wrong, obedience, and respect for authority. (2) Reproof. This is the process of pointing out what is wrong with a particular behavior. (3) Correction. This is bringing the child back to the right way. (4) Training in righteousness. This includes ongoing coaching, positive reenforcement, and day-to-day encouragement that every person needs.

Spanking is a controversial topic, but since the Bible instructs parents to use physical punishment appropriately as a part of discipline, the church needs to instruct parents in how to use this as a way of correcting their children. Much of our society wants to take spanking away from Christian parents. But the church can help expose the cultural lie that we shouldn't spank our children. Any teaching on this topic will need to include instruction on how to use spanking appropriately. My wife says spanking is "a measured amount of pain for a given act of disobedience or defiant act of the will." The next generation of parents needs this instruction.

At this stage of the parenting journey, most moms and dads will be eager to receive instruction. Here are some suggested areas for training.

- Suggest resources, seminars, conferences, and other avenues for learning how to be an effective parent.
- Consider having a parent-training weekend seminar.
- Schedule panel discussions or seminars (perhaps during the Sunday school hour) with older moms and dads to answer questions of young parents on a variety of topics—children's eating habits and sleep patterns, nursing, dealing with sickness, parent fatigue, teething, toilet training, discipline, and so forth.
- Encourage couples to consult older parents, those who have children a few years older than their own. Encourage younger parents to ask questions of the older parents about what has worked and has not worked in their parenting. What books or resources did they read? How was a schedule or routine developed for an infant? When was physical discipline initiated? How was potty training handled? What was the bedtime routine?
- Coach parents to establish discipline as early as possible. Help them realize that children need to learn through loving physical discipline properly placed (that is on the rear end).
- Hold seminars on child discipline. Discuss spanking and other forms of discipline so that young parents are not left wandering what the Bible says on this topic. Pop psychologists and talk-show hosts should not displace the Bible and the wisdom present in the body of Christ as the authority on child discipline.
- Instruct parents that when they sin against their children through anger or perhaps through an unjust punishment, they must repent, tell the child they were wrong, and ask forgiveness. They should always try to show the child in the Bible why they were wrong.
- Encourage men with young families to get together monthly (perhaps on a Saturday morning) and hold one another accountable in leading their families spiritually.
- Help couples have family worship, beginning even when their children are infants. Young children should grow up seeing and hearing their parents singing praises to God, reading Scripture,

talking about the things of God, playing the piano or guitar, listening to gospel music. By the time a child reaches age five, if family worship is done consistently and from the heart, it will be an unquestioned and accepted part of family life. Churches should encourage every one of their families with children to have family worship consistently.

- Don't ask too much of young parents, especially the moms. Lynne Richards, a pastor's wife, comments, "It was a great relief to me when God showed me life goes in seasons. Mothers with small children should not be expected to do as much or go as many places as those with no or older children."[2]

## GOALS AND STRATEGIES FOR CHILDREN

Again I urge every church not to view ministry to young children as "just baby-sitting." We need to follow Jesus' example in welcoming little children into our arms for comfort, security, and love. The following are some ways churches can nurture children during Full Nest 1.

- Consider developing a high-quality baby-sitter training center in your church for preteens and teenagers. As a part of the training, be sure these substitute caregivers are taught not only how to take care of children but also how to minister to them spiritually.
- Children should be exposed to the Word of God. Mothers should read the Word of God aloud. Audiotapes of gospel music can be played in the children's rooms as they lie down for naps and for sleep at night.
- Bible stories in age-appropriate books should be read regularly to young children. All such activities will plant spiritual seeds and will provide necessary stimulation for developing brains.
- Encourage parents to teach their children at an early age to learn how to take responsibility for their behavior, admit when they are wrong, ask forgiveness, and forgive by saying, "I forgive you."

## IDEAS FOR MENTORS

Mentors should be available to young parents to discuss topics such as dealing with expectations, shouldering the load together, sex, finances (especially for families in which the mother stays at home with the children, debt, refreshing one's relationship, and others).

Because child rearing is such an individual endeavor, I think mentoring of young parents needs to be one-on-one, as well as in small-group discussions or large-group meetings with a panel of mentors. Consider the following:

- Male mentors should pray regularly for their protégés, praying that God would develop spiritual maturity in the husbands, with attitudes of self-sacrifice and selflessness.
- Male mentors should ask questions that will elicit honest answers about how the husbands are feeling. Do they feel neglected? Are they bitter because they feel neglected? In what ways are they serving their wives during this time? What is most important to their wives? Sleep? Quality time with their husbands? Quality communication (that is, patient and compassionate listening)? What thoughts recur in the husbands' minds? Thoughts about self or thoughts about their most important "others" (wife and children)? Wise mentors can help husbands navigate through this difficult time in their lives by patiently and wisely listening to and counseling these young fathers.
- Female mentors too should maintain open lines of communication with their protégés. They should pray earnestly, ask questions pertinent to this stage of the FLC, and listen in love.
- Other questions to ask each spouse include these: Is he or she spending quality time with the children? How is family worship going (assuming the children are old enough)?
- Open dialogue about parental issues must exist in the context of a trust-based relationship between the mentor couple and the protégé couple.
- Mentors should help couples establish date nights. Offering to babysit can be a wonderful way to show the couple true love and commitment.

- Mentors should provide helpful suggestions related to marriage and parenting during this stage. For instance, mentors can remind their protégés to attend a marriage and parenting conference or seminar at least once or twice during this time period. Suggest a good book on the subject. Ideally the mentor couple will have read the book and will be able to explain how God used the books to teach them something that blessed them and their children.
- Mentors can help young families establish a family worship time in the home. Young couples can inquire as to how often family worship should be done (whether daily, every other day, weekly, etc.), and what to do in family worship (singing, sharing, Bible reading, catechism, review, acting out Bible stories, Bible memorization, discussion).

## SHARING THE GOSPEL—THE PARENT'S ROLE

Throughout church history believers have debated how old a child must be to receive Christ as Savior.[3] I appreciate what Charles Spurgeon said, "He who knowingly sins can savingly believe." Regardless of how young a child may be to be saved, parents are responsible to be the shepherds and guardians of their children and to be sure they understand God's plan of salvation.

Presenting the gospel to children begins by explaining that when they disobey or are defiant, or when they break any of God's laws, that is sin. This sinfulness is a part of their nature and is why they do wrong things.

## THE FAMILY-NEEDS SURVEY

*Full Nest 1*

*The following are the percentages of adults in this FLC stage wanting help with various needs.*

| | |
|---|---|
| Christian values in the home | 85% |
| Spiritual growth | 85% |
| Children's spiritual growth | 84% |
| Spiritual disciplines | 80% |
| Developing and sharpening parenting skills | 65% |
| Developing character/morality in children | 64% |
| Building a strong marriage | 57% |
| Developing and maintaining good communication | 57% |
| Understanding your spouse's needs/expectations | 56% |
| Disciplining a child | 55% |

*Source: The Family-Needs Survey, FamilyLife, Breakdowns by Family Life Cycle, National Database, March 2000, 89.*

---

## FAMILY LIFE CYCLE CHECKLIST

### Full Nest 1—Key Ministry Objectives for Leaders

*Topics/Issues:*

- ❑ Marriage and family expectations
- ❑ Transition to parenthood
- ❑ Sharing gospel with children (parents)
- ❑ Family worship
- ❑ Stewardship of finances and resources
- ❑ Romance and intimacy

*Actions/Activities:*

- ❏ Parenting training—overview
- ❏ Child discipline
- ❏ Parenting panel discussions
- ❏ Mini-getaways for couples with young children
- ❏ Couples' small groups
- ❏ Date night encouragement
- ❏ Men's groups—with accountability
- ❏ Marriage conference
- ❏ Parenting conference
- ❏ Marriage covenant renewal service

*Mentor Focus:*

- ❏ Help couples guard against isolation and help them move toward oneness as their careers and family demands grow
- ❏ Maintain and monitor accountability between mentors and protégés
- ❏ Encourage attendance at marriage and parenting conferences
- ❏ Encourage family worship

## RESOURCES

*For the Pastor or Mentor*

HomeBuilders Couples Series. Loveland, Colo.: Group Publishing, 2000. Easy-to-lead, interactive series of studies on marriage issues. Newly updated for the twenty-first century. (See details in the "Resources" section at the end of chapter 11, pages 121–22.)

*For the Individual or Couple*

Burkett, Larry. *Women Leaving the Workplace.* Chicago: Moody Press, 1995. Practical ideas for woman leaving the workplace to stay at home. Includes information on how to overcome traumas, fears, and financial issues, and how to start an in-home business.

Fanstone, Michael. *Unbelieving Husbands and the Wives Who Love Them.* Ann Arbor, Mich.: Vine Books, 1994. This pastor-author gives insights to women married to husbands who do not share their love for God. He offers ideas for empathy and strategy to help draw husbands to faith in Christ.

Hughes, Kent, with Dennis Rainey. "Spiritually Mismatched: Seeing Heart to Heart." Audiotape series. Little Rock: FamilyLife, 2000. Discusses multiple issues associated with relating to an unbelieving spouse. Includes five sessions.

Hunter, Brenda. *Home by Choice.* Sisters, Oreg.: Multnomah Publishers, 2000. Argues persuasively for stay-at-home moms. Backed by research showing that mothers give the best care to their children.

Rainey, Dennis, and Barbara Rainey. "Creating a More Romantic Marriage." Audiotape series. Little Rock: FamilyLife, 1995. Six sessions on recognizing and conquering the intimacy thieves in marriage and restoring passion.

Rosberg, Gary, and Barbara Rosberg. *The Five Love Needs of Men and Women.* Wheaton, Ill.: Tyndale House Publishers, 2000. Based on survey data that explodes some myths about couples' needs in marriage. Shows how to achieve a deeper understanding of one's spouse.

*Infertility, Miscarriage, and Adoption*

Glahn, Sandra, and William Cutrer. *When Empty Arms Become a Heavy Burden.* Nashville: Broadman & Holman Publishers, 1997. Gives advice and encouragement for "infertile" couples.

Howard, Terri, and Bill Howard. *Miscarriage: Heartache and Hope.* Audiotape series. Little Rock: FamilyLife, 1993. Three cassettes in which the authors relate personal experiences and God's faithfulness in working through the heartache of miscarriage.

*For Parents*

Arkins, Anne, and Gary Harrell. *Watchmen on the Walls.* Sisters, Oreg.: Multnomah Publishers, 1998. A prayer guide designed to build a child's character through parents' systematic prayer.

Dobson, James C. *Parenting Isn't for Cowards: Dealing Confidently with the Frustrations of Child-Rearing.* Nashville: Word Publishing, 1997. This classic confidence-builder for parents is designed to help achieve the intended joy of parenthood.

Farrar, Steve. *Anchor Man.* Nashville: Thomas Nelson Publishers, 1998. Explains the high calling, traits, adventure, and significance of being a father.

Glenn, Denise. *Freedom for Mothers Kit.* Houston: MotherWise, 1999. MotherWise founder offers advice for the challenges mothers face at all ages.

Guffey, Angela. *Prayers of Expectant Mothers.* Tulsa, Okla.: Honor Books, 1998. Devotional prayer book addresses new feelings and questions of expecting moms.

———. *Prayers for New Mothers.* Tulsa, Okla.: Honor Books, 2000. Mother of four shares encouragement for and prayers with new mothers.

Hunt, Gladys. *Honey for a Child's Heart.* Grand Rapids: Zondervan Publishing House, 1989. A classic guide to good books for children. This current edition has updated listing.

Hunt, Susan. *Your Home: A Place of Grace.* Wheaton, Ill.: Crossway Books, 2000. The rewards of seeking the mind of Christ and emphasizing grace instead of formulas in the home.

Morgan, Elisa, and Carol Kuykendall. *What Every Mom Needs.* Grand Rapids: Zondervan Publishing House, 1998. How to understand and care for nine needs that all moms of children under school age have in common.

Rainey, Dennis, and Barbara Rainey. "Principles for Effective Parenting." Audiotape series. Little Rock: FamilyLife, 1998. God's plan for parents on how to receive, raise, and release a child with purpose. Includes projects for parents.

White, Joe. *What Kids Wish Their Parents Knew about Parenting.* West Monroe, La.: Howard Publishing, 1998. Reveals the insecurities and fears that lurk in children, and how a parent can help overcome them.

Wilson, Douglas. *Standing on the Promises.* Moscow, Idaho: Canon Press, 1997. Presents helpful insights on biblical child rearing with emphasis on grace and covenantal blessings.

## Discipline

Priolo, Lou. *The Heart of Anger.* Amityville, N.Y.: Calvary Press, 1997. Practical ideas on how to apply Ephesians 6:4.

Rainey, Dennis, and Barbara Rainey. "A Biblical Approach to Spanking." Audiotape series. Little Rock: FamilyLife, 1993. Five cassettes on how proper discipline is both biblical and beneficial to the child. Reviews the do's and don'ts of spanking.

Tripp, Tedd. *Shepherding a Child's Heart.* Wapwallopen, Pa.: Shepherd Press, 1998. Discusses the fact that the attitude of a child's heart drives his behavior. Includes practical ways to reach reasonable objectives in parenting.

## Sex Education

Jones, Stanton, and Brenna B. Jones. *How and When to Tell Your Children about Sex.* Colorado Springs: NavPress, 1993. Helps parents prepare children to appreciate God's gift of sexuality while following biblical standards.

## A Child's Identity

Boyd, Charlie. *Different Children, Different Needs.* Sisters, Oreg.: Multnomah Publishers, 1994. Helps identify a child's "personal style"— how he or she relates to other people.

Tobias, Cynthia. *The Way We Learn.* Wheaton, Ill.: Tyndale House Publishers, 1994. Emphasizes that parents can determine a child's basic personality and individual learning style.

## Relating to a Child

Bolin, Dan. *How to Be Your Daughter's Daddy.* Colorado Springs: Piñon Press, 1993. Gives 365 ideas on how a father can make his daughter feel special.

———, and Ken Sutterfield. *How to Be Your Little Man's Dad*. Colorado Springs: Piñon Press, 1993. Gives 365 ideas for father-son activities to build a strong bond.

Campbell. Ross. *How to Really Love Your Child*. Colorado Springs: ChariotVictor Publishing, 1992. Teaches how to show unconditional love through eye contact, physical touch, focused attention, meeting emotional needs, discipline, and spiritual encouragement.

### A Child's Character Formation

Hunt, Susan, and Richie Hunt. *Big Truths for Little Kids*. Wheaton, Ill.: Crossway Books, 1999. A fun, contemporary catechism, with questions, answers, stories, Scripture, and prayers to help communicate truth about God to children.

Taylor, Helen L. *Little Pilgrim's Progress*. Chicago: Moody Press, 1982. Simplified vocabulary and concepts for children in this classic work by John Bunyan.

### A Child's Spirituality and Mission

Elliff, Jim. "How Children Come to Faith in Christ." Audiotape series. Little Rock: FamilyLife, 1996. Shows how to lead a child according to his age and stage in spiritual maturity. Specific teaching for children on sin, judgment, God's love, salvation, and forgiveness.

Smouse, Phil A. *Jesus Wants All of Me*. Uhrichsville, Ohio: Barbour Publishing, 1999. An adaptation for children ages two through seven of Oswald Chambers's *My Utmost for His Highest*. Includes full color illustrations.

### Special Situations

Taylor, Rick. *When Life Is Changed Forever*. Eugene, Oreg.: Harvest House Publishers, 1992. Candid account of parents' loss of their young son in a drowning accident. Speaks to wounded hearts about death, guilt, sorrow, frustrations of faith, and courage to love again.

# CHAPTER
# 13
## The Golden Years
## Family Life Cycle 4—Full Nest 2

I*n phase 4, the family has preadolescent children in elementary school, ages* *six through twelve.*

This is typically the calmest stage in the family experience—a nice interlude when families can be prepared for new challenges waiting just around the bend during the teenage years.

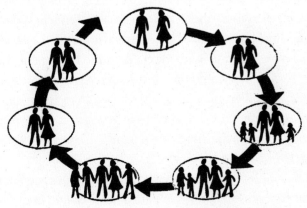

**4 FULL NEST 2**
child(ren) in
elementary school

Barbara and I like to refer to Full Nest 2 as the "golden years." I don't mean that there are no trials or difficulties, but the children are more under control and still eager to fulfill parental expectations. The hormones of adolescence have not hit. The children still spend a lot of time at home, and for the most part they enjoy it. They don't yet have "wheels" or outside jobs, and family events are easily scheduled. Parents continue to exert significant control without much resistance. Life seems more predictable and manageable than at other times.

But this is the calm before the adolescent storm. Since most parents don't fully understand what their children are facing from the culture, their peers, the media, and other forces, a church has a strategic opportunity to schedule a wake-up call by educating and equipping parents so they will understand the battlefield of snares awaiting their children. Their youngsters are about to begin a hazardous journey beset with spiritual, moral, and physical traps. If the parents can anticipate many of these traps, they can develop an offensive plan.

Parents need strong Bible-based convictions that will help them draw boundaries and define the Christian life for their children *before* they enter the mine field. They need the support of other parents who have either successfully equipped their children during these years or who are in the process of doing so.

One of the things I've done to help parents in raising teenagers is expose their preteens to a panel of older teenagers. I usually did this in the sixth-grade Sunday school class I used to teach. I invited a panel of teens to come help me "educate" both the children and the parents. I asked the teen panel to tell about temptations they had faced in peer pressure, drugs, alcohol, sex, and other issues. Invariably the youth replied with such candor that most parents were shocked at what teenagers from a typical church youth group were experiencing. These panels strongly motivate the parents of preteens to want training!

I fear that most of us in local-church Christian education don't go far enough in equipping parents. We pour lots of energy into junior high and high school youth groups. Certainly dynamic, relevant youth groups are needed for today's youth, but without realizing what's taking place the average youth pastor (who usually is not a parent of a teen himself) replaces parents as the primary spiritual teacher and influencer of the teens. Remarkably most parents don't recognize the importance of their own role. Of course, teens should be involved in youth groups. But parents should not relinquish their responsibility for the spiritual education of their youth. Families, not the church, should bear the *primary* responsibility for the spiritual development of their children and youth so long as they are in the home.

If more churches would focus on equipping parents to be better spiritual leaders of their children and youth, they would find that the ministry of the youth group would be far more effective. The youth group would be *supporting* the work of the parents at home rather than *supplanting* the parents.

## GOALS AND STRATEGIES FOR MARRIED COUPLES

In Full Nest 2 complacency in the marriage and the lure of other "good things" can take its toll on a family. Here are some thoughts on how to help men and women flourish instead of wither in this FLC stage.

A marriage that has adjusted to having children must now deal with other forces that threaten to pull the partners into separate worlds.

The husband, who is usually in his thirties, realizes his responsibility to become an even better provider than ever for his growing family. He is also at the point in his career where the combination of his energy and eagerness often provide significant advancement and earning opportunities. So he plunges wholeheartedly into his work. He is very busy.

The wife tends to give more focus to her children and the family, even though she might be facing opportunities in a career as well. She has her hands full supporting her husband, mothering the children, and keeping the household functioning. She too is very busy.

Too often these busy people increasingly lead separate lives, the children being the only significant relational common denominator. But what will be left of the marriage in ten to fifteen years when the offspring leave the nest?

The message on marriage the church must deliver to these husbands and wives is this: "Get your priorities right; eliminate the nonessentials;

slow down; win where it really counts; and work hard to stay connected to each other."

First Baptist Church of Grants Pass, Oregon, has a program called "D8 YR M8" (Date Your Mate) that helps couples do this. Pastor George Pritchard explains, "We provide a brief skill idea for strengthening marriage, as well as offering free children's programs for four hours. Couples are then free to date! This tears down walls pre-Christians have about 'church,' along with providing support for our church couples."[1]

Here are some ways to build marriages during Full Nest 2.

- These couples need time alone to recharge their relationship. Try reasonable creative ideas to help accomplish this. As suggested before, if possible have a "baby-sitter training academy" in your church, thereby ensuring a good supply of quality childcare personnel. Continually encourage activities like weekly date nights, getaway nights or weekends—anything to keep the couple close without there always being a child in the middle!
- Hold sweetheart banquets.
- As a surprise, dismiss young-adult Sunday school classes some week but insist that every couple go away alone for the hour to discuss a question or two you give them. Do everything it takes to help keep the fires burning in these Full Nest 2 marriages!
- Encourage and, if necessary, subsidize every couple's attendance at least once every two or three years at a biblically based marriage conference during this phase of the FLC.
- Small groups can provide enduring friendships that will be needed in the next phases of the family's development. This will not only keep couples accountable and offer prayer support for their marriages, but it will also become a resource later as they encounter issues with their children. Much of what was said about the importance of small groups in Full Nest 1 applies here as well. The only difference is to tailor the questions and inquiries and lesson goals to this FLC stage. If couples have established relationships with other couples who have gone before them, very often they will find that that relationship grows so that this living "resource" naturally flows from one stage to the other.

- Stress three key steps to marital oneness: purity and repentance, sanctity of the marriage covenant, and honoring God-ordained roles of husband and wife. These are essential not only to a good marriage but also to developing healthy, God-fearing children. Children experience great emotional insecurity when they see or experience disunity or coldness in their parents' marriages.

## GOALS AND STRATEGIES FOR PARENTS

Because this is a period of relative peace in most families, many parents have been lulled into passive parenting. But parents should be equipped to emphasize at least three major issues during this phase.

1. *Faith and character development.* As stated earlier, parents need to share the gospel with their children. During these years children are capable of placing their faith in Jesus Christ. They also can achieve growth in obedience to God, integrity, walking with God, and making correct choices.

2. *Conviction formation.* Parents should lead the way in helping children form convictions that will stand for a lifetime. In addition to convictions on character issues, children need to think through how they will respond to various temptations. This process of establishing convictions according to the Scriptures must certainly be well underway by the time the kids start school. These convictions should pertain to friends, TV, literature, time on the Internet, music they listen to, and time spent alone in their rooms. It's been our experience that even with these convictions formulated well in advance of facing these issues, children will continue to need their parents to help shape and develop these convictions well into adolescence.

3. *Parent-child relationship.* In their preadolescent and adolescent years children will test their parents' standards, and this may affect the relationship between the parent and child. The warmth, trust, and love in the parent-child relationship will help smooth out many tensions and conflicts. But if a good relationship is not firmly in place before adolescence, it will be tough to build it during the teenage years.

Here are some thoughts on how to help parents during the Full Nest 2 years.

- Sponsor a retreat for parents of preadolescents. (These can be led by "approved" parents of teens who have faithfully executed their responsibility and can teach others.) Get away all day on Saturday, providing childcare at the church. Have the parents look into issues such as spiritual faith and development, character formation, discipline, and conviction setting. At the retreat give parents opportunity to discuss issues with more experienced couples informally and in small groups.

- Continue helping families know how to have a family night at home at least once a week. Have a young family who is doing this model a session for the whole group.

- Put together a teenage panel, with youth who are sixteen, seventeen, and eighteen years old. Get permission in advance from the teens to ask them questions such as these: What's your conviction about drinking? What's the hardest lesson you've learned as a teen? Would you be willing to share with us how far you will go sexually with the opposite sex prior to marriage? This will be a wake-up time for parents when they hear how some older teenagers lack boundaries on important issues. Other teens will have clear boundaries and will be able to articulate them, thus serving as a model for younger youth.

- In a parents' meeting, display and discuss resources for parents that apply to this stage of the FLC. Include audiotapes, videocassette tapes, and books. (If the cost of resources such as these is an issue, purchase a set or two and create a lending library for parents.)

- Teach a twelve-week class or Saturday seminar on "preparing for adolescence." The youth pastor may not be the right one to lead this effort, particularly if he is unmarried or has no children or only young ones. He may want to select two or three couples to teach by themselves or to come alongside him in instructing the parents. Choose couples that have done a relatively good job of raising their teenagers. These couples need to be authentic, willing to share their mistakes and talk frankly about parenting teenagers.

- Sponsor ongoing activities and special events that facilitate parent-child relationship building, such as a game night, a sports league, a parent-child banquet, or wiener roast. Get dads and moms, sons and daughters interacting, having fun, building memories and relationships together.

- Encourage parents in Empty Nest 2 to teach a grade or two beyond where their own children are today. This is one reason my wife and I taught a sixth-grade Sunday school class for eleven years. We wanted to see what children were experiencing before their teenage years and thus to be better equipped in preparing our own children for adolescence. When each of our children was in the sixth grade, we continued to teach this class because it gave us a full year to instruct them "formally" with their peers. We would never have been able to teach our children at home with the same freedom we had in the class.

- Near the end of this phase encourage a "Passport to Purity" or similar weekend getaway for a mother and her eleven- or twelve-year-old daughter or a father and his eleven- or twelve-year-old son. This Friday evening and all-day-Saturday retreat is a great way to prepare preteens for issues they'll face in adolescence.

## GOALS AND STRATEGIES FOR CHILDREN

To augment what parents are doing at home, use an appropriate curriculum and develop activities that will challenge elementary-age children to grow in faith and character. When children in this part of the FLC are a bit older—ages ten, eleven, and twelve—they need to face up to issues they will encounter in adolescence.

Here are some ways to help parents with the training of their children during this time.

- I heartily recommend a Bible memory program like AWANA that combines fun activities with solid learning of biblical truth.
- As children in this age-group mature, encourage them to participate with their parents in Sunday worship.
- Be sure the church library has a good supply of the many excellent materials available for this age-group. In our family we probably

listened to every *Adventures in Odyssey* broadcast on audiotape, either while driving on vacation or by giving them videocassette tapes as gifts to our children. Other superb options include *The Chronicles of Narnia*, by C. S. Lewis (also available on audiocassette).

Churches can help parents by giving them ideas on how to maximize the child's learning with these tools. For example, parents need to be shown how to engage their children creatively in conversation about a book or movie. How do you ask the right questions and use these experiences strategically rather than haphazardly? During a meeting for parents, do some role-playing to illustrate the point.

- As children go through these years, issues such as peer pressure, lying, stealing, pornography, cheating, sibling rivalry, and others need to be dealt with repeatedly by parents.
- Work with parents to be sure that appropriate instruction in sex education is taking place. If children don't know by the time they are in the first grade about "the birds and the bees" and how babies are made, then they will certainly be told by a peer at school. Offering Bible-oriented instruction in sex education can counter what children learn from the media, at school, and from peers.
- Some churches hold rite-of-passage ceremonies for children as they move into the teenage years or even from the teenage years to adulthood. A meaningful event is for dads to plan a thirteenth birthday event for their sons, to which key Christian men in their boys' lives (i.e., pastors, grandfathers, uncles, accountability partners, or others) are invited to share wisdom and affirm the young man's move to the next stage of manhood. The goal is to launch sons into a new dimension of responsibility and accountability to the Lord and these older men.
- Moms can be encouraged to plan a similar rite-of-passage thirteenth-birthday event for their daughters.

## IDEAS FOR MENTORS

Keeping a marriage on track in the midst of the busy years of Full Nest 2 is no small task. Mentors should help couples address such issues as family values, priorities, scheduling, conflict resolution, money matters, and financial planning.

A mentoring couple can help a couple guide their children through the elementary years and help them start thinking about how life will change when teenagers are in the family.

Full Nest 2 is the time to refresh intimacy and discuss in greater detail how family values can continue to prosper in the days ahead. Mentors need to model ideas of how to handle various family situations. To make sure this happens, perhaps occasionally you could have a panel of more experienced parents tell how they do things or have a role-play, for example, of a father-daughter conversation on boys. Advice and demonstrations like this will take away some of the fear of failure from parents and give them courage to do what's right.

Much of what I said in previous chapters applies equally as well here. Mentors need to continue to focus on effective listening, which expresses true love and concern for their couples. Asking wise, properly timed questions is important. Being constantly in prayer for mentored couples is essential.

Here are a few additional suggestions for mentors during this stage.

- Get couples thinking early about preparing their children for adolescence. When their children reach age ten, parents should have a plan on how to help launch their children into adolescence.

- Engage couples in discussions about media issues, such as movies, TV, the Internet, music, magazines, and video games. What is appropriate, and what is not? How much time a day or a week is too much? These issues may become a source of intense disagreement between moms and dads. Many times one parent is more liberal than the other regarding media issues. It helps for couples to hear objective, wise third-party opinions about such issues.

- Mentoring couples should help their mentored couples regularly assess their spiritual walk with the Lord, their relationship with each other and with their children. Do their lives reflect the biblical roles of husbands and wives (Eph. 5:21–33)? Are their children more often than not obeying their parents in the Lord (6:1–3)? Are dads provoking their children to anger, or bringing them up in the discipline and instruction of the Lord (6:4)? It is always important to hold up the Word of God as a mirror before our eyes so we can see ourselves as God does.

# THE FAMILY-NEEDS SURVEY

## Full Nest 2

*These are areas where Christian adults in this stage of the Family Life Cycle say they want help.*

| | |
|---|---|
| Children's spiritual growth | 74% |
| Spiritual growth | 72% |
| Spiritual disciplines | 66% |
| Developing character/morality in children | 64% |
| Christian values in the home | 61% |
| Parenting skills | 59% |
| Understanding your spouse's needs/expectations | 54% |
| Developing and maintaining good communication | 53% |
| Building a strong marriage | 51% |
| Family communication | 50% |

*Source: The Family-Needs Survey, FamilyLife, Breakdowns by Family Life Cycle, National Database, March 2000, 89.*

# FAMILY LIFE-CYCLE CHECKLIST

## Full Nest 2—Key Ministry Objectives for Leaders

*Topics/Issues:*

- ❑ Facing family-career tensions (men)
- ❑ Facing family-marriage tensions (women)
- ❑ Shaping convictions in children
- ❑ Effective sex education (done by parents)
- ❑ Sharing the gospel with children (for parents)
- ❑ Preparing for adolescence

❏ Family worship
❏ Stewardship of finances and resources

*Actions/Activities*

❏ AWANA or other Bible training program for elementary-age children
❏ Family night training and support
❏ Older teenager panel
❏ Relationship-building events for preteens and parents
❏ Rite of passage ceremonies for boys and girls
❏ Parent retreat for parents of preadolescents
❏ Weekend getaway for parents and children entering adolescence
❏ Date night encouragement
❏ Marriage and parenting conferences
❏ Marriage covenant renewal service

*Mentor Focus:*

❏ Offer insight on the dangers of a too-busy lifestyle
❏ Coax couples to prepare early for their children's adolescent years
❏ Maintain and monitor accountability (as a spouse and a parent)
❏ Encourage attendance at marriage and parenting conferences
❏ Encourage family worship

## RESOURCES

*For Individuals or Couples*

Dillow, Linda, and Lorraine Pintus. *Intimate Issues: Twenty-One Questions Women Ask about Sex.* Colorado Springs: WaterBrook Press, 1999. Honest, Scripture-based insights on sex in marriage, with creative ideas for enhancing a wife's physical relationship with her husband.

Weber, Linda. *Mom, You're Incredible.* Nashville: Broadman & Holman Publishers, 1999. Honors mothers for their divine calling and awesome responsibility.

*Work and Travel Issues*

Hendricks, William, and Jim Cote. *On the Road Again*. Grand Rapids: Fleming H. Revell Co., 1998. Presents twelve keys for sustaining a marriage when one or both partners travel for business.

Sherman, Doug, and William Hendricks. *Your Work Matters to God*. Colorado Springs: NavPress, 1987. Presents a biblical treatment on the importance of secular work.

Wells, Peggy Sue, and Mary Ann Froelich. *Holding Down the Fort*. Minneapolis: Bethany House Publishers, 1998. Considers how to parent successfully when the other parent is away for long periods of time. Discusses the challenge of feeling close, saying good-bye, and reentry problems.

*For Parents*

Arterburn, Stephen, and Jim Burns. *Drug Proof Your Kids*. Ventura, Calif.: Regal Books, 1995. Six building blocks to keep a child alcohol-free and drug-free.

Boyd, Charlie. *"All About Boys" Discovery Profile*. Atlanta: Personality Insights, 1999. Takes a parent and child through an exercise to find out if a child is determined, softhearted, influencing, or cautious. Builds understanding. For ages five through ten.

Kimmel, Tim. *Raising Kids Who Turn Out Right*. Sisters, Oreg.: Multnomah Publishers, 1993. Lighthearted look at parenting. Explains how to set reachable goals, learn one's parenting style, and transfer Christian values.

*Young Children*

Leininger, James R. *The Beginner's Bible*. Grand Rapids: Zondervan Publishing House, 1989. Ninety-five timeless stories from God's Word, colorfully illustrated. Especially appreciated by six- to eight-year olds.

*Family Nights*

Elwell, Ellen Banks. *Christian Mom's Idea Book*. Wheaton, Ill.: Crossway Books, 1997. More than five hundred ideas, tips, and activities from more than eighty mothers of various ages.

Family Wise, 4555 Mansell Road, Suite 300, Alpharetta, Ga. 30022. 770-531-4228 or www.familywise.org. Provides various resources to help parents rediscover family time and teach children character.

Ledbetter, J. Otis, and Kurt Bruner. *Your Heritage*. Colorado Springs: David C. Cook, 2000. How to create a legacy that will make parents and children and future generations proud, with emphasis on spiritual, emotional, and social aspects of building great memories.

Weidman, Jim, Kurt Bruner, Mike Nappa, and Amy Nappa. *An Introduction to Family Nights: Creating Lasting Impressions for the Next Generation*. Family Night Tool Chest Book 1. Colorado Springs: ChariotVictor Publishing, 1998. A collection of twelve fun and meaningful family nights that have been tested and found to make a lasting impression on both children and parents. This "Family Night Tool Chest" includes a number of other titles.

"What If . . . ?" Audiotape series. Little Rock: FamilyLife, 1995. Vignettes use stories, drama, and music to spark discussions in family devotions. A fun way to teach values and build godly character in children.

*Conviction Formation*

Lewis, C. S. *The Chronicles of Narnia*. New York: HarperCollins, 1994. Classic series of seven books that take children and adults to a magical kingdom with mythical characters. Stretches the imagination.

*Adventures in Odyssey*. Videocassette series. Nashville: Word Publishing, 1990–. Based on the popular radio program *Adventures in Odyssey*. Classic animation of exciting stories that teach moral messages.

*Big Idea Veggie Tales.* Videocassette series. Nashville: Word Publishing, 1994–. Humor, catchy songs, and strong animation for younger children. Bible stories and principles presented in creative and memorable fashion.

### Parent-Child Relationships

McDowell, Josh, and Dick Day. *How to Be a Hero to Your Kids.* Nashville: Word Publishing, 1993. A fun way to see and build parent-child relationships and impact the next generation positively.

### Sex Education

Rainey, Dennis, and Barbara Rainey. "Beyond Abstinence." Audiotape series. Little Rock: FamilyLife, 1997. Abstinence is not the primary goal of sex education but should be the result of moral excellence, character development, and positive sexual identity.

————. "Foundation for Moral Purity." Audiotape series. Little Rock: FamilyLife, 1987. Teaches children about sex from a biblical foundation. Helps children learn responsible behavior, moral excellence, and how to make right choices.

————. "Passport to Purity." Audiotape kit with material for parents and children. Little Rock: FamilyLife, 2000. A guide for a weekend retreat for parents of children who are nearing adolescence. Helps their children prepare to make wise decisions on sex, dating, peer pressure, and other issues.

### Preteens

Barner, Leslie, and Nancy Butkowski. *My Heart Belongs to Him.* Multiproduct kit. Little Rock: FamilyLife, 2001. Discipleship program for mothers and daughters. Teaches daughters the meaning of true beauty, how to choose friends, how to use their time wisely, and how to manage peer pressure.

Lewis, Robert. *Raising a Modern Day Knight.* Wheaton, Ill.: Tyndale House Publishers, 1999. A biblical pattern for shaping a boy into a man by equipping him with three essential elements.

Moore, June. *You Can Raise a Well-Mannered Child.* Nashville: Broadman & Holman Publishers, 1996. Clarifies basic manners for junior high children, both inside and outside the family.

Rainey, Dennis, and Barbara Rainey. "Deadly Traps." Audiotape series. Little Rock: FamilyLife, 1998. Four cassettes on how to train children to avoid traps (see the next item) of the coming teenage years.

————, and Barbara Rainey, with Bruce Nygren. *Parenting Today's Adolescent.* Nashville: Thomas Nelson Publishers, 1998. Discusses how to help children avoid traps such as peer pressure, drugs, sex, media. Includes sections for single parents.

Sapp, Brent. *Teknon and the Champion Warriors.* Multiproduct kit. Little Rock: FamilyLife, 2000. Discipleship program for fathers and sons, to help boys learn to live with courage, honor, and integrity.

# CHAPTER

## 14

## Encounter with Adolescence
## Family Life Cycle 5—Full Nest 3

D*uring this season children are in their teenage years and attending junior high school or high school. This stage continues until all children have left the nest.*

The house is full of teenagers or near-teens. The lights come on early and go out late. Cars pull in and out of the driveway regularly. This feels like a beehive. Welcome to Full Nest 3!

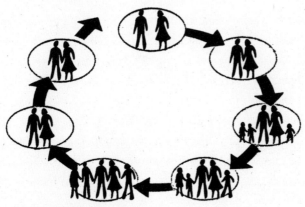

5 FULL NEST 3
child(ren) in junior high
school and high school

During this stage of the Family Life Cycle, it's more important than ever that a family have clear goals and an understanding of its mission. If not, because teenagers are so involved outside the home these days, the average parent may feel like a cat that never catches up with its tail.

The family's pace must be planned and monitored. Otherwise parents will spend their days in a reactive mode, responding to one minicrisis after another. Gone are the golden years. Gone is the daily schedule that "easily" allowed the entire family to gather at the appointed time for dinner. Now family times have to be carefully planned, and flexibility is the key. Time with children increasingly has to be taken on their terms, often at the most unexpected moments.

We all need to offer more encouragement to both teenagers and their parents. Let's not buy into the negative messages from our culture on young people. These last years when children are in our homes need not be filled with fear and frustration. These are years of great opportunity in which to enjoy the results of years of labor in parenting, as well as to apply the final touches to young men and women who will soon be on their own.

## GOALS AND STRATEGIES FOR MARRIED COUPLES

Marriages can grow stale during Full Nest 3 because of simple neglect. Teenagers take a lot of time and energy. There is the pressure of ongoing decision making as teens encounter endless choices and opportunities. And adolescence can be something of an emotional teetertotter for both teens and parents. A couple must carve out time for themselves to communicate and stay emotionally close.

Couples in Full Nest 3 also are entering midlife. At the very moment they need to be stable and strong in helping their adolescents reach maturity, they may be asking deeper questions than before about their own goals and meaning in life. Alert church leaders will include instruction for adults on midlife issues.

Here are two ideas on how to keep marriages in your church vital during this last stage before the nest empties. First, sponsor marriage-enhancing events for couples. You may need to consider activities that consume less time—a one-evening miniseminar as opposed to a full weekend marriage retreat. Because these couples are often involved with the activities of their teens, it's more difficult for them to get away for a long period of time. Make it as easy as possible for them to fit into these church functions. Second, if you have these husbands and wives in a small group or Sunday school class, consider discussing marital and parenting topics every twelve weeks or so.

## GOALS AND STRATEGIES FOR PARENTS

I believe that most parents in the church, as they enter this phase, do not have strong enough convictions, so they are caught off guard by many of the issues their teenagers face. But if adequate preparatory work has been done in Full Nest 2, this will not be the case. Too many moms and dads end up being defensive and reactive to their teens rather than spiritually guiding them on sound biblical principles through the teenage mine field. Encourage parents to help their children to continue developing their own convictions and boundaries around moral and spiritual choices. If the parents are not united in their convictions, the teens may win the day by "dividing and conquering."

The core parenting focus in Full Nest 3 should be on character testing. As young people gain more freedom to make their own choices—some good, some bad—while they are still at home, parents have a superb opportunity to coach and instruct them. To do that well, parents need to know what I call the "Golden Rule of Raising a Teenager": *Don't allow your teenager to push you out of his life.* Given his own way, a teenager will deny access relationally or instructionally to a parent. But if there is ever a time when parents need to love their teens, pursue a meaningful relationship, and refuse to be shut out of a child's life, it is during the ages thirteen to eighteen.

Although a youth group can supplement what teens are getting at home, the primary spiritual resource for teenagers still needs to be mom and dad. Parents should be encouraged to continue some kind of family night or formal instruction on a regular basis to help guide their teens in their spiritual development.

In Full Nest 3 many parents get tired of correcting their young people on issues of sibling rivalry, foul language, bad habits, movies, Internet use, the telephone, dress, and disrespect. So these parents tend to give up, just at a time when they should not. The teens need their parents to remain solid and keep their standards in place, giving grace when appropriate but continuing to train them on an ongoing basis.

Another important focus during this FLC stage should be the affirmation of male and female identity in each child by the same-sex parent. Our culture is creating immense confusion on this topic. Who better to affirm the goodness of being created a man or a woman than a dad or mom? As the homosexual movement continues to make inroads into our society, affirming one's male or female identity is increasingly important. What better place to embrace this God-given identity than in the family?

Even though parents of teenagers have been at this for a long time, there still are critical things to learn.

- Many parents, even of children this old, still struggle with how to do spiritual training. One way to leap over this hurdle is to have a men's group of dads of teenagers decide that they will each lead individual Bible studies with their own children, and to encourage each other through prayer and accountability relationships. A women's group could do something similar.

- Give parents devotional material appropriate for teenagers. These might be short items for daily use or longer material a parent and teen can discuss once a week. Daily material options are listed at the end of this chapter, but one that we found effective was a devotional (called *On This Day*, see p. 169) that contains stories of missionaries who performed heroic deeds. We encouraged one of our teenagers to read from it daily. Another option we found effective is to read a chapter a week from the Book of Proverbs or selected verses from Proverbs on a given topic. Coach parents to be flexible in matching the teen's schedule and turf—perhaps this kind of study could be done together by parent and teen at a favorite doughnut or bagel shop. I have found that these studies work best during the child's junior-high and high-school years.

- Set up short-term mission endeavors involving both parents and teenagers. Involving the family in a Third World country can enable parents and teens to look at the needs of the world through the eyes of Christ. You don't have to go long distances. Consider options in the inner city, at a teenage pregnancy center, or a home for runaway children.
- Strongly consider a POTS (Parents of Teenagers Support) group. Parents in this stage need to be involved with other parents of teenagers.
- Encourage parents to volunteer as teachers or helpers in their teens' youth group. This will help keep them informed of what's going on among young people today and will also enable them to know their own teenagers better.
- Consider challenging parents to give leadership with their teens in establishing a spiritual outreach to your teens' junior high or high school. Student Venture is an organization committed to equipping volunteers to begin such outreach. For information and help on starting one of these groups, call 1-800-699-4678 or visit www.studentventure.com.
- Encourage parents to schedule time with each of their teenagers. As this relationship is in transition from parent/child to parent/child-friend and perhaps (hopefully) to a more conscious relationship of brother or sister in Christ, it is critical that parents and teens "connect" in communicating with each other.
- Again emphasize to parents the importance of praying for their teens. Parents too often try to remedy things with their own wisdom, resources, and strength. But God alone alters hearts and brings about lasting change. Parents should be on their knees regularly, recognizing their dependence on God.
- Parents should remember that love covers a multitude of sins. Teenagers will sin boldly at times. Other times they will sin without deliberately intending to do so. Parents should let their teens know that they love them, no matter what.

## GOALS AND STRATEGIES FOR CHILDREN

Most church youth groups do an excellent job of teaching the faith and providing wholesome activities that allow teenagers to "hang out" together.

This needs to continue, but I would suggest that with teenagers we give more emphasis to what the Bible teaches on the appropriate roles of men and women. Hopefully teens have seen husbands and wives, dads and moms model biblical roles in their homes. If not, then the church must fill in the gap for those teens who have not had such modeling. Because the issues surrounding such biblical roles may seem irrelevant to young people, church leaders will need to be creative as they seek to impact youth in this area.

## PRODIGALS

During this stage of the FLC, some families will have an unusually difficult or rebellious child. Some of those teens will leave home, but a more likely scenario is that the teenager will be a child acting out rebellion but still living at home.

The church can help parents know what to do in these situations, and mentors can be unusually helpful. Parents may need the church's help in knowing what limits to set for a teen if he or she continues living at home.

Pastor Bill Parkinson and his wife, Anne, went through this with one of their children. They developed an excellent contract that they established with their rebellious son. A copy of this is included in the booklet *When Your Child Breaks Your Heart,* available from FamilyLife (1-800-358-6329).

### The Youth Pastor–Parent Team

Churches should not measure their success in building spiritual faith in the next generation based on the number of teens who attend their junior high or high school youth groups. Rather, churches must measure their "success" based on how well they are equipping parents to prepare their children spiritually at home.

Grant Osborne, pastor of Grace Community Church, Sanderton, Pennsylvania, says, "We have built into the church the value of the parent/teen relationship, emphasizing the father, not the pastor, as the primary influence upon his children."[1]

If I were a youth pastor, I would seek to establish a fellowship group of teens' parents. And whether the adults met weekly or once a month, I would encourage the parents to support the youth group, and vice versa. This is what Carlsbad (Calif.) Community Church has done. Pastor Scott Koop comments, "We have a Parents of Teens Fellowship. They meet weekly to pray and share and to support each other. They have common goals and experiences. It is our largest fellowship group."[2]

Also I would encourage every parent of teens to have some kind of involvement in the youth ministry of the church as their children are in their teen years. This will foster better connections among teenagers, parents, and church. It will also open parents' eyes to many issues about which they are ignorant. We need to team up so that youth will emerge at the end of their teenage years with their spiritual faith in Christ intact.

These are some ways to continue equipping youth during Full Nest 3.

- Give instruction, both at home and in church, on sex roles. Instruction on these roles takes place in our home church based on the book *Rocking the Roles*, by Robert Lewis and William Hendricks (Colorado Springs: NavPress, 1991).
- Continue instructing youth on relationships and issues related to sexual purity. One key biblical passage is 1 Thessalonians 4:1–8, which is perhaps the clearest expression in the New Testament on how Christians are to live in relation to their bodies. Teenagers should be confronted with this text in a variety of contexts over time and encouraged to memorize it.
- Consider having a seminar for older teens on "the Christian worldview." Many young people are not properly prepared for the onslaught against their ideas and values that may occur when they go to college or leave home to enter the workplace.
- Hold rite-of-passage events (such as a banquet) for teens who are leaving home. Encourage parents to make the entrance of the young person into adulthood a meaningful event. Church leaders and parents should pray over their youth as they leave for college or elsewhere.

- Encourage them to obey God's spiritual mandate to be involved in the Great Commission. The First Presbyterian Church of Nashville, Tennessee, holds a banquet for graduating seniors to which their parents are also invited. Pastor Mark DeVries says that these graduates are thus surrounded by "a cloud of witnesses."
- Another idea is for parents to take a graduating senior to breakfast and ask some adults influential in the teen's life to share insights. At the conclusion parents and the others can place hands on and pray over the teen.

## THE TRAPS OF ADOLESCENCE

My wife and I have identified the following as the major traps that every adolescent faces. Use this as a resource for discussion with youth, parents, and youth workers. (The topics are explored at length in our book *Parenting Today's Adolescent* [Nashville: Nelson, 1998].)

| | | |
|---|---|---|
| Peer pressure | Unresolved anger | The Tongue |
| Sex | Appearance | Mediocrity |
| Dating | Deceit | Pornography |
| Attitudes | Substance abuse | False gods |
| Media | Busyness | |

## IDEAS FOR MENTORS

The best mentors for couples in Full Nest 3 are dads and moms who are one step ahead in the FLC in Empty Nest 1. These are parents who have recently "released" a teenager to college or work away from home. Other good mentor candidates are those parents who have a larger family and have faced the teen years several times.

Couples in Empty Nest 1 share with parents in Full Nest 3 how they came through the teenage years and solved various problems. These mentors should coach parents to let their teens make an ever-broadening range of choices, and to see how those choices—both right and wrong ones— can be the basis for further instruction and guidance.

A major goal of the mentor during this phase is to encourage parents not to give up and not to loosen their standards or stop instructing teenagers in the way they should live. Mentors need to explain how the teenage years can produce new strains on a marriage, as teenagers exert independence and perhaps rock the stable family boat.

A mentoring couple could discuss a book on adolescence with parents of teens.

Mentors are aware that many marriages falter when the nest empties. Now is the time to prepare married couples for Empty Nest 1. Mentors can observe whether or not the marriage has been built around children. The entry into the empty-nest phase will be a jolt if preparation does not begin before the youngest child leaves the home.

A final goal for mentors is to consider asking husbands and wives in Full Nest 3 to consider how they can become mentors themselves.

## THE FAMILY-NEEDS SURVEY

### Full Nest 3

*The following are the percentages of adults in this stage who said they want help from the church with their needs.*

| | |
|---|---|
| Spiritual growth | 70% |
| Spiritual disciplines | 66% |
| Children's spiritual growth | 64% |
| Releasing a child | 54% |
| Developing and maintaining good marital communication | 51% |
| Family communication | 51% |
| Understanding your spouse's needs/expectations | 50% |
| Christian values in the home | 48% |

| Developing character/morality in children | 47% |
| Building a strong marriage | 43% |

*Source: The Family-Needs Survey, FamilyLife, Breakdowns by Family Life Cycle, National Database, March 2000, 89.*

## FAMILY LIFE CYCLE CHECKLIST

### Full Nest 3—Key Ministry Objectives for Leaders

*Topics/Issues:*

- ❏ Midlife challenges (men and women)
- ❏ Parent prayer for teenagers
- ❏ Character testing of teens (for parents)
- ❏ Male and female identity (for teens)
- ❏ Spiritual coaching of young men and women (by parents)
- ❏ Youth pastor-parent support team
- ❏ Christian world-view (for older teens)
- ❏ Becoming a mentor (for those in "Empty Nest 1")
- ❏ Family worship for the family with teenagers
- ❏ Planning for empty nest (God's call, ministry options, etc.)

*Actions/Activities:*

- ❏ Relationship training for teens, with emphasis on sexual purity
- ❏ Parent-teen, short-term mission opportunities
- ❏ Parents of Teens support group
- ❏ Rite-of-passage ceremony for children leaving home
- ❏ Minigetaways for couples
- ❏ Marriage covenant renewal service

*Mentor Focus:*

- ❏ Help parents navigate their final home years with their children
- ❏ Help parents prepare for the empty nest
- ❏ Encourage parents to maintain accountability (as a spouse and as a parent)

❏ Encourage attendance at marriage and parenting conferences
❏ Encourage family worship
❏ Emphasize the importance of building romance and intimacy in marriage apart from the children
❏ Encourage spiritual oneness

## RESOURCES

*For Individuals and Couples*

Arp, Dave, and Claudia Arp. *Fifty-Two Dates for You and Your Mate.* Nashville: Thomas Nelson Publishers, 1993. Ideas on how to enrich a marriage and create years of special memories.

Chapin, Alice. *Four Hundred Creative Ways to Say I Love You.* Wheaton, Ill.: Tyndale House Publishers, 1996. Ideas on how to add spice to any marriage—young or mature.

LaHaye, Tim, and Beverly LaHaye. *The Act of Marriage after Forty.* Grand Rapids: Zondervan Publishing House, 2000. Help on nutrition and the effect of supplements on sex life, and discussion of physical fitness, sexual desire, impotence, female hormonal drugs, and menopause.

Stanley, Scott M. *The Heart of Commitment.* Nashville: Thomas Nelson Publishers, 1998. Noted marriage researcher explains secrets of great marriages.

Yates, Susan. *How to Like the Ones You Love.* Grand Rapids: Baker Book House, 2000. Emphasizes that God did not make a mistake when He assembled your family. Discusses solutions for building covenant commitment and family policies that work.

*Midlife*

Buford, Bob, Peter Drucker, and Terry Whalin. *Halftime.* Grand Rapids: Zondervan Publishing House, 1997. How to experience a fresh vision at midlife, emphasizing that the second half of life can be more rewarding than the first half.

*For Parents*

Campbell, Ross. *How to Really Love Your Teenager*. Colorado Springs: ChariotVictor Publishing, 1993. Instruction for parents on unconditional love and how to help teenagers develop intellectually, set goals, learn to cook nutritionally, and handle money and anger.

Rainey, Dennis. "Hidden Traps." Audiotape series. Little Rock: FamilyLife, 1999. Four cassettes on subtle pitfalls teenagers sometimes ignore, including appearance, attitude, deceit, mediocrity, busyness, the tongue, and false gods.

————, and Barbara Rainey, with Bruce Nygren. *Parenting Today's Adolescent*. Nashville: Thomas Nelson Publishers, 1998. Discusses how to help children avoid traps such as peer pressure, drugs, sex, and media. Includes sections for single parents.

Solomon, Jerry, Kyle McGraw, Sara Peebles, Dennis Rainey, and Bob Lepine. "Preparing Your Teen for College." Audiotape series. Little Rock: FamilyLife, 1998. Four cassettes on preparing young adults for the intellectual challenges of college.

Rainey, Dennis, and Barbara Rainey. "Preparing Your Teen for Life." Audiotape series. Little Rock: FamilyLife, 1996. Six cassettes on life skills every parent wants a teenager to have before he or she leaves home for college, work, or military service.

Rohn, Robert. *I Sight*™. Minneapolis: Carlson Learning Co., 1996. A helpful test for teens to know themselves and their personal attributes better.

*Character Testing*

Rainey, Dennis. "My Soapbox." Audiotape series. Little Rock: FamilyLife, 1998. Discusses teenage issues like appearance, drinking, profanity, movies, music, friends, sports, part-time jobs, curfews, limits, and other hot topics.

### Devotional Times

Morgan, Robert. *On This Day: 365 Amazing and Inspiring Stories about Saints, Martyrs and Heroes.* Nashville: Thomas Nelson Publishers, 1998. Twenty centuries of faith have produced many uplifting stories that give insight into the history of the church and its heroes. Excellent discussion starter with teenagers.

### Problem Children

"Encouragement for Brokenhearted Parents." Little Rock: FamilyLife, 2000. Includes a daily prayer guide, knowing your teenager, listening to a teenager when you don't like what you're hearing, writing a contract with a teenager.

### Short-Term Mission Trips

Student Venture of Campus Crusade for Christ. 1-800-699-4678 or www.studentventure.com. Domestic and international short-term opportunities for high-school students.

Summer work camps. Group Publishing. 1-800-774-3838 or www.groupworkcamps.com. Summer U.S. missions experience for teenagers. One-week intensive work on repair projects for needy families.

### Releasing a Child

Kuykendall, Carol. *Give Them Wings.* Wheaton, Ill.: Tyndale House Publishers, 1994. Practical ideas for parents of children who will soon leave the nest.

Mehl, Ron. *Just in Case I Can't Be There.* Sisters, Oreg.: Multnomah Publishers, 1999. Wisdom from a father to any child leaving the nest. Topics include faith, choosing a mate, integrity, and managing finances.

# CHAPTER

## 15

### Free at Last
### Family Life Cycle 6—Empty Nest 1

In this stage the last child has left home but at least one parent is still em-ployed full-time. Children often marry during this phase, and the first grandchild may arrive.

This stage of the life cycle should be the most fruit-filled chapter in a married couple's life.

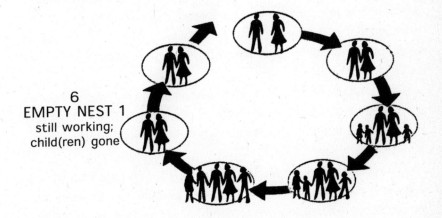

6
EMPTY NEST 1
still working;
child(ren) gone

Many adults are entering this stage at a young age, with nearly a third of their lives yet ahead of them. This is the stage when the parents' huge time commitment to their children reduces drastically. With fewer children in the average family, the nest often empties when a couple is in their late forties or early fifties. Grandchildren reclaim some of the focus that was formerly captured by children.

As the Baby Boomers move toward empty-nest status, this is a strategic moment for the church that is prepared. Many of those adults can become mentors for younger adults.

But this won't happen by itself. These couples are accustomed to concentrating on the needs of their own family, and they do have legitimate needs of their own—adjusting to children being gone, strengthening their marital relationship, facing health problems, making decisions on how to use their time, learning the new role of grandparenting, and others. They need equal doses of compassion and challenge.

I think churches need to make an all-out effort to stir the souls of laypersons who are in their fifties and are still hard at work but are in need of a new purpose and mission. If we don't challenge them with specific ministry opportunities, the lure of hobbies, outside interests, and the world may consume their attention.

Paul wrote in Titus 2:3–5 that older woman are to teach younger women how to love their husbands at home. And older men need a similar assignment with younger men. There's a great need for older men to reach down and call younger men "up" to their responsibilities in the family.

This is the time to challenge empty-nest couples to consider becoming mentors, ministering to the younger generation—first to their own adult children, but then also to those who will not receive such guidance from their own parents.

Churches need to initiate formal training for couples who want to move into various kinds of lay ministry. In 1996 the first Baby Boomers turned fifty, and by the year 2014, 76 million will find themselves evaluating their mission and purpose.[1] The church needs to capitalize on the vast experience of this group and their availability. They represent a massive amount of wealth, resources, and volunteer manpower.

Another challenge I would issue to couples in this stage is that they consider mentoring and ministering in "both directions." Those who are older and in Empty Nest 2, particularly as they near the end of their earthly life, do not need advice on how to live, but they do need assistance and companionship. Couples in Empty Nest 1 could help minister to them.

## GOALS AND STRATEGIES FOR MARRIED COUPLES

This season for a husband and wife should be like newlywed days when there was more time to enjoy each other. But unfortunately for too many couples, this time in their lives becomes a nightmare of broken dreams and cold isolation because attention has been focused primarily on the children.

I have noticed that many couples enter into Empty Nest 1 as individuals. By that I mean the husband has his career, civic responsibilities, and hobbies, and the wife has her civic responsibilities, Bible studies, responsibilities at home, interests, and often a career. These couples do not have a common vision and plan.

Certainly two people can have an impact as individuals, but a couple who have been married thirty or more years can have a greater influence if they are living life purposefully for God and see themselves as life coaches for the next generation. This is a time to call couples to "step out" in faith and embrace a cause or a mission that is worth giving their lives to.

Here are some thoughts on helping marriages be reinvigorated during Empty Nest 1.

- Encourage and facilitate romantic marriage-enrichment opportunities for empty-nest couples. They need these times to reconnect and talk through their "new life" together. Perhaps consider a dual-purpose getaway couples' retreat—some marriage instruction tailored to empty nesters, along with fellowship, recreational, and entertainment options.
- Emphasize the need for each believer to have a part in evangelism and missions. Encourage older couples to share testimonies about their ministry, of how God has given them the privilege and pleasure of being used by Him to see people's lives redirected and legacies

changed. Publicly honor couples, as well as individuals, who are using this phase of their lives and gifts to address family needs in your church. Encourage couples to spend some of their vacation time on short-term missions activities.

- Challenge couples to embrace a "cause" that would impact families in your church. This could include mentoring, teaching classes, and receiving training that would help equip newly marrieds and new parents.

- Hold an Empty Nest Fair each fall—an evening devoted to offering a seminar or two on making the shift to the empty nest, as well as a presentation of the many ministries in your church that need the help of empty nesters.

- Instruct those in this stage of their lives on how to honor and care for the needs of their aging parents. This can be a huge concern for couples in this phase, called the "sandwich generation"—those who are concerned for the needs of their older children and also their aging parents.

## GOALS AND STRATEGIES FOR PARENTS

Couples frequently are caught off guard during this phase by the needs of their children as they begin their own marriages and families. Parents are never finished parenting. The children may be away, but most likely they still receive financial and emotional support during college years or in their transition to adulthood.

It is important that couples in Empty Nest 1 devote time to their adult children, continuing to invest in them for the benefits that will come to their own family. Parents must never surrender their responsibility to pray for their children and to offer *appropriate* assistance and advice. These involvements must be gentle and usually at the adult child's request.

The reality of the empty nest strikes when a young man asks a parent for his daughter's hand in marriage or a son announces his upcoming marriage plans. After marriage the child may come back to the parent for godly counsel and advice in areas that were not relevant in the past. It may be as simple as helping get a newborn to sleep through the night or may be as profound as providing counsel for a couple who are struggling to get along.

Note these ideas for equipping Empty Nest 1 dads and moms:

- A church provides a tremendous service to families if it gives some instruction to parents on what it means to release children—first as they leave home, then more critically as they marry. Older mentor couples can be invaluable in exhorting Empty Nest 1 parents to "cut the cord" and dissuade them from "lengthening it."
- Parents should be coached to have some individualized, instructive messages in mind for each of their children as they begin their own families. Appropriate grace-filled mentoring of adult children *before they marry* should be suggested. When Ashley, our daughter, and Michael decided to marry, I met with Michael once a month for six months in preparation for their wedding. I talked about issues such as the differences between men and women, the purpose of marriage, commitment, the honeymoon, and sex. This helped cement our relationship too.
- Have a seminar for empty nesters on how to be effective grandparents. Grandparenting is increasingly becoming a lost art in this culture, and we need to exalt the high and holy calling of these "generational connectors."
- A growing number of parents are getting divorced and are turning the care of their children over to the children's grandparents. Other parents ask their parents to care for their children while the husband and wife work. So consider teaching a class for those in Empty Nest 1 who are rearing grandchildren.

## GOALS AND STRATEGIES FOR CHILDREN

Of course in every church there are adults—some single, most married—who are the children of empty nesters.

Issues that single adults face include establishing their own identity, managing their finances, adjusting to jobs, and finding suitable housing. A growing number of singles continue to live at home. These young single adults need to be taught that they must still honor their parents whether they live at home or not.

Also married children, although they are now independent from their parents and are concentrating on their own marriages and families, should be reminded that the command to "honor your parents" holds as long as a mom and dad are living.

The "children" of empty nesters are adults—but they do need coaching as their role in relation to their parents is changing.

- In teaching and preaching include positive challenges for adult children to stay connected to their parents.
- As the baby boomers become older, many parents may need some type of assistance from their grown children. A church can help guide individuals in Full Nest 3 and Empty Nest 1 on how to care for aging parents appropriately.

## IDEAS FOR MENTORS

Mentors need to help their protégés with the most radical transition in the life cycle of a family (other than the death of a spouse)—making the once-in-a-lifetime transition from full nest to empty nest. Obviously the mentors must be people who have experienced this phase or who are fully in Empty Nest 2.

While helping mentees adjust to a new way of life, mentors should be talking to their protégés about becoming mentors themselves, if they aren't already. With good training, a couple in Empty Nest 1 can step in at any one of the four previous life cycles and coach others effectively.

Mentors at this stage should seek to impart to the couples they are mentoring a broader vision for ministering to families and others in the family of God.

# THE FAMILY-NEEDS SURVEY

## Empty Nest 1

*Percentages of those in Empty Nest 1 wanting help with their needs:*

| | |
|---|---|
| Spiritual growth | 62% |
| Spiritual disciplines | 56% |
| Developing and maintaining good marital communication | 41% |
| Understanding my spouse's needs/expectations | 37% |
| Healthy living and eating habits | 35% |
| Rekindling romance | 30% |
| Having a ministry | 34% |
| Establishing adult friendships | 30% |
| Family communication | 27% |
| Adjusting to my season of life | 26% |
| Managing my time | 26% |

*Source: The Family-Needs Survey, FamilyLife, Breakdowns by Family Life Cycle, National Database, March 2000, 89.*

# FAMILY LIFE CYCLE CHECKLIST

## Empty Nest 1—Key Ministry Objectives for Leaders

*Topics/Issues:*

- ❑ Releasing children
- ❑ Empty-nest orientation
- ❑ Being an effective grandparent
- ❑ Becoming a mentor
- ❑ Reconnection, communication, and intimacy in the mature marriage
- ❑ Parenting the adult child

❏ Housing an aged parent
❏ Vision and planning for ministry, not retirement
❏ Financial planning with focus on Christian ministries

*Actions/Activities:*

❏ Empty-nest fair
❏ Seminar on identifying one's call and ministry passion
❏ Short-term mission opportunities
❏ Marriage covenant renewal and tributes
❏ Tribute to parents

*Mentor Focus:*

❏ Monitor progress in adjusting as an empty-nest couple
❏ Encourage involvement as mentors
❏ Give tribute to parents
❏ Maintain accountability regarding life, finances, and career
❏ Maintain accountability regarding spouse, children, and grandchildren
❏ Encourage life-mission planning

## RESOURCES

*For Individuals or Couples*

*Affairs*

Carder, Dave, Duncan Jaenicke, and David Seamands. *Torn Asunder.* Chicago: Moody Press, 1995. Specific realistic counsel for recovery after an extramarital affair.

Rabey, Lois Mowday, Dave Carder, and Dennis Rainey. "Affairs: Before and After." Audiotape series. Little Rock: FamilyLife, 1996. Tells how to avoid getting trapped in an adulterous relationship and how to rebuild a broken covenant after an affair.

Rabey, Lois Mowday. *The Snare: Understanding Emotional and Sexual Entanglements.* Colorado Springs: NavPress, 1994. Explains the subtle danger signs in a relationship that can lead to an immoral path with devastating results.

*For Women*

Rainey, Barbara, and Ashley Escue. *A Mother's Legacy*. Nashville: Thomas Nelson Publishers, 2000. A mother and her adult daughter share reflections of their relationship and stories of other mothers and daughters. Demonstrates how family traditions and values can be passed on to the next generation.

Rabey, Lois Mowday. "Coming of Age." Audiotape series. Little Rock: FamilyLife, 1995. Author tells her own story and gives spiritual encouragement.

Mayo, Joseph, and Mary Ann Mayo. "Managing Menopause." Audiotape series. Little Rock: FamilyLife, 1998. A doctor and his wife discuss menopause issues—including the medical and homeopathic options and how to maintain a strong marriage through changes.

*For Parents*

*Daddy, I'm Pregnant*. Joplin, Mo.: College Press, 1998. How a father, faced with his teenage daughter's pregnancy found his faith, family, and ministry stretched to the breaking point before grace appeared.

Rainey, Dennis, Anita Worthen, Bob Davies, Robert Lewis, and Stephen Arterburn. "Understanding Homosexuality." Audiotape series. Little Rock: FamilyLife, 1997. Three cassettes in which individuals tell how people near to them found God's love after having lost their God-given sexual identity.

*For Adult Children*

Rainey, Dennis, with David Boehi. *The Tribute and the Promise*. Nashville: Thomas Nelson Publishers, 1994. Encourages love for and honor of parents, and includes practical helps and examples on preparing a "tribute" for a parent.

# CHAPTER

## 16

### Sunset
### Family Life Cycle 7—Empty Nest 2

$T$*his last stage of the Family Life Cycle occurs at about age sixty-five (or when the individual retires), when there are no more day-to-day career or job responsibilities. During this season of life a spouse may die, and the grief and loneliness of widowhood are encountered.*

7  EMPTY NEST 2
    retired

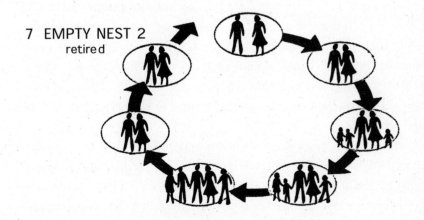

Consider the value these Scriptures place on those who are nearing the finish line of life.

> Grandchildren are the crown of old men, and the glory of sons is their fathers. (Prov. 17:6)

> The glory of young men is their strength, and the honor of old men is their gray hair. (Prov. 20:29)

> Listen to your father who begot you, and do not despise your mother when she is old. (Prov. 23:22)

> Honor your father and mother (which is the first commandment with promise) so that it may go well with you, and that you may live long on the earth. (Eph. 6:2–3)

Unfortunately senior citizens are seldom thought of as individuals of experience and authority, people to whom others go for wisdom and counsel. The Christian community desperately needs to restore the dignity of our elders in the faith.

Of course, seniors should have time to rest and enjoy favorite pastimes. But this is also a time for service—the last lap in finishing strong, which means a deeper service than golf, a loftier calling than the crossword puzzle, and a higher agenda than daytime TV. We must challenge those at this stage to stay involved, as long as they are physically and mentally able, to reach out to younger generations and impart values, insight, and love.[1]

Those in Empty Nest 2 often buy into the idea of their own obsolescence. "Well, I guess I don't understand this younger generation. I guess I don't have much to offer. My old ways are for the old days." Many elderly persons speak as if their past is of no value. Many have developed a pessimistic attitude toward life instead of a treasured view of the past that embraces lessons learned and family memories.

The Bible pictures old age as a time of contentment and satisfaction as adults approach the end of the course and are ready for heaven. Instead of thinking of the twilight years as days of cynicism, ugliness, and self-focus, adults should enter their older years with dreams and new vistas—looking forward to tomorrow, and expecting God to work in and through them.

We should not view Empty Nest 2 as a time of decay and shutting down. Inevitably age catches up with everyone, and the physical body wears out. But let's go against the culture and do what Scripture teaches— honor the elderly by making use of their gifts and wisdom to help extend the Lord's work. By doing this we can pass a vision on to succeeding generations, to people who need to know how to grow with dignity, grace, purpose, and mission as disciples of Jesus Christ.

If we raise our expectations for this season of life, families, churches, and society as a whole will benefit.

## GOALS AND STRATEGIES FOR MARRIED COUPLES

In this stage of life the marriage covenant should represent its finest hour with spouses caring tenderly for each other. For many couples the time comes when one spouse must provide sacrificially for the physical care of the other spouse. In such cases both persons will need encouragement and support from outsiders. What a beautiful testimony to those watching when a husband or wife supports and ministers to a spouse who will soon depart for heaven.

Certainly a portion of that care should include spouses sharing with each other their final wishes regarding property, personal possessions, and funeral arrangements. Finances should be mutually understood and in order. One's last will needs to be reviewed and updated. The better the shape of these matters, the less anxiety and tension the couple will face.

Here are four ideas for serving these elderly covenant keepers in the body of Christ.

- Do not take senior marriages for granted, as though there are no unresolved issues or any need for growth in their relationships. Go out of your way to honor older couples every year on their wedding anniversaries. These long-married wives and husbands should be recognized as the decorated veterans of a family reformation.

- Couples in Empty Nest 2 stage should be encouraged to continue mentoring. Younger couples should be encouraged to seek them out, to question them about their lives, their experiences, their burdens, their hopes.
- Church leaders and families should esteem these older couples. When seniors enter a room, the younger generations should be taught to stand in their honor. Words of thanks and gratitude should be shared regularly. Once or twice a year, honor older Christians in your church for their faithfulness and obedience to Christ. Perhaps a potluck dinner can be the setting for this. Have others in the church comment on what the honored person(s) has meant to them personally and to the ministry. Also allow the honored individual(s) to share wisdom and insights God has given them over the years. This type of activity will encourage the older believers, and it will also help them appreciate what God has done in their lives and to persevere. And younger believers will benefit from "older" wisdom that otherwise might be missed.
- These couples should seek out ministry opportunities. Prayer ministry is perhaps the most obvious, for empty nesters make great prayer warriors. These couples should actively seek out others for whom they can pray. They should ask their pastors, their protégé couples, their children and grandchildren, friends, missionaries, and others how they can pray specifically for them.

## GOALS AND STRATEGIES FOR PARENTS

Even at this stage of the FLC, parenting is not complete. The children have been adults for many years and may even have an empty nest of their own. However, as they are able, parents in Empty Nest 2 should still encourage and share wisdom with their children. And they have a great opportunity to exert considerable positive spiritual and emotional influence on their grandchildren and perhaps even great-grandchildren. With kind acts and encouraging words, older people can influence the course of their family's future. The opposite is true as well: A bitter, cynical old person can sow a legacy of low self-esteem, despair, and pessimism.

The following are ideas for helping dads and moms who are in Empty Nest 2.

- One of the lost arts that needs to be revitalized among Empty Nest 2 folks is letter writing. In a "Peanuts" cartoon strip, Charlie Brown once moaned, "Nothing echoes like an empty mailbox." In this age of cyber communications and instant messaging, handwritten letters from even a shaky hand will become treasured artifacts for generations that follow. Encourage senior Christians in their sixties and seventies to write letters to younger people about their own beliefs and values. Although it is not necessary to wait for a significant milestone (birthday, wedding, birth, graduation, anniversary) to do this, such occasions do provide a good opportunity.

  I have kept nearly every letter that I received from my father after he turned sixty. There weren't many, but I have them all. If those letters had been more instructive or informative in reference to values, wisdom, and advice, they would be even more valuable.

- I think we need to give a little more time in our church services or Sunday school classes for members of the older generation to relay stories of how they weathered emotional, physical, and spiritual storms, and to give testimonies on how they lived for the Lord and how He answered prayer.

## GOALS AND STRATEGIES FOR CHILDREN

These "mature children" need to be prepared to play a special role in honoring their parents in their sunset years. Christians have a great platform from which to show the world how much God cares about human life.

Although older Christians may have the resources and health to live by themselves for many years, there will come a time when most of them will require more intense assistance. Their children need to be ready to take on this responsibility. This may not mean that the parent will live with the child, although that may happen. If the parent ends up living in a care facility, children need to provide emotional, spiritual, and physical support. We must break the pattern of Christians abandoning their older parents to an existence of loneliness and in some cases neglect. How can this possibly be "honoring" our parents?

Here are a few ideas for helping equip adult children.

- Every church needs to respond to the biblical admonition to care for widows (and widowers). With the "extended family" more extended than ever, even conscientious children may not be able to fully support a widowed person who lives across the country. Younger families need to be encouraged and supported by the church to adopt a "grandpa or grandma" to love and help care for. Both parties in this arrangement will reap benefits, and God will be glorified.

- A church's efforts to educate adults on issues related to caring for their aging parents will be well received. Perhaps a special seminar once a year, coupled with some books or tapes available in the church office or library, would be adequate. Also consider having a "mentor on call" to help adult children deal with specific issues that come up—sometimes unexpectedly, as when a parent has a sudden health emergency.

- Consider one service a year near Mother's Day or Father's Day when adult sons and daughters can take a few minutes and publicly give their parents a written and verbal tribute for what they did right. These tributes are minisermons in themselves, communicating the value of marriage and family and the impact of our choices.

- Encourage adult children to write letters to their elders. They should also train their children and grandchildren to write to their grandparents and great-grandparents on a regular basis, thanking them and blessing them with words of love and affirmation.

Children and grandchildren of these empty nesters should seek opportunities to approach their parents and grandparents to ask questions and seek counsel—to adopt them as mentors.

## IDEAS FOR MENTORS

Mentors of individuals in Empty Nest 2 will be of two types. The first type is the more traditional—someone a bit older and who has more experience—possibly a person who has already gone through losing a spouse to death. The relationship is one of friendship, in which they help bear each other's burdens.

The second type of mentor was explained more fully in the previous chapter. This "mentor-minister" is someone younger, ideally in Empty Nest 1, who now ministers to an older person, a kind of "child in absentia." This mentor may have legal or financial expertise to help the individual solidify matters of his or her estate. The mentor can provide friendship to a senior who may be alone and in need of companionship. The mentor may also help accomplish simple household chores or run errands. The essence of this mentoring is service and the honoring of parents.

## CASE STUDY: A WIDOW'S SERVICE

In the 1970s I met Kitty Longstreth, a remarkable woman who in many ways personifies the potential people have during Empty Nest 2 for impacting future generations.

When we met nearly thirty years ago, I had no idea that a challenge I gave Kitty would have such a profound influence. Kitty's husband had passed away a few years earlier, and I saw a woman with a heart for impacting others. I challenged Kitty to pour the rest of her life into ten women. At last count that ten has grown to several hundred, and Kitty is still finding new women to whom to minister. Her life illustrates what can happen when people do not retire in God's work. Here's a brief sketch of Kitty's story.

The Longstreth nest emptied in 1965 when the last of two daughters left home. Kitty had been a long-time Christian who was looking for something deeper in her walk with God. In 1969 she attended an evangelism conference led by Bill Bright and found what she had been looking for spiritually.

For two years Kitty cared for her ailing husband at home. After he died in 1972, Kitty was now not just an empty nester but a widow as well. She was fifty-four years old, and with her financial needs covered, she could have chosen a number of ways to occupy her time. But excited by her expanding faith in Christ, she listened to God's call and began to use her home as a place to minister to others.

About this time I urged her to share her life with young women. About thirty years later the door to her home still remains open. Kitty says now, "Hardly a day goes by when there isn't a note from someone from some-where in the world telling me something about our past."

There never was a particular plan or agenda to Kitty's ministry. She simply remained available to do what God wanted in her life. A young woman once told Kitty, "It's like you're just sitting on the side of the road, Miss Kitty." Kitty responds, "That's really what I do! I just sit there in that house and God just brings all these strangers. And I welcome them in."

Most of her guests were young students or women busy in their careers but who were empty for one reason or another. Kitty says, "God made it possible for me to teach the Word out of my home and out of my heart to a few women who really wanted to know a better thing to do with their lives than what they were doing at the time.

"They just needed what God had given me—and that was a big home. I could afford to have them; I could afford to cook. And I had the time. I loved doing that. And they were ministering to me. God brought those people in my home for me!"

These young people learned at least as much from Miss Kitty's example as from her teaching. She says, "It was my lifestyle they liked. I wasn't try-ing to remarry. When a girl came to see me, my whole focus was to try to let her see that God was sufficient for all her needs. Whatever her need was, I would always say to her, 'God is sufficient. Look at my life!' "

Along the way Kitty also found time and energy to participate in the founding of a new church—Fellowship Bible Church in Little Rock. Her home has been used for numerous church events through the years. FBC now has over five thousand people in attendance and has a ministry for Christ that reaches throughout the world. Kitty has always been one of the church's behind-the-scenes prayer warriors.

For thirty years Kitty followed the same routine. She got out of bed at 5 A.M. and prayed until 6. Then no matter the season or the weather, she set out for a two- to three-mile walk. Now at age eighty-two Kitty is not able to walk as much, but her loving heart is in fine working order. One of her latest personal ministry projects is to teach groups of married women how to host teas for single moms.

Not long ago a woman phoned Kitty and told her to be at home the next day. The woman and her husband arrived with papers in hand and took Kitty to the door to see a gift. "This car is yours," the woman said. She was another of the women who had spent several years studying and praying with Kitty, and the experience, she said, had "changed her life." Now she wanted to give something back to Kitty. In a few minutes the papers were all signed and notarized and Kitty owned a newer car—free and clear.

Kitty knows from experience that ministry is not complicated, no matter how old a person may be. After touching thousands of lives over a thirty-year span, she sums it all up this way: "Prayer and believing God for everything is my whole approach to life."

Individuals like Kitty make me very excited about the potential of ministry during the final years of every believer's life. May their tribe increase!

## THE FAMILY-NEEDS SURVEY

### Empty Nest 2

*Percentages of those in Empty Nest 2 wanting help with their needs:*

| | |
|---|---|
| Spiritual growth | 51% |
| Spiritual disciplines | 44% |
| Developing and maintaining good marital communication | 33% |
| Having a ministry | 27% |
| Understanding your spouse's needs/expectations | 27% |
| Establishing adult friendships | 26% |
| Healthy living and eating habits | 26% |
| Adjusting to my season in life | 22% |
| Family communication | 19% |
| Managing my time | 17% |

*Source: The Family-Needs Survey, FamilyLife, Breakdowns by Family Life Cycle, National Database, March 2000, 89.*

## FAMILY LIFE CYCLE CHECKLIST

**Empty Nest 2—Key Ministry Objectives for Leaders**

*Topics/Issues:*

- ❑ Passing vision on to the next generation
- ❑ Influencing values of grandchildren
- ❑ Housing an aging parent
- ❑ Caring for an ailing spouse
- ❑ Mentoring
- ❑ Vision for life ministry

*Actions/Activities:*

- ❑ Tribute events for senior parents
- ❑ Events honoring elderly saints
- ❑ Support for widows and widowers
- ❑ Physical need services for the elderly
- ❑ Observation of wedding anniversaries for older couples
- ❑ Ministry opportunities for senior saints—intercessory prayer, praying for an "adopted teenager," peer support, etc.
- ❑ Activities involving youth with seniors (honoring seniors)

*Mentor Focus:*

- ❑ Providing companionship
- ❑ Making sure that affairs of the elderly are in order
- ❑ Identifying physical, emotional, and spiritual needs of widows and widowers
- ❑ Encouraging accountability regarding life, finances, and career
- ❑ Encouraging accountability regarding spouse, children, and grandchildren

## RESOURCES

*For Individuals or Couples*

McQuilken, Robertson. *A Promise Kept*. Wheaton, Ill.: Tyndale House Publishers, 1998. The true story of love and devotion as a husband leaves his career to care for his ailing wife.

*For Grandparents*

Endicott, Irene M. *Grandparenting by Grace*. Nashville: Broadman & Holman Publishers, 1994. A grandmother addresses issues including divorce, single-parent households, and grandparents raising grandchildren. Packed with grace principles and fun ideas.

Schreur, Jerry, and Jack Schreur. *Creative Grand Parenting*. Grand Rapids: Discovery House. 1992. Gives guidance on how grandparents can have a positive impact on their grandchildren through unconditional love and nurturing of self-esteem.

# PART
# 3
## UNIQUE FAMILIES

# CHAPTER
# 17

## The Adoptive Family

At the conclusion of a worship service in a church my wife, Barbara, was visiting, a pastor excitedly invited his wife to bring up front their recently adopted infant daughter. He introduced the child, then spoke eloquently about what this recent addition meant to him and his family. At the conclusion of the pastor's words, Barbara expected the congregation to stand and give the couple and child a rousing cheer. But there was no standing ovation, not even polite applause.

The service ended, and feeling a bit sad that she had not been more demonstrative, Barbara rushed forward to congratulate and encourage the pastor and his wife. She moved quickly, because she assumed there would be a long line of well-wishers. But again she was surprised. Only one couple came forward. Obviously the enthusiasm for adoption was not shared widely in that congregation.

Perhaps everyone was just having a bad day, but I think there are more profound reasons for this "underwhelming" response. Adoption is probably one of those revered ideas that are too often ignored by most Christians. In their defense the topic is not often discussed in the pulpit, and to my knowledge there are no best-selling books extolling adoption. Many people, perhaps, have been negatively influenced by a sad story of how an adopted child just "never really fit into the family." Maybe it's one of those "things" that happens to someone else, and because we haven't experienced it, we don't applaud the courage and compassion of a couple when they adopt a child as their own.

In spite of the many reasons for not focusing on adoption, the church as a whole and individual believers must attempt to fulfill what Jesus said in Matthew 25:45: "Truly I say to you, to the extent that you did not do it to one of the least of these, you did not do it to Me." Though the Lord was not speaking of homeless children, we should not think that these children are excluded. Throughout Scripture we encounter this theme that God is the "helper of the orphan" (Ps. 10:14) and "the father of the fatherless" (68:5). Can we do any less?

Barbara, who has a passion for children in need of adoption, once said, "I have thought for years that there really should be no children in need of adoption—ideally there would be no children anywhere living in orphanages or permanent foster homes. There should just be a sense within the church that we as believers are available—to reach out to those who are in need. We often think of other types of needs, but I don't think as a whole the church is very sensitive to needs of children who have no home." This comes in spite of the apostle James's admonition, "Pure and undefiled religion in the sight of our God and Father is this: to visit orphans and widows in their distress, and to keep oneself unstained by the world" (James 1:27).

The Christian community has long mounted a crusade against abortion, which it should. But we have not been as eager and visible in showing tangible love to homeless and needy children. I think there is no question that our witness for the unborn will be strengthened if we become more proactive in adopting children or providing foster care for those who need a family and a place to call "home."

The concept of caring for the abandoned and homeless appears explicitly and implicitly throughout the Bible. Moses was adopted by Pharaoh's daughter (Exod. 2:7); Samuel was in a sense adopted by the priest Eli (1 Sam. 1:28); and Esther was adopted by her uncle, Mordeccai (Esth. 2:7).

The supreme biblical example of adoption is God's work of adopting into the family of God those who receive Christ as their Savior. Paul wrote triumphantly, "For all who are being led by the Spirit of God, these are sons of God. For you have not received a spirit of slavery leading to fear again, but you have received a spirit of adoption as sons by which we cry out, 'Abba! Father!' The Spirit Himself testifies with our spirit that we are children of God, and if children, heirs also, heirs of God and fellow heirs with Christ, if indeed we suffer with Him so that we may also be glorified with Him" (Rom. 8:14–17).

Since our Father in Heaven has so graciously reached out to spiritual orphans like us, we need to follow His lead in welcoming homeless children—"strangers" (Matt. 25:35)—into our families in a similar fashion, in His name.

## WHO SHOULD CONSIDER ADOPTION?

Adoption is not for everyone. Some families may not have the gifts or resources to accept a child who may present unusual challenges. But such families are probably the exception rather than the rule. Yet the Christian community often seems to make adoption an option reserved for a select few who are uniquely called.

I would encourage church leaders to ask *every* Christian family to consider adopting at least one child, regardless of the number of natural-born children already born or desired. With millions of children worldwide who have no home, I believe this is an appropriate heart attitude. This is what my wife and I did. We prayed for a couple of years about the possibility of adopting. God then opened the door eighteen years ago and gave us the privilege of welcoming a little baby girl named Deborah into our family. Why not ask God to open the adoption door in your home and in the homes of your congregation?

Obviously, many couples are childless because of infertility. They should seek God's direction in prayer in the same way that those who have children should pray: "God, is it Your will that we adopt a child?" I would never minimize the importance or blessing of bearing natural children. But God did not say that only those naturally born are a "gift of the LORD" or that our quivers should be stocked only with tykes that are born into our families (Ps. 127:3–5).

Increasingly in the United States adoptions are made by single parents, in some locales as many as 25 percent of the total.[1] I have some reservations about this trend. We know that children do best in a home where both a loving father and mother are present. There are challenges in raising adopted children, challenges best met by the strength and wisdom of a mom and dad. But there may be unique circumstances in which a single-parent adoption makes sense, perhaps a situation where a blood relative provides the only good opportunity for a child to have a home. We must always commit matters like these to the Lord and let the Holy Spirit orchestrate what's best in particular cases. Barbara and I know of instances where this has occurred and the results were excellent.

If you have an opportunity to help a young woman with an unwanted pregnancy, do not forget to explore with her—and/or her parents—the possibility of releasing the child for adoption. Surprisingly many pregnancy counselors do not present adoption as a good option to the women they assist. Since so many American couples are waiting to adopt a baby, let's be sure this choice is always considered seriously.

## ADOPTION OPTIONS

If a couple is reasonably qualified—with good character references, in acceptable health, without a criminal record, economically stable, and with no record of child abuse—they may have an opportunity to adopt a child.

Adoptions take place either privately, such as the placement of an infant born to an unwed mother, or through a variety of state or private agencies supervising the placement of children who are legally free to leave the foster-care system or to come from a foreign country. Children of certain races or with special physical or mental needs are often easier to adopt because fewer prospective adoptive families are available. A huge amount of information on adoption is available via the Internet. One excellent source is Bethany Christian Services at 1-800-238-4269 or www.bethany.org. This agency has offices in many states. There are many other fine organizations helping with adoptions. If someone desires to pursue adoption, abundant assistance is available.

Sadly, because of the effects of all kinds of sin and evil, the world is highly populated with homeless children. Wars are a primary culprit in producing orphans. The first significant surge of international adoption in America did not happen until after the Korean War. In the United States, at any given time, there are about five hundred thousand people seeking to adopt a child, but there are five to six adoption seekers for every adoption that actually occurs.

Of the half million children in the United States who are under state-run programs like foster care, about fifty thousand are legally free to be adopted.[2] Of this group, around seventeen thousand are adopted each year.[3] Added to this number are private adoptions, usually in which the child of an unmarried woman is adopted soon after birth.

America leads the world in adopting children from other countries, and the rate of adoption of international children more than doubled during the 1990s to a total of nearly sixteen thousand in 1998. Over half of these children came from Russia and mainland China.[4] I have been told by adoption authorities that up to 4.5 million children currently reside in orphanages in the former Soviet Union alone. These boys and girls will be turned loose at age sixteen or seventeen, and many will become gang members, criminals, and prostitutes. Millions of other homeless children await adoption in other countries. I realize there are obstacles and risks in pursuing an international adoption, but how can we in America who have so much abundance turn our backs on these children?

I'm confident that Christians are responsible for a sizable percentage of the estimated fifty to sixty thousand adoptions each year in the United States. But we're only scratching the surface. My wife has a great idea worth considering: "A church could target a country in South America, Asia, or elsewhere, see what the orphan needs are, bring this need to the congregation, and begin to pray. Initially, only the childless couples might be very interested, but later others may become interested too. This could become a mission of the church! Instead of merely sending items to that country, we can bring some children to the States and to Christian homes."

## AN ADOPTION MINISTRY

If you choose to make adoption a featured opportunity for service and ministry in your church—something I urge not just for the benefit of children but also for the blessings that will accrue to the parents and others in your church—three important activities should take place: raising the challenge, supporting adoptive parents, and supporting adopted children.

### Raising the Challenge

As with any need, little will happen in any church until someone raises the issue. This is probably even more the case with adoption, because many people have misconceptions and fears about the subject. Ideally someone who is a respected leader (such as the senior pastor) needs to teach, preach, and exhort on the critical importance for the family of God to welcome and nurture children who do not have homes.

Adoption is not to be feared, but neither should it be treated as a fairy tale in which there are no problems and everyone lives happily ever after. Adoption does result in enormous benefit to the child and a host of benefits to the parents. But often unique challenges occur, and these must be faced squarely. Although many adopted children adapt quickly and effortlessly into their new family, this is not always the case. And a situation that seemed idyllic when the child was young may develop into something less than ideal as the child heads into adolescence. None of this is beyond God's intervention and provision, but it's important that parents and children not be naive about potential hurdles.

Once the members of a local church know and embrace the conviction that adoption is highly valued, then information on the subject needs to flow on a regular basis, including information on how interested families can pursue the possibility of adoption. Starting and maintaining this emphasis in the church does not have to become a burdensome process. It just takes some initiative by the pastor and the involvement of a few lay couples who have a heart for this ministry.

But the first and perhaps most important step is to present a clear challenge that God can use to stir the hearts of men and women with compassion for our contemporary orphans.

### Supporting Adoptive Parents

Couples who adopt will need a community of believers who will encourage them as they raise their child.

At first the adoption process may seem complex and scary. Some individual in the congregation should be designated as a point person, one who can distribute basic information, answer questions, and give guidance on an individual basis. Once the process is underway, the church's support may shift, for example, toward giving some financial assistance to help cover the often significant out-of-pocket expenses of adoption. (In 1999 the cost of adopting a child born in the United States ranged from "nothing" if handled by a public agency to twenty thousand dollars if arranged by some private agencies. The cost of adopting a child from China, for example, ranged from twelve thousand to twenty-five thousand dollars.[5] Private placement adoptions can cost substantially less.)

At a minimum, ongoing and specific prayer should occur for families in the adoption process. Often the delays and detours encountered are wearing and stressful for a mom and dad who want to provide a home for a child. Such a family needs an abundance of spiritual and emotional support.

The arrival of the child may seem like the dramatic conclusion in the process, but adoptive parents still face challenges. The best thing a church can do is encourage and facilitate networking among parents of adopted children. If the church is small, this probably will mean networking with parents from several churches; perhaps a lay leader can arrange this. Such support groups should assemble parents by the age of their adopted children—one group for children up through elementary school age and another for children in the teenage years. Breaking up the groups is good because the needs related to the child can change dramatically with age. A "one-group-fits-all-needs" approach may frustrate and discourage participants. However, if multiple age groups are impossible, then be sure at least one group is functioning.

On occasion these groups may want some outside "expert" to share information, but the most important purpose is simply to give parents opportunity to share experiences and gain support from others who are walking the same path.

### Supporting the Children

One adopted child described her childhood as "feeling like a zebra in a herd of giraffes. . . . It was not that I wasn't loved. I just felt separate."[6]

Adopted children have unique needs. If a community of believers recognizes this, ministry to such children is well underway. Perhaps the best thing to be done for adopted children is to help their parents with their needs so that they in turn can be effective with their children. Churches need not set up special church programs for adopted children. The one exception to this would be to encourage occasional adoptive family gatherings. This will give the children opportunity to see and know others who are adopted. Often just the awareness that "I am not the only one" reduces insecurities. And then as the children grow older and become more independent, they will know other adoptees with whom they may associate.

Leaders and pastors who work with children of elementary-school age and older need to understand the particular needs of the adopted, especially in attachment to others and struggles with self-identity. Again adopted children should not be singled out, but a teacher or youth worker who is aware of a child's background will be better able to minister to unique needs.

Personal issues related to adoption will probably intensify as adopted children grow older. "Adopted children tend to act out, as a group, more than other teens," Lynn Franklin wrote. One adopted child stated, "It wasn't until I was in my later teens and early twenties, when I was struggling for an identity, that adoption issues became a big part of my life."[7]

Ultimately between 60 and 90 percent of adopted children will show some interest in finding information about their birth families.[8] The church that understands how normal this is will be better prepared to support those children, their adoptive parents, and the birth parents.

As my wife put it, "Adoption is not easy, but it's God's idea." More churches need to investigate how to turn God's idea into a living reality in many of their families.

# HOW ONE CHURCH LOVES ORPHANS

Jorie Kincaid is passionate about adoption. For good reason. She was adopted at birth, and she and her husband, Ron, pastor of Sunset Presbyterian Church, Portland, Oregon, have adopted a boy and girl themselves. But her ongoing, deep interest in orphaned children is more than personal; it has grown primarily through her involvement with a ministry enthusiastically supported by a local church.

About ten years ago Jorie and Ron visited Romania shortly after the fall of the communist government. The Kincaids returned to America not only with a precious adopted daughter but with memories of thousands of homeless children—many of them reaching tiny, imploring hands through the bars of their cribs for help and attention.

These images prompted Jorie and others to convene a prayer team to learn how they could do something for orphans around the world. The result of several months of prayer was a foundation called Orphans Overseas. The mission statement of the new organization was simple—to love orphans the way God loves them and to accomplish ministry with integrity.

Since then this agency, which operates separately from the church as a nonprofit entity, has prompted a number of members in Ron's church to become involved in orphan ministry. Besides funding and sponsoring a variety of humanitarian activities, Orphans Overseas has helped facilitate nearly three hundred adoptions. The church provides office space, the mission board gives financial support, and the Sunday school department spearheads collection drives. Volunteer teams travel to foreign countries to support indigenous churches in helping orphans. According to Jorie the key to being effective is to work with local churches in foreign countries.

When asked how a local church might initiate a similar outreach, Jorie listed these important action steps:

- Begin with seeking God's will through a prayer team.
- Network with other similar agencies—such as Orphans Overseas.
- Work with the local church overseas.
- Stay flexible—the rest of the world often operates differently than we do in America.

It is important to understand that actual adoption is only a small part of ministry to the world's needy children. Since about 85 percent of needy children in other lands are not eligible for adoption anyway (these children have parents who have not relinquished legal rights), Orphans Overseas invests money on site to help relieve the physical needs of orphans, pays for inoculations and other types of medical care, and operates a sponsorship program that emphasizes not just money but also prayer. Since overt sharing of the gospel is not possible in many countries, praying for orphans is a significant way to reach them for Christ.

Jorie's passion for orphans cannot be contained. "My heart says that if every family could reach out to one orphan, we would wipe out the need for orphanages around the world." Why not consider such a ministry in your church? If you need help getting started, contact Jorie Kincaid and Orphans Overseas at 1-503-297-2006.

## RESOURCES

Eldridge, Sherrie. *Twenty Things Adopted Kids Wish Their Adoptive Parents Knew*. New York: Dell, 1999. An adoptive parent sheds light on hidden issues in the lives of adoptive children.

———, with Dennis Rainey and Barbara Rainey. "Twenty Things Adopted Kids Wish Their Adoptive Parents Knew." Audiotape series. Little Rock: FamilyLife, 2000. Instructive interviews on adoption issues.

# CHAPTER

## 18

## The Singles Ministry

When a church begins to focus on building stronger marriages and families, someone usually asks, "What about all the singles? Where do they fit in a family-friendly church?"

That one question—"What about the singles?"—has left some churches paralyzed, doing less than needed to strengthen families because they don't want anyone to be hurt or offended. But the response to the question should not be to diminish the help we give to couples and families. Instead, we should help families and *also* address the spiritual and relationship needs of singles in the church. Let's build a community where singles play a vital role in serving, in growing, and in interacting with other singles and with married couples and their children.

Singles represent one of the largest untapped and unreached "people groups" in America. Open to the gospel and hungry for community, singles present a challenge for most churches. But because the approach of many local congregations doesn't fit the needs of this group, many singles tend to avoid church.

This is a tragedy of significant proportions. In the nineteenth century and through the first half of the twentieth century, less than 5 percent of the American adult population was single (never married, widowed, or divorced). By 1996 this had skyrocketed to 43 percent.[1]

The fastest growing household type, according to 1997 census data, is the single-adult household. [2]

Because singles represent such a huge demographic portion of the American adult population, much commercial enterprise focuses on their needs. This is frequently revealed in advertising for products like automobiles, beer, and clothing, in which the single lifestyle is presented.

Many employers value single over married staff because the single person is able to devote more time and emotional energy to his or her job. Also single people tend to be more receptive to unusual work schedules or a geographical move, which is cheaper for a business than moving an entire family.

Even though the major institutions of our culture have accepted the fact that singles are a huge societal force, churches may be lagging behind. A report in 2000 revealed that only 31 percent of singles attend a church on a typical weekend, compared to 49 percent of married people.[3]

In the next chapter I will discuss ministry to single *parents*. Here I want to issue a specific ministry challenge concerning the "never-marrieds," those who are divorced and without children, and the widowed. Instead of discussing the full spectrum of a singles ministry, I will focus on how a church can help equip singles relationally—a tremendous benefit for the present as well as for the future when most singles will marry and lead their own families.

## SINGLES BELONG IN CHURCH

The Bible blesses both the married and the single state, and we know from Scripture and church history that a number of the great molders and defenders of the faith were single. Many single people will have more time and energy to devote to Christian ministry than do married people. The apostle Paul made this point clearly: "But I want you to be free from concern. One who is unmarried is concerned about the things of the Lord, how he may please the Lord; but one who is married is concerned about the things of the world, how he may please his wife, and his interests are divided. The woman who is unmarried, and the virgin, is concerned about the things of the Lord, that she may be holy both in body and spirit; but one who is married is concerned about the things of the world, how she may please her husband" (1 Cor. 7:32–34).

Jim Talley, who has ministered to singles for decades, once said on our "FamilyLife Today" radio broadcast, "We have to realize that singleness is an opportunity for us to focus on our spiritual walk. . . . Many married people are not as focused on service to God as are singles."[4]

Too often today, single people are made to feel as though they are incomplete human beings who will never find fulfillment until matched up with their "other half." Certainly the vast majority of Christians will experience the blessings of marriage. But the Scriptures teach that some are called to singleness, so they can be "concerned about the things of the Lord" (7:32) and "be holy both in body and spirit" (7:34). I agree enthusiastically with Nancy DeMoss, a dynamic woman of God who is single: "Tireless, reckless abandon to the will and work of God ought to characterize the Christian who is single."[5]

Our marital state, as important as it is, is not the most critical issue in the Christian life. Pursuing God and living in obedience to Him are the goals. We all start out single, then most of us marry. But eventually we will again be single when our spouse dies. Our goal should be to serve God passionately, whatever our marital state.

Each local congregation must help its members understand that God calls singleness a gift. Churches must get in agreement with God's plan for singles and recognize the important contribution singles can make in the life of the church.

Now may be one of the more difficult times in history emotionally and socially to be a single adult. God designed us for meaningful connection to others, something that is becoming increasingly difficult to achieve in contemporary society.

Steve Woodrow, a singles pastor for many years, offers some penetrating insights. "Being single is getting tougher and tougher in America because of the pressures, because of our increased degeneration of morals and temptation, the fragmentation of community. . . . More and more singles are traveling. Companies look to them to carry heavy travel schedules, which pulls them away from community. These travel schedules are just crazy, and it's killing singles in a lot of ways. More and more singles lack strong intimate relationships, even with the same sex. That makes relationship with someone of the opposite sex even harder when there's not a friendship support base. Very few singles will even say that they have a best friend today."[6]

We should not overly generalize about single adults, but a definite picture that emerges is of a large group of people eager to find friendships who, because of the pace and fragmentation in contemporary life, often end up not just alone but also lonely. This represents what should be the dramatic intersection of a human need with the provision available in what is the greatest inclusive, expansive, resourceful community ever created: the church of Jesus Christ.

## IS THE CHURCH A RELATIONSHIP INSTITUTE?

Perhaps the greatest opportunity for the church to affect the lives of singles dramatically is in their relationships. Dick Purnell, leader of a nationwide ministry to singles, notes, "I really believe the church can be at the forefront of helping singles to meet the challenges of life. [Churches] have what they want, which is community."[7]

Many people today—including singles—do not know how to form and maintain a healthy relationship, even at the most basic level of friendship. The church that takes this issue seriously and provides teaching and coaching on the topic will find a large, eager audience. Jim Talley comments on what he considers to be the relational ineptitude of so many single Christians: "The typical evangelical friendship [among singles] in our country today lasts about three hours. That is the length of a date. At the end of the date they are doing relational things—holding hands, hugging, kissing, something. The friendship at that point stops. . . . When you begin to do things with the opposite sex you wouldn't do with the same sex, you are no longer friends. All the roles have changed and you are in a relationship."[8]

There are three reasons singles desperately need and want this relational training. First, they are a generation that has been crippled, relationally speaking, by divorce. They need "relational rehab." They are unhealthy, relationally speaking, and many of them know it. They are scared of commitment, the opposite sex, and marriage.

Second, many singles have lost faith in the institution of marriage and the family. Increasingly Christian singles mirror our culture by sleeping together before marriage and not thinking anything is wrong with it.

Steve Woodrow explains how a church should address issues related to sexuality and purity: "Present people with something that satisfies far greater than sex outside of marriage—a romantic, intimate, vibrant relationship with Christ. . . . There is something far greater out there—the abundant life. And if somebody is involved in sex, then obviously they are seeking for something. Communicate that they won't find it in sex; they will just find destruction and death."[9]

I regularly receive letters from singles who know something is terribly broken in our world's approach to marriage and family. Many are looking for a model of love and commitment that they never had at home in hopes that they too can love and be loved in a meaningful marriage.

Third, experts tell us that over 90 percent of all singles will eventually marry.

Helping singles develop basic relationship skills ought to be part of the agenda of every local church. But the focus should not be on building those skills so that the singles can hurry up and get married! The focus needs to be on helping singles live more effectively in a spiritual community—to fulfill the "one another" commands found in the New Testament.

I think the average singles group in most churches today needs to be given a much greater challenge about spiritual maturity. Nancy DeMoss observes, "Those singles whose lives are characterized by chronic loneliness probably have not discovered their place in the Body of Christ. The fact is, we are not alone. We are part of an incredible family of faith. And that family includes far more than just other singles!"[10]

One word of caution: Don't apologize for training singles in marriage and family. Singles groups can be "controlled" by a few who will never marry and who are "offended" that we would spend time teaching on marriage and family relationships. I fear that a small number of people can keep us from doing what is vitally important for the larger group.

## A SINGLES EQUIPPING MINISTRY

Singles populate every stage of the Family Life Cycle. It would be ludicrous to think that one set of teaching and ministry opportunities and social activities will appeal to them all. "There definitely is a generational aspect to things," says Steve Woodrow. "The twenty-year-old single today definitely has a different mind-set than the upper thirty- or forty-year-old single."[11]

Sometimes the most innocent actions in a church can send the wrong or hurtful messages to singles. For example, in the area of financial giving, most churches issue reports based on "family units." A common way of encouraging fellowship is to organize dinners in homes of members, often advertised as "dinners of eight"—that screams "couples only." Sometimes even innocent small talk causes hurt, such as teasing comments that can sting: "You're not married yet?" "What's wrong with you! You're obviously a great catch!"

Here are some ideas that can help churches serve their singles as they grow relationally and—in many cases—prepare to marry.

- Use every opportunity to involve singles with families. Two single authors have commented that "the more we get inside homes of married people and families, the more we feel connected,"[12]
- Don't turn your singles group into a "marriage hunter" group. Singles need to be pointed toward God, personal holiness, and spiritual maturity.
- Call singles to relational accountability. Moral holiness and biblical standards need to be lifted up. Instruct them on aspects of godly dating.
- Teach on the biblical definitions of manhood and womanhood. Singles will not understand the fullness of being a man or a woman by getting married and merely taking on the titles of husband and wife. Also teach singles the basics of fatherhood and motherhood.
- Instruct them on how to know God's will for finding a life mate and how to make a good decision in selecting a spouse.

- Emphasize the value of children—if for no other reason than to encourage singles to minister to children and youth in their church.
- When appropriate, get singles tied in with some of the single-parent families for the purpose of discipling and loving kids whose fathers or mothers are not involved.
- Help singles understand and resolve emotional issues with their parents—what does it mean to love and honor them while not living at home?
- Teach the importance of being concerned for their nieces, nephews, and other relatives.
- Consider banding together with other churches in your community if maintaining a singles ministry in your own church is overwhelming. As Dick Purnell observes, "Singles ministry . . . will be a spearhead uniting a whole community."[13]

## A GREAT OPPORTUNITY

Instead of turning singles off and away, let's turn them on and bring them in by including them in all aspects of church life. Steve Woodrow explains what happens when we do this well: "There are single men and women out there who are hungry and desperate for pastors and leaders to take them under their arm and equip them and unleash them in the church and to take ownership and strong roles in the church to build His church. . . . We need to reeducate them and define church. They are the church. We are not here to entertain but to equip them. They are the ones to carry out the work of the ministry of the church. . . . I believe single adults are the wave of leadership the church needs to bring about revival and renewal."[14]

Will you see and seize the opportunity to minister to nearly half of the adult population in the United States? Instead of allowing singles to drift toward extreme self-absorption and too much emphasis on finding a mate, let's challenge them to use the advantages of their single state for God's glory.

Tommy Nelson, senior pastor of Denton Bible Church, Denton, Texas, commutes forty miles to Dallas to teach a "Metro Bible Study" for singles. This started with a small group of single professionals, but he ended up having two to three thousand single people showing up for this basic Bible study on relationship training related to marriage. I think this illustrates the enormous hunger among single people for clear, solid biblical truth around the issues of how a man and a woman are to relate to each other.

## RESOURCES

DeMoss, Nancy Leigh. *Singled Out for Him.* Buchanan, Mich.: Life Action Ministries, 1998. Discusses singleness as a blessing and gift from God.

Purnell, Dick. "Single Life Resources." Seminars and resources for ministry to Christian singles by an authority on such ministry to singles. 1-919-363-8000 or www.slr.org.

# CHAPTER

## 19

## The Single-Parent Family

$S$ome are moms, some are dads, some have never been married, and some are divorced. A very small number are widowed. Some are just teenagers, others are grandparents—parenting again in their senior years. All of them have one thing in common—they are raising children by themselves.

In 1998, 28 percent of all children lived in single-parent families (for African-Americans, the figure was 55 percent), a total of 19.8 million children under age eighteen. This total has increased threefold since 1960, when only 9 percent lived with a single parent. The overwhelming majority of single-parent families today are headed by the mother—84 percent. However, the percentage of father-led, single-parent families has increased from 9 percent in 1970 to 16 percent in 1998. Of the single-parent families with mothers, 40 percent of the women have never married—up from just 4 percent in 1960. The number of female single parents who have never married now exceeds the number of female divorcées.[1]

Single parents are often the most desperate, hurting, and lonely people in our congregations. We must step in and be a father to the fatherless, to help the "widows" in their distress (James 1:27), to walk beside these single parents in one of life's toughest assignments. We need to enlist people in our congregations to shoulder this load of ministering to single-parent families.

The single-parent phenomenon is not as unique to our generation as we might think. Lynda Hunter, editor of Focus on the Family's *Single-Parent Family Magazine*, made a profound observation. "A century ago, there were almost equal [percentages] of single parents. At that point, it was due to desertion or death as opposed to divorce and never married situations. . . . But what they had in those days that we don't have now is extended families. . . . They had community. Today there is so much mobility in our society that [single-parent families] not only don't have a dad in the home, they don't have grandparents, they don't have aunts and uncles to help. So, where does that job fall to become family to that individual? There is only place where that can be done. That's the church."[2]

Churches don't necessarily need to add programs for single parents. Instead, church leaders should encourage church members in intact families, the empty nesters, and others to include single-parent families in their lives. Intact families will have to take the initiative—you must give them the vision for this opportunity to serve others and how it will be of particular help to children. It means calling others in the congregation to step into the life of a single mom or dad with financial support, assistance with children, giving wisdom, supporting by prayer—all given in a spirit of service that demonstrates Christ's love.

But as the church assumes more and more responsibility for caring for the emotional, spiritual, and physical needs of single parents, it is also important that single parents understand the need to be involved in meaningful fellowship with others.

When we minister to this segment of society, we are being like God Himself, who is "a father of the fatherless and a judge for the widows, . . . [who] makes a home for the lonely" (Ps. 68:5–6).

## MINISTRY TO SINGLE PARENTS

Make single parents feel welcome. They have enough to handle without our making them feel excluded.

Although we should not shrink from holding up the intact family as the ideal—which it is—we should never imply that a single-parent family is not a family. In fact many of these families have qualities that would enhance intact families. Single parents present opportunities to show the true family—the family of God—at work.

Gary Richmond, pastor and expert on the needs of single parents, has put together this helpful list (I've modified just a few words) of the typical needs of single parents.

1. Emotional support
2. Practical help (car maintenance, mowing the lawn, fixing the garbage disposal, etc.)
3. Rest (a weekend off from the demands of parenting can bring much-needed refreshment)
4. Baby-sitting
5. Gifts of money
6. Help with child discipline
7. Adult conversation
8. Counsel for major decisions
9. Guidance on future relationships
10. Someone to relax with
11. Someone to cry with
12. A good listener
13. A good role model of the opposite sex for children
14. Help in reentering the job market
15. Reassurance that they and their children will be all right.[3]

What follows is a summary of ways in which the church can minister to single parents—formally and informally, regularly or as needs arise. Ministering in these and other ways can help single parents and their children feel accepted and loved.

*Physical Needs*

Single moms especially are often at the brink of physical exhaustion and need someone to give them a break. Every church can provide at least informal relief, perhaps by providing childcare on a regular basis. Another superb way to help is to enlist fix-it men and women in your church who will agree to be on call when a single mom needs a leaking sink repaired, a tire changed, windows washed, and so on.

The possibilities and opportunities are limitless. They might include helping a boy without a dad learn how to throw a football, put together a plastic model, or buy a present for mom for Mother's Day or her birthday.

Single parents often need financial help. I recommend that every church set aside a portion of its benevolence fund for single-parent family needs. Appoint a wise, sensitive, caring person to keep in contact with single parents to assess their financial needs. Sometimes single parents are too busy or embarrassed to seek assistance.

Dick Purnell, who ministers throughout America to singles, has said, "One of the greatest things you could do for single parents is to help a single woman to know how to raise a boy . . . and how a single father can raise a little girl."[4] Let single parents know that your church wants to be their first contact when they need help of any kind. You may not always be able to meet all their needs, but position yourself aggressively. A single parent needs to know that resources and wisdom are there for the asking.

Once Barbara and I found ourselves helping a single-parent mother whose child had gotten into difficulty. We knew this single-parent mom needed an objective opinion, some kind of advice or game plan from outside her family. Since Barbara and I did not have the expertise to help her on a long-term basis, I encouraged her to go to her church and say to her pastor or elders, "We have a situation that perhaps could end in death. I need your counsel as my spiritual leaders in this church to guide me." She did that and was helped immeasurably as she worked through the crisis.

*Spiritual Health*

Catherine Marshall became a widow when her husband, Peter Marshall, chaplain of the U.S. Senate, died unexpectedly. She wrote about her subsequent experience as a single parent: "In my situation the best answers to the sense of helplessness and frustration came through my early morning quiet time when in prayer I would seek God's guidance for my son."[5]

Related to this, prayer support for single parents is crucial. How about setting up a support team for single parents, a group of individuals who will pray for single parents' specific needs? This group could also coordinate care for the physical needs mentioned above.

## Ex-spouse Issues

For a person who has been emotionally mangled by an ex-spouse, the only appropriate response is to extend kindness and forgiveness. As the apostle Peter wrote, "To sum up, all of you be harmonious, sympathetic, brotherly, kindhearted, and humble in spirit; not returning evil for evil or insult for insult, but giving a blessing instead; for you were called for the very purpose that you might inherit a blessing" (1 Pet. 3:8–9).

No one can predict or control what an ex-spouse will do. But with the Lord's help, the single-parent can control actions and seek to do what is right. When anger and bitterness are not allowed to fester, God's promise of blessing will be obtained.

## Custody Matters

Lynda Hunter told our "FamilyLife Today" radio audience, "In custody situations, no matter who wins or who gains the custody, there are no winners or losers. You must realize that in all studies that are done, the best circumstance within the divorce—except for abuse situations—is that both parents maintain a constant relationship with that child."[6]

Sometimes a single parent will wish the noncustodial parent would disappear—the hassles hardly seem worth it. But children need to know their parents. And in those situations the single parent needs to apply grace and not compete with a former spouse.

In addition, simply because a mom or dad has "dropped the ball," so to speak, parentally, that does not mean children have the right to violate God's command by not honoring their parents. Christian single parents must be careful to guard their children from wrong attitudes and to encourage them to seek ways to honor the other parent despite his or her sin and rebellion against God.

The noncustodial parents in our churches, most of whom are men, also need to be encouraged to do what's right. They need to avoid the temptation to be a "Disneyland Dad" who only gives his child gifts. Instead he should offer the soul-to-soul experience only a father can give a child.

Both parents—custodial or not—must recognize their responsibility to battle for the spiritual well-being of their children, to help them grow spiritually.

## Child Support

Urge the divorced men in your church to do their honorable duty and make their child support payments. When I speak to men's audiences, such as at PromiseKeepers, I often call on the divorced men in the crowd to do two things: "First, speak no evil of your spouse. Second, pay your alimony and child support on time." Every time I've made that statement the entire stadium or arena breaks into applause as the other men challenge the divorcés to fulfill their sense of duty.

After pastoring thousands of single parents, Gary Richmond offers this advice: "I always tell the moms to press it [child support] to its limits. We get what we tolerate. If you tolerate the dad not paying child support, you're going to be in a difficult circumstance very quickly. So don't tolerate it, don't let him get late, and don't let him get behind."[7]

Single parents need to realize that the law is on their side when it comes to child support. David Sims, an attorney on our FamilyLife staff, says, "Motions for contempt for nonpayment of support work very well in most cases. Judges do not tolerate nonpayment of court-ordered support. After one or two warnings, most judges will put nonpaying spouses in jail and award attorney's fees for bringing the motion for contempt."[8]

## Friends and Mentors

Like the rest of us, single parents must avoid getting isolated, which will tend to happen when they are exhausting nearly all resources of time, finances, and energy in seeking to make a living and raise their children alone.

Single parents need a solid cadre of godly friends and wise advisers who will speak God's Word to them, who won't shrink back from telling the truth when they need to hear it or when they get emotionally off-base. Having good friends with whom to share concern will prevent any unhealthy tendency of a single parent to make a child something of a "soul mate," what is sometimes called emotional incest or in psychological terms "enmeshing." Judges and psychologists alike view this as emotionally unhealthy for children.

Because of the demands on them, single parents may need some help in connecting with those who could serve as mentors. This task should be the responsibility of a layperson or someone on the church staff. "Single parents don't want two-parent families to treat them with an annual good deed," says Mike Yorkey. "They really desire friendship. But some . . . are so exhausted or have been so wounded that they can't take the first step toward getting together."[9] Unfortunately many times the wounds have come from churches and church members.

## A Single-Parent Support Group

One way to provide some organized support for single parents is to organize a support group. But such a group should not be a place where singles vent their anger or criticize their ex-spouses. The emphasis should be on learning from one another, sharing needs, and praying together.

Gary Richmond tells of his experience in helping single parents and children at the First Evangelical Free Church in Fullerton, California. "We try to put them into . . . a great support group network that will become their extended family, the uncles and the aunts, brothers and sisters, mothers and fathers who are missing in their own lives and give them a sense of support and cohesiveness."[10]

## Dating Relationships

Unfortunately many single parents remarry too quickly. The stepfamily may provide some relief for the adults, but children often suffer more in such situations than when their parent was single. The relational dynamics are so complicated, the environment so chaotic, that the children may receive less attention than in the one-parent home. Of course, there are exceptions, but often it is better for the single parent to complete the task of raising children before considering remarriage.

After experience with thousands of single-parent families, this is what

Gary Richmond wisely advises: "A blended family is not an easy thing to put children in. There is coming and going; there is uncertainty; and there are different values coming in and out of the house. . . . Very few people do it successfully. Second marriages have only a 22–24 percent chance of lasting five years. Statistically it is better to raise your children and then think of marriage later. . . . Research shows that if children watch two relationships break, especially extended relationships, the children lose their ability to bond. They have already watched [one] marriage fail, and if they watch a continuation of serious relationships break, then what's planted into the young mind is that relationships are disposable and they don't work."[11]

### Pre-remarriage Counseling

We may be tempted to think that individuals wanting to remarry do not need premarital counseling. But they probably need it more! Make the process rigorous for those who want your blessing on a second marriage, especially in light of the impact on children.

People in such situations must be counseled and challenged to evaluate their own spiritual condition carefully and to grapple with what the Bible has to say about their lives and how they will apply what the Bible says, particularly regarding the selection of another mate.

Ron Deal, a family-life minister and specialist in ministry to stepparents, is acutely aware of the importance of this topic. He says, "Pre-remarriage counseling [for those previously divorced] is another thing the church really has to pick up on. Churches overlook the significance of preparing couples for stepfamily life. They [churches] think, 'We'll just provide remarrieds the same premarital training that we did before.' But that's totally inadequate. . . . I really challenge these couples to examine their spiritual condition and their scriptural permission to seek a remarriage. I also challenge them tremendously with the realities of stepfamily life. I don't want them going in blind or they are sure to be blindsided."[12]

## CHILDREN OF SINGLE PARENTS

Children are the most severely wounded family members in a divorce or other loss of a parent. One pastor related an incredible story of how one child responded to the breakup of her family.

> This [single parent's] girl decided to start stealing clothes from the mall. She had never done this kind of thing before in her life. She was just a good Christian girl. When I asked her in the privacy of my office and she felt safe (we had known each other for some time), "Do you have any idea why you did this?" she said, "Yes."
>
> I said, "Why?"
>
> "I wanted to do something to get in trouble," she said. "I wanted to get taken to the police department because I knew both my mom and my dad would show up. I hoped that when they saw each other and looked into each other's eyes, they would fall in love again and we would have our family back."[13]

That makes me ache every time I read it. It also serves as a parable you can remember as you think about the needs of the children of single parents in your church. Although these kids may look, talk, and act like other children, they have within them an open wound that may never completely heal. Although you need to be subtle so that you don't cause shame and embarrassment, the children of single parents *do* have unique needs that require some special insight.

Here are some guidelines on ministering to single parents in raising their children.

### Remember That Children of Single Parents Are Depraved Too

Children in a single-parent home often take advantage of tired, emotionally worn parents and skillfully manipulate them. If you think the old "divide and conquer" game works well for a child in an intact family ("But Dad said I could do it!"), just think of the possibilities when one parent is seen only on weekends! Encourage single parents to avoid creating an environment in which "anything goes" and in which discipline and proper instruction are lacking.

### Encourage Single Parents to Set Boundaries

Related to the last point, single parents should set boundaries for their children in relation to movies, curfews, dating, and related matters. These guidelines need to be made clear to the child, and then the single parent needs to begin shaping that young person's convictions around those standards or boundaries. If the single parent needs help in setting these limits, he or she should be encouraged to have a same-sex friend who can listen and provide advice and encouragement.

### Facilitate a Parent Community

Parents with children in the same age group need to band together to assist each other in watching out for each other's children. This will be particularly helpful to the single parent who lives in a family with only two parental eyes instead of four. Encourage these groups of parents to get together to talk about reenforcing one another's standards. Then if a child veers off the path, other parents will be able to come alongside that child—not to condemn him, but to express love, belief, and affirmation—to put an arm around him and even pull him away from negative peer pressure.

### Provide Opportunities for Adults to Be Role Models for Children

Be sure to provide opportunities for children of single parents to receive mentoring from godly adults. In the vast majority of cases this means men in the church will need to be recruited, exhorted, and trained for this role. Help men see the opportunity they have to make a tremendous impact on fatherless boys and young men.

Gill Duncan IV, pastor of Covenant Church, Pittsburgh, helps lead a "Brothers' Keepers" mentoring program for sons of missing fathers in their congregation and community. Boys between the ages of eight and eighteen are coached to become responsible individuals. The mentoring men accompany mothers to school meetings, assist in home interventions, and build relationships and attend special events with the boys.

Catherine Marshall wrote, "It takes a great deal of masculine companionship to make up for missing a father's steady presence in the everyday-ness of life."[14]

Women, too, should take the opportunity to help "parent" children of single parents, because often the single mom is so exhausted that extra support is welcome and necessary.

## GIVE SINGLE-PARENT FAMILIES HOPE

I am impressed by the courage and tenacity of many single parents. I believe some of the greatest rewards in heaven are being stored up for single-parent moms and dads who are facing steep obstacles but are fighting the fight of faith and finishing their parenting assignment well.

I encourage single parents to consider three ways to stay focused. First, like all parents, their hope must be in God. "Unless the LORD builds the house, they labor in vain who build it" (Ps. 127:1). Single parents may be more aware of their need for God's sustaining guidance than those in two-parent families.

Second, single parents need to pursue a relationship with a fellow burden-bearer, someone who can support them in their struggles of raising children.

Third, single parents need to make prayer a daily discipline in protecting their children spiritually.

The good news is that just as single parents have a unique opportunity to grow and mature spiritually and in other ways, the same holds true for their children. We have heard many stories of how some of the most outstanding kids in a youth group, for example, are growing up in single-parent homes.

Aren't you glad we serve a God who offers hope to everyone, regardless of the mistakes we have made and misfortunes visited on us in a fallen world? Make your church the place where single parents receive this message and the support that goes with it—and you will be host to a large, important, and thriving work of God to a very needy group in today's society.

The story of a boy named Alex is a poignant reminder that we have a great God who cares for us. Alex was three years old when his mother's divorce from his dad became final. Two psychologists testified in his mom's final divorce hearing. They had been seeing Alex for about a year because of some rather bizarre behavioral problems. When Alex threw a temper tantrum, he screamed and yelled. But he also assaulted his mother with fists, teeth, nails, knives, and whatever else he could use to inflict physical damage, as best a three-year-old could. Alex had seen his daddy beat his mother many times.

Alex's psychologists testified that his was the worst case of child physical abuse they had ever seen. Alex's mother thought her son was hopeless.

Twelve years later she learned that she was wrong. Alex loves the Lord. He's followed him in baptism and desires to become a missionary to Mexico. He has been on several missions trips to Mexico already, and he and his mother have moved to a Texas town on the Mexican border so they can be more effective missionaries to the Mexican people.

Our God is good, full of hope and mercy!

## RESOURCES

Gangel, Kenn. *Ministering to Today's Adults.* Swindoll Leadership Library. Nashville: Word Publishing, 1999. Includes a helpful chapter on single parenting, entitled "Flying Solo in the Family."

Hunter, Lynda. *Parenting on Your Own.* Grand Rapids: Zondervan Publishing House, 1997. Gives practical advice and encouragement from a single mom.

———. *Single Moments.* Wheaton, Ill.: Tyndale House Publishers, 1998. A weekly devotional written by a single mom, with fifty-two devotions that give spiritual insight into single-parenting issues.

Richmond, Gary. *Successful Single Parenting.* Eugene, Oreg.: Harvest House Publishers, 1990. An experienced parent and pastor addresses struggles single parents face with finances, work, needs of children, visitation, and social activities, and discusses the feelings of children of divorce.

# CHAPTER
# 20
## The Stepfamily

A number of years ago I received a letter from a stepparent that may be an extreme case, but it made me realize that my compassion for stepfamilies must be matched by a solid understanding of their family dynamics.

I separated from my second wife. It was a blended marriage. She had two teenage boys, and I had a daughter from my first marriage. I tried to be a leader of the home, but my wife would not let me. One of her boys is in a gang and was suspended from school several times. Her other son is into satanic rock and self-mutilation, and has ended up in the hospital. I tried to address these issues as a family, but my wife refused and thought that by ignoring them they would go away. Then she brought some older members of her family to live with us. I soon began to detach and hide myself in my work. I left the house early in the morning and did not return until after ten each night. I was a stranger in my own home. Finally I was kicked out of the house and we divorced.[1]

The stepfamily may be the most needy of all kinds of families. But the unique problems of stepfamilies are often overlooked or sentimentalized by what might be called the "Brady Bunch" stereotype—a smiling, giggling love fest of "his-hers-ours."

In fact the stepfamily can be a dangerous place for children. One study found that the presence of a stepparent in the home is "the best . . . predictor of child abuse yet discovered."[2]

The struggles of the typical single-parent family do seem more obvious—often a single mom struggling alone to hold life together for her children and herself. Then when that single parent remarries, it is tempting to think that her family's problems are over—she has a new mate, she is in a new nuclear family, the crisis has passed. However, the reality is that the issues facing such a combined family are significant, and if they are not addressed quickly and effectively, they will seriously hamper the marriage before it has a good chance to succeed. The divorce rate is about 60 percent for all second marriages, of which a significant number include children.[3]

In the United States, which has the highest remarriage rate in the world, more than 40 percent of all marriages are remarriages for one or both partners.[4] (Of course not all remarriages involve divorced people, and often one person in the relationship has not been married before.) The number of stepfamilies increased 36 percent from 1980 to 1990, and the U.S. Census Bureau reports that one out of every three Americans is now a stepparent, stepchild, stepsibling, or some other participant in a stepfamily.[5] About half of the sixty million children under age thirteen in the United States are currently living with one of their biological parents and that parent's current partner.[6]

Some predict that by 2010 the stepfamily will be the most predominant family form in America[7] and that more than half of all Americans living today will be part of a stepfamily sometime in their lifetime.[8] This single statistic alone is proof that churches need to be ready to address the needs, issues, and problems that result from the formation of stepfamilies.

Few local churches seem to be focusing on stepfamilies, and yet these families represent one of the greatest opportunities today for church ministry. Not only should we minister to those already within our doors—the Family-Needs Survey has found that of those who have children, 22 percent report having kids from a previous marriage or relationship[9]—but also to the many stepfamilies on the outside. Both groups represent incredibly great opportunities for ministering "the glorious gospel of the blessed God" (1 Tim 1:11).

## UNDERSTANDING THE STEPFAMILY

Why am I calling the "blended family" the "stepfamily"?

One of the things I learned early in studying this topic is that experts in the field do not like the more popular term "blended family." Ron Deal says, "Most stepfamilies do not blend. Consider a cooking analogy. If you blend ingredients, what do you have when you're finished—one fluid mixture in which everything is the same. While that's a connotation we might talk about regarding Christian marriage (that is, becoming 'one'), that's not an appropriate way to describe stepfamilies. They are not one. Stepfamilies can develop meaningful close relationships, but there will always be a difference between biological and step relationships."[10]

This hints at a key point in understanding these families: Even though they may look from the outside like traditional nuclear families, the dynamics on the inside are different.

Two unique family cultures, two sets of traditions must now reach happy (or at least truce-ful) coexistence in one family. Roles for everyone are jumbled and confused. Virtually every activity has to be evaluated, as will important issues like discipline, money, recreation, and media choices. Even something as basic as what titles to call each other has to be decided. This takes a lot of time and emotional energy, and yet the basic responsibilities of life, work, school, meal preparation, shopping, and home chores must go on.

A stepparent wrote, "Soon after our new family was created, I discovered what millions of other stepparents have learned already. The stepfamily has little in common with the traditional family. Since the stepfamily is comprised of fragments from two or more traditional families, the conflicts are different, more complex. A different set of guidelines is needed to make it work. . . . No matter what experts say, it is not the traditional family and the perplexities cannot be handled in the same way."[11]

The sheer number and complexity of relationships are mind-boggling.

Where first marriages have family trees, stepfamilies have family forests! For example, a typical three-generational stepfamily has from three to six-plus coparents managing two to three-plus linked homes, coraising three to six (or more) minor children with forty to more than one hundred extended relatives. Full stepfamilies have up to thirty roles (like stepgrandmothers and stepcousins), compared to fifteen roles in normal three-generational biological families. Maintaining such a multitude of relationships is a challenge and can be incredibly frustrating. One child who was attempting to gain a positive perspective said of her stepfamily, "You get to love more people, you know!"[12]

A stepparent noted, "The stepfamily is a tangled web of communication difficulties; stepparent and stepchild, stepparent and spouse (stepchild's parent), stepparent and absent parent, parent and absent parent, parent and child, child and absent parent; not to mention the extended family of aunts, uncles, and grandparents. Any one problem and the whole household feels the negative effects."[13]

Because of the unusual pressures that exist because of stepchildren and these multiple, often demanding relationships, the new husband and wife in the stepmarriage have virtually no honeymoon period in which to concentrate on solidifying their own marriage. It's no shock that of the stepfamilies that fail, most will crash on the rocks and experience divorce quickly—within the first two years of the marriage.

Also each person in the stepfamily faces a unique set of "personal" emotional hurdles, often best summed up as grief or loss. "One of the most overlooked emotional processes in stepfamilies, by the families themselves and by clergy," says Ron Deal, "is the fact that loss had to take place for this home even to be born."[14] This fact is a critical pastoral clue for ministering to stepfamilies.

Typically one or both of the parents have suffered the trauma of a divorce, one of the most devastating emotional experiences anyone can experience. Furthermore children experience another loss as they orient themselves to the fact that their mother or father has married someone else. This is the case even if the previous parent died.

In addition, children themselves are working through their own sense of grief and loss, as well as anger, guilt, and fear. One boy, whose parents divorced when he was about ten years old, told his mother at age sixteen that for the past six years he thought the divorce was his fault. When he found out that the divorce happened because of his father's infidelity, a torrent of emotions erupted in the young man. As a result, he has struggled for years with anger and has had recurring difficulties with obeying his mother, stepfather, and even the law.

To help us grasp just how staggering the emotional ramifications are for stepfamilies, here's a look at some of the realities facing the core participants.

### Stepchildren

Children experience great difficulties in adjusting to a stepfamily situation. Stepparents Edward and Sharon Douglas write, "Feelings of disappointment and anger may surface in children who are suddenly forced to adjust to a new family after separating from their biological parent whom they deeply love and care for. . . . The loss of a special relationship is one of the deepest psychological losses experienced."[15]

Although we might think that children—especially those a bit older—would welcome another adult into their home, someone who will be a companion to their mom or dad, this is often not the case. James Eckler reports on how children may feel after having adjusted to their roles in a single-parent family. "The children who worked so hard to make life pleasant for their parent are not ready to surrender the duties they have enjoyed. The son is no longer needed to be the man around the house after the second marriage. And the teenage daughter who tried to fill mom's shoes, cooking and taking care of the younger children, finds herself replaced by a stepmother."[16]

Even in an intact family, children try to "divide and conquer" their parents. Just think of the possibilities for this in a family where one parent has to endure "you-are-not-my-real-dad" kinds of statements. Jim Talley, who grew up with separated parents, tells how he "worked the system" to his advantage.

> I was twelve years old. I knew my mother and father were fighting. I also knew they were not communicating very well. I'm just a normal twelve-

year-old, and I have an eighth-grade field trip. This is in 1956, and the hourly wage for the working man was $1 an hour. So 40 hours equals $40, a week's wages.

I went to my mother and said, "I need $20 for the field trip." She gave me $20. I knew they were not communicating, so I went to my father and I said, "I need $20." I went to that eighth-grade field trip with more money in my pocket than any of the teachers! Kids will work both ends of those things against the middle . . . and take advantage of the situation as well. . . . And once they start into this process, there is a battle over who the child is going to be faithful to. And it depends on who pays the kid the most or bribes him the most.[17]

### The Stepmother

Of all the roles in a stepfamily that of stepmother is typically the most demanding. Much is expected of the mother in any family, but in a stepfamily the variety and complexity of the demands placed on her can become overwhelming. Eckler lists these cutting terms often associated with stepmothers: wicked, intruder, home wrecker, part-time mother, daddy's new wife.[18]

Eckler adds, "When a woman marries a struggling widower, the public and his children see her as far short of the saint who has died. If she marries a divorcé who tried everything to hold his marriage together, she is looked upon as the destroyer of a happy home. Whatever the situation, the new stepmother becomes the bad guy. . . . The expectations of her new responsibility seem endless; fit in with the new family, solve problems, get along with the children's father, greet their mother with a smile, handle the finances, and help with the bills left over from her first marriage. She has to learn to receive a little and give a lot."[19]

### The Stepfather

Stepfathers also have some unique challenges as they seek to exert godly leadership in their home. Eckler describes expectations placed on a stepfather this way: "Be a good male role model for the children, but don't overstep the bounds; develop good relations with the wife and strive to meet her needs; when the children's father arrives to pick them up, be nice to him; and when the grandparents . . . come to visit don't overdo the father routine, you're just the kids' stepdad. . . . The stepfather lives the life of a family man, but he also lives in the shadow of the family before he came along. There is no way he will be a father to the children whose natural father shows up on weekends to take them away, sends them money and buys them clothes, and is the father image they want to maintain."[20]

Another stepfather said, "I brought two sons to my marriage. My [present] wife had never been married. After five years, my teenagers and my wife still haven't bonded. She's constantly critical of them. I'm afraid that once my sons are grown, they'll avoid coming home so they won't have to be around my wife."[21]

Not every person living in a stepfamily has all these experiences. But we should not be naive or fooled by appearances. The stepfamily is not the ideal. Much of God's grace and the hard work and perseverance of all concerned are required to make a stepfamily successful. Pastoral awareness of these realities is the first step to an effective ministry on behalf of these families.

## MINISTRY TO STEPFAMILIES

Why do churches focus so little on stepfamilies? Perhaps some congregations are afraid of the message that may be sent if stepfamilies are significantly "legitimized." Ron Deal answers this objection as follows:

"Whenever I go to speak to any group of ministers, I make this clear—for me, working with stepfamilies is not about condoning their past. It is about preventing the pressures and peculiarities of stepfamily life from keeping people from serving their Lord. Stepfamilies need a message of hope and redemption. There needs to be a very strong balance, however, in our public messages about remarriage. God's ideal of one man and one woman for life must always be taught foremost. God's plan must be held high. Yet remarried couples need to know that God expects their covenant to last. Our part is to give stepfamilies special help to avoid a family breakdown.

Churches must be just as serious about preventing divorce in second (or subsequent) marriages as we are in preventing divorce in first marriages."[22]

A lack of receptivity on the part of the church is not the only reason stepfamilies do not flourish. The husband or wife or both may be struggling with "postdivorce syndrome," with a personal sense of shame and failure that makes it difficult for them to set foot in church. But if they have this attitude, it is even more important that we make them feel welcome. No doubt one of Satan's tools is isolation, to get a family fending for themselves while cut off from other Christians.

Here are six suggestions on how to do stepfamily ministry in the church.

### Educate Your Pastoral Staff and Lay Leaders

Beware of embarking on a ministry to stepfamilies unless you've done your homework. Family expert William Doherty writes, "Remarried families require the highest levels of intentionality of any form of family life in our culture. Otherwise the forces of entropy will push them apart rapidly."[23]

Locate helpful resources (some are listed at the end of this chapter), talk to individuals in your community who work with stepfamilies, learn from stepfamilies themselves—and include church staff and lay leaders in this orientation. Hold stepfamily forums. Prayerfully enlist lay leaders to coordinate meetings, socials, Bible studies, seminars, and workshops for stepfamilies. Put stepfamily ministry in the church budget. And make sure that those who are serving in the church—especially those who are teaching children and youth—understand the unique needs of these families. Issues as elementary as who has the authority to pick up the kids must be clearly understood by those in church childcare or Sunday school.

### Make Stepfamilies Feel Welcome

Most stepfamilies feel out of place in church, as Deal observes: "When stepparents go to parenting classes, the things they are taught often backfire if stepparents try to implement them too quickly. What they experience in the educational environment of a local congregation oftentimes doesn't fit their life experience."[24]

If you understand that stepfamilies tend to see themselves as outsiders, even a small gesture like acknowledging stepmoms on Mother's Day or stepdads on Father's Day will bring down many barriers. A pastor making practical applications for stepfamilies during his sermons can also be encouraging. Keep in mind that somewhere between 15 and 30 percent of your audience on Sunday mornings (and even higher in some areas) may be members of stepfamilies. And the number of stepfamilies is increasing.

### Be Positive and Patient

Stepparents need huge doses of encouragement and hope. Widowed Catherine Marshall recalled her own early misgivings about remarrying. "How do you put families broken by death or divorce back together again? How can a group of individuals of diverse backgrounds, life experiences and ages ever become a family at all? I did not have the answers, but I knew Someone who did. . . . I remembered that during His [Jesus'] time on earth, He Himself had had to get along with at least six other children in a humble Nazareth household. What a comfort to know that He has experienced what families are up against, sympathizes, and stands waiting and available with the wisdom and help we need."[25]

That's the essence of the message stepfamilies need to hear. If we don't cheer them on and urge them to persevere, failure looms. One expert reports that "adjustment in a stepfamily takes an average of seven years or more."[26] Some would argue that the adjustment is never complete.

### Emphasize Spiritual Matters

The husband and wife in a stepfamily must be grounded spiritually, for their family situation provides an incredible opportunity for spiritual maturation. A biblical challenge to put before stepfamilies is this: "You have a tremendous opportunity to show how God can work to make a less-than-perfect situation something that shows the wonder of His grace, power, and restoration. Remain committed—to the glory of God!" Stepfamily couples and entire families need to be urged to pray together.

### Provide Support Groups and Other "Services"

Give your stepmoms and stepdads an opportunity and place to come together regularly for mutual support. Identifying with each other's struggles brings comfort and encouragement. Hearing how another person handled a messy, less-than-perfect situation in their stepfamily will help reduce the tendency for stepfamilies to isolate and deal with problems on their own. Godly maturity of those who lead these classes is a prerequisite. This ministry in many cases needs the wisdom of Solomon.

Another simple but effective idea is to have a Sunday school class for remarried couples.

Remarried couples must have time alone (especially if there are stepchildren). Even more than in a first marriage, the husband and wife need concentrated time to communicate, bond, work out solutions to family issues, and be intimate. Yet such time may be nearly impossible to find because of the unceasing demands related to the children. Also such time alone is dangerously akin to walking through a land mine, because stepchildren may resent their mother or father spending such focused time with their stepfather or stepmother. The stepchildren may even engage in subversive tactics to undermine and thwart the parents' time alone. Being aware of such realities in a stepfamily gives church leaders great opportunities to help the stepfamily. Through dedicated childcare services or other programs oriented to children, be sure stepparents have opportunity to establish an "island" of peace and love.

### Go Online

One of the great needs in the church today is for a generation of "pioneers" in stepfamily ministry to step forward and carve out church-based solutions and encouragement for this group of families. By means of the Internet we can benefit from one another's ingenuity and Spirit-led creativity. (For more information contact FamilyLife at www.familylife.com.)

## TIPS FOR A SUCCESSFUL STEPFAMILY MINISTRY

At Mother's Day (and Father's Day, too) one of the traditions at our church is having the Bible class teachers take time before Mother's Day to help kids make cards for their moms. Then we hand them out during the worship service. Give the kids an option of making a mother's card and a stepmother's card. It's an option—you don't force them to make two cards; they may not want to, but if they do, then have the materials available.

Another thing is youth ministry: Unless a formal adoption has taken place, stepparents have no legal rights to their stepchildren. So if your youth ministry is taking kids on a camp retreat and is having stepparents sign a medical release form, legally it is not binding. Don't walk away with a false sense of security about having medical consent. You don't.

Also, when church chaperones travel with kids, they need phone numbers for both biological parents—not just for the home in which the kids live. Acknowledge that there's another biological mother or father in another household, maybe on a different side of the country. You need to have those numbers in case of emergencies.

—Ron L. Deal, Jonesboro, Arkansas

### RESOURCES

Anderson, Sharon. *And the Two Became One Plus*. South Easton, Mass.: Bridges of Hope, 1994. A mother in a stepfamily of eight discusses complex issues of remarriage with children.

Deal, Ron L. "Building a Successful Stepfamily" seminars and resources. Deal, a licensed family therapist and seminar leader, ministers to stepfamilies in local churches. Write to Ron Deal, 1601 James Street, Jonesboro, AR 72401, or contact him at 1-870-932-9254 or www.swfamily.org/stepfamily.

_____. "Seven Steps to Stepfamily Success." A video presentation on the key aspects of successful stepfamilies. Useful for Bible classes, study groups, and church leadership training sessions.

Douglas, Edward, and Sharon Douglas. *The Blended Family*. Franklin, Tenn.: Providence House, 2000. Parents in a stepfamily of eight offer biblical insights on complicated situations involving discipline, finances, outside influences, roles, and privacy.

# PART
# 4

## A TIME FOR COURAGE

# CHAPTER
## 21

### Declaring War on Divorce

Divorce is killing us.

Many pastors—especially of smaller churches—often feel consumed, overwhelmed, and exhausted by the strain of dealing with even one crumbling marriage and family.

Divorce is a monster. If you don't believe this, ponder this "tip of the iceberg" set of statistics:

- The president of the National Institute of Healthcare Research has said, "Being divorced and a nonsmoker is only slightly less dangerous than smoking a pack or more of cigarettes a day and staying married. Every type of terminal cancer strikes divorced individuals of either sex, both white and non-white, more frequently than it does married people."[1]
- The risk of suicide is 290 percent higher for the divorced individual compared to a married person.[2]
- The percentages of persons who suffer from any type of psychiatric disorder by their marital status are as follows:
  Married, never divorced or separated—24%
  Single, never cohabited for one year—33%
  Divorced or separated—44%
  Unmarried and cohabited—52%[3]

- The incidence of depression in divorced women is more than 270 percent higher than that reported for married women. And the rate climbs to over 380 percent higher for women divorced twice.[4]
- Percentages of adults who will battle alcoholism over a lifetime by their marital status are as follows:
  Intact marriage—8.9%
  Never married or cohabited—15%
  One divorce or separation—16.2%
  More than one divorce or separation—24.2%
  Cohabited only—29.2%.[5]
- More than half of the children born in 1994 will spend some of their childhood in a single-parent home.[6]
- Currently about one child in ten lives with a stepparent, and about one-third of children will live with a stepparent before reaching the age of eighteen.[7]
- Children living in a situation other than with both of their biological parents are 20-35 percent more likely to experience some type of general health vulnerability.[8]
- Boys raised outside of an intact nuclear family are more than twice as likely as other boys to end up in prison, and this is true regardless of the boys' social or economic backgrounds.[9]
- Children who grew up in a single-parent home are twice as likely to get divorced as children who grew up in a two-parent biological family.[10]
- Young people in single-parent families or stepfamilies are two to three times more likely to have had emotional or behavioral problems than those with both biological parents in the home.[11]
- The likelihood of a daughter experiencing sexual abuse from a stepfather is at least seven times greater than her chances of experiencing such abuse from her biological father.[12]
- According to four surveys of high school dropouts (all data adjusted for factors of race, sex, parental education, number of siblings, and place of residence), the rate for students from two-parent homes ranged from between 9 and 15 percent, and for single-parent families the range was between 16 and 29 percent.[13]

- The same four surveys of high school students found that the risk of teen births for unmarried women ranged from 11 to 20 percent among two-parent families and from 19 to 31 percent in one-parent families.[14]
- The U.S. Census Bureau reported in 1997 that in married families in which one partner works full-time, less than one in fifty families is classified as poor. But nearly one in three families headed by a single woman is poor. And almost one in seven headed by a single man are classified as poor.[15]

The litany against divorce could go on, but the bottom line is this: There is no such thing as a "good" divorce. Divorce unnaturally dismantles the most basic unit that God created, the family.

This must change if we are to serve as salt and light in our culture. On "FamilyLife Today" we interviewed Steve Grissom, founder of an effective ministry called DivorceCare. He said this: "I think the only way to substantially dent the divorce rate and aid in the healing of the divorce problem is through the church. It is the body of Christ that God has called to this ministry, and we've got to activate it."[16]

We need to do everything we can through prayer, counsel, and, if necessary, exhortation and rebuke to confront the evil of divorce, especially in the church. But how?

First, the Christian community is in a deep ditch on the issue of divorce. We are playing defense, and as a result we have lost much of our influence in calling people to keep their marriage covenants.

Second, recognize that many people in our churches are divorced. Therefore if you address the subject of divorce, you risk enormous fallout.

Third, no cookie-cutter answers exist for the epidemic of divorce. The solutions offered in this chapter are given in a spirit of wanting to help, but with the realization that ultimately pastors must stand and courageously implement what they believe the Scriptures teach and what is best for their congregations. And because leaders come at this issue from a variety of experiences, some of the recommended solutions may sound simplistic to some and courageous to others. After being in a ministry to married couples and families for more than twenty-five years, I know there are no simple answers to the issue of divorce.

Fourth, because of space limitations I am not writing a theological statement about divorce, but rather one that recognizes that since God hates divorce (Mal. 2:16), we need to take steps in the church to make divorce rare instead of routine.

This chapter addresses divorce prevention through both long-range and short-term strategies. We need to remember that divorce—like all relational chaos—is a result of sin. When the Pharisees tried to trap Jesus with their questions about divorce, He quickly pointed out the real, under-the-surface, irreconcilable issue in so many hurting marriages is hardness of heart (Matt. 19:8). Divorce in the church would be a rare event indeed if the words "repentance" and "sacrifice" carried more weight than the words "rights" and "ambitions."

As we fight the divorce epidemic and minister to those wounded by a broken marriage, we must make sure we are preaching grace and forgiveness, while encouraging our people to examine humbly the condition of their hearts.

## PREVENTING DIVORCE

Divorce is an emotional topic. In the few messages that I have heard preached from the pulpit on divorce, I can feel the discomfort of the pastor as he begins with a lengthy set of statements trying to let the congregation know that he loves them and that he understands the pain that many have experienced.

Most pastors know their people. They have looked into the pain-filled eyes of couples in humanly "hopeless" situations, some of which are abusive and even dangerous. Many pastors have invested hours, month after month, in hopes of seeing a stone-cold marriage resurrected, only to be an unwilling witness to another divorce decree and the death of a family.

Unfortunately many Christians have accepted our culture's attitudes and standards about divorce. We observe an inappropriate "relationship" being formed between a married coworker and a single secretary. We look the other way and say nothing. A friend separates from his wife and files for divorce. And we say nothing. The easiest thing to do is nothing. And that is exactly what far too many Christians have done for too long. Nothing!

We need fresh courage. We need to start pointing out God's expectations as set forth in the Scriptures instead of lowering our standards to that of the culture. Here are some ideas that if consistently practiced may help turn the tide against divorce in our churches and communities.

## Have a Plan

It is important that pastors and other church leaders have clear convictions about what they believe about marriage and divorce. A number of years ago the Family Manifesto became our ministry's statement about marriage and divorce. Here is the clause on divorce in that statement.

> We believe God's plan for marriage is that it be a lifelong commitment between one man and one woman. We believe God hates divorce. We believe divorce brings harm to every person involved. Therefore, reconciliation of a marriage should be encouraged and divorce discouraged. We also believe that God allows for divorce in certain situations, not because He wills it, but because of the hardness of people's hearts. We believe the Bible teaches that God allows for divorce in the case of adultery and in the case where an unbelieving spouse has chosen to abandon the commitment of marriage.
>
> We believe, however, that it is God's priority that marital oneness be restored and that, through the power of the gospel of Jesus Christ, forgiveness and reconciliation be experienced. We believe that in the unfortunate cases of abuse and abandonment, God has provided protection for an abused spouse and provision for child support through the church, civil law, godly counselors, prayer, and other practical measures. We believe God can restore broken people and broken marriages by His grace, by the power of His Spirit, and by His practical truths found in the Bible (Malachi 2:16; Matthew 5:31–32; 19:3–9; Mark 10:6–12; Luke 16:18; Romans 7:1–3; 13:1–5; 1 Corinthians 7:15).

The remainder of the Family Manifesto is in appendix A. It is can also be viewed at www.familylife.com.

In addition to a statement of beliefs, establish a set of guidelines on how you will handle marriage-related issues in your church. This should be agreed to by the governing board, understood by all staff members, and communicated openly and frequently to all members of the congregation. In too many churches today, there is a high level of confusion on how to handle various situations, including cohabitation, spouse abuse, divorce, abortion, and remarriage. If your convictions related to marriage and family issues are clear, there will be less confusion and a clear standard for your congregation to evaluate and embrace.

### Lift Up the Marriage Covenant

I have already emphasized this in chapter 3. But on any checklist of items related to opposing divorce, an emphasis on the marriage covenant must have a high priority. If church leaders don't start holding up a high view of marriage commitment, who will? Preserve, protect, and exalt the dignity of the marriage covenant among all those in your church. Let those who are divorced know that you love them, but that you must uphold God's view of the marriage covenant.

Also, by promoting the marriage covenant, your church will be better positioned to help prevent divorce. So many times we in the Christian community are known by what we are against. But it's difficult to criticize an organization that stands for permanence in marriage.

I think we would be shocked to learn how many people in our churches signed prenuptial agreements before they got married. I encourage you to call on those who have these "escape clauses" to burn them. And challenge those who are single never to marry a person who insists that a prenuptial agreement be signed.

### Speak and Preach the Truth about Marriage

In talking about the advantages of lifelong marriage, let's be careful not to present a romantic, sentimental view of marriage that creates unrealistic expectations. Marriage is wonderful, but it has its ups and downs, and sometimes it is downright tough. Yet married people need to know that troubles in marriage, like any trial in life, can be used by God to drive us closer to Him.

For some people marriage will not turn out quite the way they had hoped. Others live in unusually difficult situations, but if God is honored through the keeping of the marriage covenant, He will bless those families.

## Speak and Preach against Divorce

More of the truth about divorce needs to come from our pulpits in order to avoid hearing more stories like this one from Barbara Dafoe Whitehead.

> After I spoke to a mainly evangelical audience, a woman came up to me and said, "I'm a Baptist and I go to church. My husband left our marriage because he met someone he liked better, and she left her marriage because she liked my husband. My husband married this woman, and they broke up two marriages involving five children. And now they go to my church. They sit in a certain pew at church, and I sit there, too, next to my kids. And my church doesn't have anything to say about the right or wrong of their actions." She wasn't asking for the pastor to thunder condemnation from the pulpit. But she wondered why it wasn't possible for her own church to address the moral dimension of breaking up marriages and ignoring the first spouse and the children. . . . By not talking about it, the church sanctions it.[17]

Whitehead continues, "There is a feeling among clergy that to speak frankly about marriage is to be judgmental and unsupportive of all the people sitting in the pews who are divorced. This means those who have the most to say about the commitments of marriage are keeping silent."[18]

But we dare not remain silent. Divorce is offensive to God. We need to do everything we can to keep people from breaking their marriage covenant in the first place, because this is a serious spiritual issue with enormous generational and societal consequences. Regardless of the high divorce rate in our contemporary situation, God simply does not want people to divorce. (A sermon outline on divorce is included in appendix C.)

## Provide Premarital Counseling

Most people still want to get married in a religious ceremony; an estimated 73 percent of all marriages are still held in a church or synagogue.[19] But amazingly, only 20 percent of all engaged couples receive premarital counseling.[20] In our society, where authority means little, this is one situation where the church still has some clout. Churches ought to use it effectively to give couples the very best preventive premarriage checkup possible. (Chapter 10 discusses ways to minister to premarried couples.)

## Support Community Marriage Policy Efforts

In a number of communities, pastors from many denominations are banding together and agreeing to basic requirements that engaged couples ought to meet before they can be married in a church. Michael McManus, of Marriage Savers, has done a wonderful job in leading the way in this campaign. In Modesto, California, the first community in America to adopt a community marriage policy, divorce fell by 35 percent from 1986 to 1997. But the *national* divorce rate declined only 1.3 percent in the same time period. Other communities have not had such dramatic improvement, but these efforts are saving marriages everywhere.[21] (To learn more about Marriage Savers, see www.marriagesavers.org on the Internet.)

## Train and Assign Marriage Mentors

This idea has already been discussed, but it deserves mentioning in any "divorce prevention" checklist. Most people have only sporadic contacts with their extended family. Thus every marriage at every stage in its life cycle will benefit from the advice, encouragement, friendship, and accountability provided by a mentoring couple.

## Conduct Marriage Seminars

I could fill an entire book with stories of how God has impacted couples dramatically in just one weekend marriage seminar. God has touched many lives and changed many families at these weekend conferences on married life. A number of organizations sponsor such seminars, and many churches do their own. Strongly encourage all your couples to go to a weekend seminar at least once during their married lives—the earlier in their marriage the better. (Call 1-800-FL-TODAY for information.)

## Coach Men

As a rule, men seem more caught off guard by marital problems than women are. Perhaps a woman's intuition and her relational bent uncover growing isolation in the relationship before it's announced verbally. A man may be oblivious to them because of giving his life to his job, hobbies, and other pursuits outside the family.

Several years ago I talked with a man who was at the top of his profession, experienced and successful in his business. There he sat, with his marriage about to fail and unable to relate to his wife and son. Both he and his wife desperately needed training in knowing how two selfish, sinful human beings could live together in the most intimate of human relationships. The church is the ideal place for this training to occur on an ongoing basis.

Recently I had the privilege of teaming up with pastor Dan Jarrell in teaching a twelve-week course called "Men's Fraternity II—A Man and His Wife." Between five and six hundred men met each week at 6:00 A.M. In this course we attempted to equip men with the basics of loving, serving, and leading their wives while fulfilling their marriage covenants. At the end of this chapter is a list of the topics we covered.

## Responding to Crumbling Marriages

Often when a couple faces marital problems, they think some magic wand can be waved over their relationship to lift them instantly out of the ditch and put them back on the road. But that is not the way God normally solves problems. Instead we grow through our repentance, our learning and obeying Scripture, and allowing fellow believers to help us.

But as much as people need to understand the often-crushing reality of sin and bad choices, they also need to be reminded that following Christ brings opportunity for abundant hope. Never stop saying, "Come on, you can do it. You can stand courageously for this marriage. You don't have to give up as everyone else does." Obviously we must be careful not to control, judge, or condemn them, but instead to try to call them out of sinful choices.

Researchers Paul Amato and Alan Booth wrote, "From our own data we estimate that less than a third of parental divorces involve highly conflicted marriages. Only 28% of parents who divorced during the study reported any sort of spousal physical abuse prior to divorce, 30% reported more than two serious quarrels in the last month, and 23% reported that they disagreed 'often' or 'very often' with their spouses. Thus, it would appear that only a minority of divorces between 1980 and 1992 involve high-conflict marriages."[22]

This means you need to discern carefully what is really happening in a troubled marriage. It may be that issues are not as serious as the couple thinks. Do the parents realize that a divorce might bring much greater harm to the children than a low-conflict marriage?

### Lay Crisis-Intervention Team

One of the most effective ministries of a local church can be a team of godly couples whose purpose is to "do battle" for marriages in crisis. This team can be composed of those who have experienced grave difficulties in their own marriages and were rescued by God and His church. These may include those whose marriages experienced and survived adultery, abuse, emotional difficulties, job loss, and more. This team may also include some adults who have experienced divorce and can share the "real" story about its impact on their lives.

This is a special-forces group deployed to work on behalf of marriages that are in trouble. Besides relieving the pastor's load, this team can have a positive ministry in the lives of those they help.

## Separation

Although I have recommended physical and even legal separation in certain situations (such as emotional or sexual abuse of the wife and children), the word "separation" should always sound an alert. Separation suggests that "the train has begun to move and is leaving the station." Slowing or stopping the train is much easier early in the process, before forward momentum builds. Early intervention is critical.

The term "legal separation" means that a court has ordered it or both parties have consented to living apart under terms described in a written agreement. Often a legal separation is obtained so that issues like financial support for the wife and children, for example, are enforceable.[23]

Since dealing with a couple in crisis requires so much time, consider assigning a lay mentor who can give intensive one-on-one attention. It is critical that mentors/counselors be those who are committed to working hard to keep the marriage together. I fear that far too many vocational counselors give "lip service" to the marriage covenant but advise couples to move toward divorce.

Often when a Christian couple separates, one spouse shows up at a Sunday school class without the other spouse. The church needs a predetermined plan to guide folks through this awkwardness—without isolating either spouse from much-needed spiritual support and fellowship.

Godly intervention and counsel are essential if marriages are to regain hope. The following e-mail describes how the church can be part of the problem.

> The sad news is that the churches we've attended didn't help much. Often when I opened up to people in the church, they seemed to be pushing me toward divorce, especially if the problem I described was bigger than they thought they could handle. Even pastors didn't have the courage to say, "Stay married. Keep your covenant."
>
> Often people encouraged divorce, because they were divorced themselves (I didn't know it until we started talking about marriage problems) and wanted me to be as happy as they felt they were in second marriages. Other people offered me biblical loopholes to try to justify divorce. I wasn't looking for a way out. I was looking for a way through, and it's so sad that

so many Christians don't have a high view of marriage. Also, they minister more to the hurting divorced person in some churches than to the hurting married person.[24]

### Spouse Abuse

Abuse of one kind or another is much more common in Christian homes than we might think. Statistics probably do not tell the whole story, because this is a problem that exists for the most part behind closed doors. However, one study reported that about 13 percent of adult men had physically abused their wives. And over one-third of these aggressive acts were classified as severe, including punching, beating up, or threatening with a knife or gun.[25]

Sexual, financial, verbal, and emotional abuse can be as damaging as physical affliction.

Regardless of their social, economic, racial, or religious background, women are often hesitant to speak openly about their husbands' abuse, or they may not think that certain behaviors are even abusive. The inclination to remain silent exists among many Christian women who believe, through a twisted understanding of Scripture, that they are to take a husband's abuse as a part of their "submission." It is important to listen with discernment when dealing with a woman who you suspect may be receiving abuse.

When possible, involve others in gathering the facts—both men and women who have experience or are aware of the woman's situation.

After discovering an abusive situation, the first task is to make sure the wife and children receive adequate protection. After physical safety is guaranteed, then a whole range of issues must be addressed: anger and conflict management, finances, counseling with both spouses, and a host of other day-to-day matters.

Situations like this require a churchwide commitment; certainly the pastor can't and shouldn't carry this burden alone. Usually there is someone in a church who has experienced abuse and has established a track record of trust and renewal. These couples should be considered as possible mentors with other couples who are experiencing similar situations.

## Reconciliation

As already noted, divorce is not God's first choice in any situation. His desire is for a couple to forgive one another, to work through their pain, to be reconciled, and to come back together as one. Jim Talley told our radio audience, "Reconciliation is a supernatural event. It is not something society does. The ability to forgive is a biblical, godly activity. . . . Your spiritual life has to be growing and maturing—time in the Word, time in prayer, sitting under good preaching, being around people who will get you going spiritually."[26]

Too many couples give up, get divorced, and end up even more frustrated and unhappy in a second marriage. Also now they have to deal with the wounds and issues left over from the first marriage.

Steve Grissom, who experienced divorce, comments, "In the end you have got either the choice of anger or the choice of reconciliation. You've got the choice of divorce or the choice of God's ideal, which is restoring your marriage. There are no other choices. You either forgive each other for the wrongs you've done and rebuild your marriage, or you proceed down the path of dissolution, anger, bitterness, unforgiveness, and resentment."[27]

## Referrals to Counselors

A counselor or marriage therapist can help struggling couples, but professionals must be chosen carefully. Therapists can be influential, so make sure you agree with his or her approach. Michele Weiner Davis, author of *Divorce Busting,* says there is no such thing as a neutral therapist. He or she is almost always a major player in the outcome of the relationship. "A lot of times a couple comes to therapy when they are at the final stages of a decision about their marriage. The therapist's role is incredibly pivotal."[28] Be sure the counselor is biblically competent and committed to the restoration of marriages and families. Just bearing the title "Christian counselor" does not ensure godly counsel.[29]

Someone representing your church in an official capacity needs to continue to monitor the situation, ideally receiving frequent reports from the counselor. (Legal permission for these reports to be released will be needed from both the husband and wife who are being counseled.) Do not abdicate the church's responsibility to seek healing and restoration of marriages in trouble.

### Lawyers

Many fine Christian family-law attorneys are doing what is right. Family law is tough and exhausting, especially for attorneys who are committed to obeying Scripture. However, too many divorce lawyers have little intention of saving hurting marriages. In fact, opposing lawyers often fuel the fire by creating a combative situation that in turn causes the fees to run up and encourages the couple to divorce. But as Psalm 1:1 advises, "Blessed is the man who does not walk in the counsel of the wicked." Every local church should have access to a godly lawyer who is willing and capable of offering biblical counsel. If a couple finds a godly legal adviser, the marriage may still have a chance to survive.

Ideally the church should settle disputes between two Christians, including a married couple. First Corinthians 6 makes it clear that Christians are not to go before an unrighteous judge to have him settle their disputes. But marriage is not just a legal commitment. It is a spiritual covenant between three persons—God, a husband, and a wife. And so churches should exercise appropriate authority over couples wanting to "dissolve" their covenant. Shouldn't churches be ready to offer a better solution when a couple is struggling over their relationship?

Another option is to obtain the services of a Christian conciliator. One I recommend highly is Peacemaker Ministries at 1-406-256-1583 or www.HisPeace.org.

### Don't Give Up

If you try to rescue someone who wants only to end his or her emotional pain and dissolve the marriage, you need to prepare yourself spiritually for a battle.

After experiencing the emotional beating that comes from trying to help people resolve marital problems, you may be tempted to conclude,

"This just isn't any of my business. I need to steer clear of this couple. Let them go ahead and dissolve their marriage. I'll just pray for them. Why get involved and dirty my own life up and risk causing further problems?"

I fear that too often today in the Christian community we are giving up "one lap around Jericho" too soon. Of course we all can grow weary in well doing. But when I want to surrender and retreat, I think of a couple who showed me a picture of their four children and said, "None of these children would have been born if you hadn't gone to battle on behalf of our family!"

I realize it isn't easy. But who knows what legacy is at stake in these families that we counsel?

## DIVORCE RECOVERY

Casualties will occur. Even after our best efforts, divorce will result, often because at least one spouse is rigidly hardhearted. And Scripture indicates that there are situations where there is the freedom to divorce, even though it is not God's first choice. In fact, I think divorce should be the very last choice.

When this point is reached, be sure that both the couple and the congregation understand the implications of their divorce. This may mean exercising the public aspect of church discipline (see chapter 22). It may mean "breaking fellowship" and separating from a friend who refused biblical counsel.

Some obvious responses to divorce include encouraging both spouses to work toward civility, friendship, and an amicable parting. Especially if there are children, this broken "family" needs to function as harmoniously as possible. This will require grace and forgiveness from all sides.

The wounded will always need bandages for their wounds, and we must put our arms around the divorced and help them recover from what they have experienced. God hates divorce, but He certainly doesn't hate the divorced—and neither should we.

There are many aftershocks to the earthquake of divorce. Adults and children need help with these.

- *Emotional trauma.* Those who have been through divorce often cannot find adequate words to describe the range of feelings. The following piece, entitled, "I Am Divorced," gives us a little peek into what a person experiences when the marriage covenant is severed. "I have lost my husband but I'm not supposed to mourn. I have lost my children—they don't know to whom they belong. I have lost my relatives. They do not approve. I have lost his relatives. They blame me. I have lost my friends. They don't know how to act. I feel I have lost my church. Do they think I have sinned too much? I'm afraid of the future. I'm ashamed of the past. I'm confused about the present. I'm so alone. I feel so lost. God, please stay by me. You are all I have left."
- *Financial hardship.* One of the realities of divorce is that if children are involved, typically the result is that a single-parent woman may face some severe financial needs as she has to maintain a separate household on a less-than-adequate income. While the husband may not have to bear as many day-to-day financial burdens, he too may experience financial pressure and a reduced standard of living.
- *Effects on the children.* Since 1971 I have worked with youth and families in all fifty states, and I can say without reservation that children are dramatically impacted by divorce. The lie that children will "get over it" is utter nonsense.
- *Impact on the community.* Harvard University sociologist Armond Nicoli II wrote, "The evidence is conclusive. Divorce, because it destroys families, destroys a culture. Divorce is not a solution but an exchange of problems."[30] How true. A divorce may solve the unhappiness of one or both spouses in a marriage, but if there are children, new weeds of unhappiness will sprout in them. The ramifications ripple out from the immediate family to impact grandparents and other relatives. The functioning family that previously could help others is now itself in need of support.

## REMARRIAGE

Three-fourths of divorced men and two-thirds of divorced women eventually remarry.[31] When a divorced single mom with two young children comes hand in hand with her "Mr. Right" (himself divorced), this potential new couple and family present spiritual, emotional, and physical challenges for pastors and church leaders.

A number of experts issue strong warnings about the potential problems of the type of remarriage I just described. Statistically the odds of success in a second or subsequent marriage are sobering. Although emotionally we have difficulty admitting this can be true, children of such a union may end up more distressed and damaged from a hurting step family than from living with a single mom or dad. As suggested in an earlier chapter, two people in this situation need to allow a significant amount of time to elapse before remarrying. Churches need to recognize the steep mountain such a couple will face. Premarital counseling for those remarrying needs to be even more extensive than what is given to couples marrying for the first time. Mentors need to be required and assigned for the first two or three years of the new marriage.

The problems surrounding divorce and remarriage can be some of the most difficult issues pastors have to deal with. Yet pastors are called to provide biblical counsel to all who seek it (and at times to those who don't want it).

Many remarried couples carry extraordinary guilt, shame, pain, and a host of other emotional wounds or baggage that arise from the spiritual issues surrounding their divorce and remarriage.

## WHY WE FIGHT DIVORCE

I close this discussion with two letters. The first is entitled, "Divorce from a Kid's Point of View," written by a thirteen-year-old girl. Basing her thoughts on the experience of her own parents' divorce, she said this to all dads:

Dear Fathers. If you are a father thinking about leaving your family, I don't believe you truly know in your heart what your child is going through. I may seem to be a normal thirteen-year-old girl. I smile on the outside and show a positive attitude, but inside I'm crying out so loud for a normal family life. You see, my father left my mom and me when I was eighteen months old. Oh, sure, he probably thought I was too young for the divorce to affect me. But oh, how he was wrong. What happened to the commitment and the promise that he made to my mom and most importantly to God? Will he ever realize that has scarred me for life? I just want to be a normal kid. What's so wrong with that? I've sat in restaurants the last ten years staring at the complete families around us, wondering, wondering what it would be like to have a father at home, to have a father kiss me goodnight and listen to my prayers; a father to be there at my volleyball games, to look at my report cards, to meet my teachers or maybe even tell me, "I love you." But all the waitress sees is the smile on my face. Doesn't my dad know how much he has hurt me? If God gave me one wish, and one wish only, I would wish for my father to watch me grow up. He wasn't there when I had my birthdays. He wasn't there for my school events or for my Girl Scout Awards programs. He never met any of my teachers and never saw a report card. My father got what he wanted. He couldn't face the responsibility of me. He got his freedom. He gambled. What he doesn't realize is that he has lost his little girl.[33]

While finishing this book I received this second letter from a woman in her twenties.

> I just listened to your broadcast . . . and felt compelled to write. You mentioned that you received a letter from someone concerned that you are "too hard" on divorce and my heart broke.
>
> I am a twenty-eight-year-old single professional woman. I grew up in an unstable, non-Christian home. I have had five parents and three sets of siblings. My mother called me just this past Sunday to inform me that she is about to bestow upon me a sixth parent and a fourth set of siblings. I understand in the very depths of my being why my God hates divorce and why we should, too. No good thing comes from it. Ever. Divorce has not only stolen from me a family, but also a trust that marriage is a good and desirable thing. The grapes my parents ate with relish have set my teeth on edge. Divorce answers no question, solves no problem, resolves no conflict, gives no respite, restores no dignity and grants no peace.
>
> Divorce cannot be dealt with too harshly, especially in the church of

Jesus Christ. I bless God that He knows no divorce in this marriage covenant He has established between Himself and His bride! We must teach husbands and wives to honor the covenant they made before God, if for no other reason than the sake of the next generation.[33]

Let's work together to win the war in the battle for a marriage that lasts a lifetime.

## MEN'S FRATERNITY II
### A MAN AND HIS WOMAN

*Syllabus*

1. The Husband You Were Designed to Be
2. Understanding Your Wife
3. Communicating Love to Your Wife, Part 1
4. Communicating Love to Your Wife, Part 2
5. Dating and Romance
6. Sex
7. Forgiveness
8. Resolving Conflict
9. Reestablishing Trust
10. Setting a Healthy Pace for Your Family
11. Small Group Project Day (meet off campus to finalize and/or celebrate your quest)
12. The Covenant and Our Legacy

*The Quest*

Your challenge in this semester of Men's Fraternity is to do a "personal quest" for your wife or for the woman who is to be your wife. The quest is a specific action you take on behalf of your wife, which requires that you exercise personal courage and discipline. Your quest must honor your wife as a woman and as an essential helper and partner in your life. It will likely involve some specific sacrifice on your part. It may be as simple as addressing a habit which you know she longs for you to address or as complex as renewed wedding vows and a second honeymoon. We will celebrate the planning and accomplishment of "personal quests" throughout this semester.

## RESOURCES

Adams, Jay. E. *Marriage, Divorce and Remarriage*. Phillipsburg, N.J.: Presbyterian and Reformed Publishing Co., 1980.

Anderson, J. Kerby. *Moral Dilemmas*. Swindoll Leadership Library. Nashville: Word Publishing, 1998. Pages 129–42.

Clark, N. K. Lowther, "The Exceptive Clause in Matthew," *Theology* 15 (1927): 167–86.

Clinton, Timothy. *Before a Bad Good-bye*. Nashville: Word Publishing, 1999. Gives Christian insights and helpful tools on how to save a troubled marriage.

Cornes, Andrew. *Divorce and Remarriage: Biblical Principles and Pastoral Practice*. Grand Rapids: Wm. B. Eerdmans Publishing Co., 1993.

Davis, John Jefferson. *Evangelical Ethics*. Phillipsburg, N.J.: Presbyterian and Reformed Publishing Co., 1985. Pages 92–105.

Ellisen, Stanley A. *Divorce and Remarriage in the Church*. Grand Rapids: Zondervan Publishing House, 1980.

Ewald, George R. *Jesus and Divorce: A Biblical Guide for Ministry to Divorced People*. Scottdale, Pa.: Waterloo Press, 1991.

Feinberg, John S., and Paul D. Feinberg. *Ethics for a Brave New World*. Wheaton, Ill.: Crossway Books, 1993. Pages 299–344.

Fitzmyer, Joseph A. "The Matthean Divorce Texts and Some New Palestinian Evidence." *Theological Studies* 37 (1976): 213–21.

Geldard, Mark. "Jesus' Teaching on Divorce: Thoughts on the Meaning of *Porneia* in Matthew 5:32 and 19:9." *Churchman* 92 (1978): 134–43.

Grenz, Stanley. *Sexual Ethics: A Biblical Perspective*. Dallas: Word Publishing, 1990. Pages 99–125.

Grissom, Steve. "Before You Divorce." Audiotape series. Little Rock: FamilyLife, 1998. In two tapes this author, who has experienced divorce, gives excellent counsel for a couple struggling or even considering separation or divorce.

————, ed. "Choosing Wisely before You Divorce." Videocassette series. Wake Forest, N.C.: Church Initiative, 1996. Marriage experts, including Norman Wright, Jim Talley, and Tony Evans, explain the effects of divorce—financially, physically, legally, spiritually, and emotionally.

House, H. Wayne, ed. *Divorce and Remarriage: Four Christian Views*. Downers Grove, Ill.: InterVarsity Press, 1990.

Keener, Craig S. *And Marries Another: Divorce and Remarriage in the Teaching of the New Testament*. Peabody, Mass.: Hendrickson Publishers, 1991.

Laney, J. Carl. *The Divorce Myth*. Minneapolis: Bethany House Publishers, 1981.

Leeming, Bernard, and R. A. Dyson. "Except It Be for Fornication." *Scripture* 8 (1956): 75–81.

Montefiore, Hugh. "Jesus on Divorce and Remarriage." In *Marriage, Divorce and the Church: The Report of the Archbishop's Commission on the Christian Doctrine of Marriage*. London: SPCK, 1971.

Murray, John. *Divorce*. Phillipsburg, N.J.: Presbyterian and Reformed Publishing Co., 1961.

John Piper, Senior Pastor of Bethlehem Baptist Church, Minneapolis, Minnesota, has written two papers on divorce and remarriage entitled, *Divorce and Remarriage: A Position Paper on Divorce and Remarriage in the Event of Adultery* and *A Statement on Divorce and Remarriage in the Life of Bethlehem Baptist Church*. This second paper is the guide for membership and discipline at Bethlehem Baptist Church. See www.DesiringGod.org.

Schillebeeckx, Edward. *Marriage, Human Reality and Saving Mystery.* London: Sheed & Ward, 1999.

Talley, Jim. *Reconcilable Differences.* Nashville: Thomas Nelson Publishers, 1991. This marriage counselor tells how couples can reconcile successfully even after an extramarital affair or other serious dilemma.

_____. "Relationship Resources." Assistance and tools for marriage and divorce reconciliation. Write to Dr. Jim Talley, 11805 Sylvester Drive, Oklahoma City, OK 73162-1018, or contact him at 1-405-720-8300 or www.drtalley.com.

Vawter, Bruce. "The Divorce Clauses in Matthew 5:32 and 19:9." *Catholic Biblical Quarterly* 16 (1954): 155–67.

# CHAPTER

## 22

## Church Discipline

I once spoke at a large national denominational conference of church leaders. The speaker who preceded me was the former NFL football great, Reggie White, who in his short talk received three well-deserved thunderous standing ovations for his statements and public courage against homosexuality.

Then I spoke and passionately challenged the audience to declare war on divorce, and as a part of this battle, to revive church discipline in local churches. A polite smattering of applause eventually occurred. I suspect the crowd's tepid response was because my message hit a bit too close to home.

The truth is that church discipline is almost nonexistent today. I think the reasons include the cultural climate, fear (of man and litigation), and negative experiences on the part of pastors and church leaders who often choose to ignore the topic, which leads to embarrassment—even shame—for not doing what the Bible so clearly commands.

Also some leaders have given up on church discipline because they don't consider it effective. After speaking once on the need for the church to uphold the sacredness of the marriage covenant, I was approached by a woman who had been divorced by her husband. Her husband, an assistant pastor in one of the fastest-growing churches in the country, had run off with a woman he was counseling and had filed for divorce. When the wife talked to the senior pastor and asked if church discipline could occur, he responded, "We don't do church discipline here. I have never been involved in a single situation where church discipline worked."

Why am I raising this topic in a book on family ministry? I believe strongly that if we do not reinstate the means of lovingly correcting wrong, sinful behavior in the body of Christ, it will be increasingly difficult to resolve marital conflicts and bring peace and healing to our families. When people believe that they will not be held accountable to anyone for how they treat their spouses, children, and others, what is to stop them from committing relational mayhem?

Often leaders back away from church discipline because they do not want to be labeled judgmental, legalistic, or "anti-grace." Of course grace must abound, but as John Wesley said, "Before I can preach grace, love, and forgiveness, I must first preach sin, law, and truth—judgment."

"Much of the weakened state of the churches in the present time is the direct result of a failure in church discipline," writes Jay Adams. "Divorces occur, church splits take place, false teaching is introduced and the like, because the means Christ outlined for forestalling such things, the process and application of church discipline, is no longer intact. . . . One of the greatest tragedies resulting from the failure of church discipline is the wreckage of homes strewn across the land. Had discipline been in place and properly functioning, few of the marriage failures and the child/parent problems now facing the church would have occurred."[1]

Many pastors may want discipline in their churches, but the process is time-consuming, intimidating, and frightening from a legal perspective. Ken Sande, president of Peacemaker Ministries and one of the church's most knowledgeable experts on conflict resolution, said, "Most churches don't get involved in the final stage of discipline—the place where you might be disfellowshipping someone—until things have gone so far—it's almost too late anyway. So the person doesn't repent and leaves the church. And then the pastor says, 'See, it doesn't work.' The whole definition of success is skewed. Pastors don't realize that when they carry out church discipline—even if the person doesn't presently repent, they don't know what will happen two years down the road."[2]

The Scriptures make it clear that God uses discipline.

> How happy is the man whom God reproves; so do not despise the discipline of the Almighty. (Job 5:17)

> Blessed is the man whom You chasten, O LORD. (Ps. 94:12)

> My son, do not reject the discipline of the LORD or loathe His reproof, for whom the LORD loves He reproves, even as a father corrects the son in whom he delights. (Prov. 3:11–12; see also Deut. 8:1–3, 15–16; Heb. 12:4–17)

> If your brother sins, go and show him his fault in private; if he listens to you, you have won your brother. But if he does not listen to you, take one or two more with you, so that by the mouth of two or three witnesses every fact may be confirmed. If he refuses to listen to them, tell it to the church; and if he refuses to listen even to the church, let him be to you as a Gentile and a tax collector. (Matt. 18:15–17)

> Those whom I love I reprove and discipline. Therefore be zealous, and repent. (Rev. 3:19)

Church discipline is even more difficult now because for decades many churches have not practiced it. That means there are many people sitting in our churches on Sunday mornings who have done what they wanted to and gotten away with it, or they have watched others make significantly wrong choices and receive just a wink and blink from church leaders. This situation is painfully reminiscent of a family where the kids are out of control—and everyone knows it—but the parents are turning their heads and acting as though all is well.

Obviously all is not well in our churches concerning church discipline, and especially in areas related to the family. Why?

## WHY SO LITTLE DISCIPLINE?

Without question the mood of our society has made church discipline much more touchy than a generation or two ago. For one thing, there are serious legal concerns. Ken Sande, a lawyer, states, "The civil courts' deference toward the church has declined dramatically in recent years. At the same time, the traditional reluctance most people have toward suing a church has all but evaporated. As a result, churches that exercise biblical discipline today are often threatened with lawsuits, some of which have resulted in shocking awards against the church."[3]

Also our culture is generally unreceptive to any person or organization that seeks to make individuals accountable for their actions. But God isn't all that impressed with our cultural proclivities. He just wants us to obey the Scriptures. Leaders must courageously stand up for what is right. Laypersons must be called back to biblical standards and convictions. The Christian community has to regain a nonjudgmental, yet intolerant attitude toward sin.

John 3:16 used to be the most-often quoted Bible verse. But now, Josh McDowell observes, the favorite is Matthew 7:1, "Do not judge or you too will be judged." This attitude of tolerance dominates our society. The only thing that is intolerable in America today is the perceived intolerance of being judgmental. But God is not tolerant of disobedience. When we fail to correct our children or our church members, we are disobeying His clear instructions. His fierce love requires that we care enough about sheep to discipline them properly, which the Bible indicates responsible shepherds will do: "Obey your leaders and submit to their authority. They keep watch over you as men who must give an account. Obey them so that their work will be a joy, not a burden, for that would be of no advantage to you" (Heb. 13:17).

It's time for the church to dust off one of God's most effective techniques for helping individuals achieve spiritual maturity: discipline administered lovingly by the local church. And to overcome our fears and reluctance, we need to keep Joshua 1:9 in mind. "Have I not commanded you? Be strong and courageous! Do not be terrified; do not be discouraged, for the LORD your God will be with you wherever you go."

How does a church change its actions and start exerting some discipline on members without looking inconsistent or foolish?

## RESTORE CHURCH DISCIPLINE

The word *discipline* in the church context usually conjures up a scary image of some browbeaten individual being paraded up front in a Sunday worship service for public disfellowshiping. Such a dramatic scene is possible, but discipline needs to occur in and through a wide variety of spiritual activities, such as personal devotions, study, and prayer; teaching and preaching by church leaders; small-group mutual care; individual discipleship; informal conversations to encourage and admonish; private confrontation; small-group confrontation; pastoral confrontation; and public admonishment and rebuke.[4]

We need to think of church discipline much as we think of discipline in a healthy family. When parents set up clear boundaries for behavior, administer abundant and grace-based guidance, apply rules consistently, and punish lovingly and judiciously, the entire family experiences greater harmony. And in such a context there is much less need for extreme disciplinary measures.

Discipline in the local church should be like that—as much or more emphasis on instruction and guidance as on correction. This is called formative church discipline. It is like preventive medicine. One reason church discipline has been discredited is that far too often it is administered unfairly and capriciously. The reaction from church members is similar to what occurs in the home when one child receives punishment while another gets by with the same infraction. The result is anger, bitterness, and rebellion.

Church discipline needs to be taught and practiced in ways that are obviously positive and that emphasize prevention. It is to be done by those in authority who are worthy of receiving submission (Heb. 13:7), with tender love (2 Cor. 2:6–8), with gentleness (Gal. 6:1), and with the goal of building up the individual (2 Cor. 10:8).

Here are nine steps to take in carrying out church discipline effectively.

## Assess Your Church's Situation Related to Discipline

A plan for discipline in the church must cover any sin that may be destroying an individual or harming the church.

Ken Sande tells of a survey of local-church minutes from about one hundred years ago. "The issues churches felt they had a responsibility to talk to people about, wasn't just adultery, but things like debt, breaking contracts, defaming someone else in the community. The church took these matters very seriously."[5] One church today lists these offenses for which a member can be disciplined: denial of the Christian faith, immoral or scandalous conduct, persistent troublemaking, especially within the congregation. Church leaders need to ask some hard questions: Is our church practicing biblical discipline? Are we administering discipline fairly? Why or why not?

## Get Expert Help in Evaluating Your Church Bylaws and Procedures

Because of our contemporary cultural climate, church discipline has become a thorny legal issue. I strongly recommend that you use expert help in evaluating whether your church has the appropriate foundation from which to initiate discipline of any member. We can't let the legal climate stop us from doing what God wants, but yet we need to be wise. Otherwise great loss can occur to a local church. (One of the best sources of assistance on topics relating to church discipline is Peacemaker Ministries. Their materials and services are described at www.HisPeace.org, and their telephone number is 1-406-256-1583.)

## Evaluate Current Policies on Church Membership

Again, because of the changing legal environment in the United States, if your church does not require church membership, you can essentially forget being able to carry out any kind of substantive church discipline that would stand up legally if a disciplined individual became angry and sued the church and its leaders. Ken Sande explains, "Many churches do not place a strong emphasis on formal membership. . . . When problems with a nonmember arise, these churches are caught in an awkward position. If they attempt to minister to the person as though he were a member, they can face devastating lawsuits. On the other hand, if they decline to confront sinful conduct or warn others of it, the nonmember generally continues in his destructive behavior and often goes on to injure other people, either in his own family or in a new church to which he flees. In either case, God is dishonored and the church as a body suffers."[6]

*Your Church* magazine stated that "churches must precisely define membership. Review the definition of a member in your church's constitution or bylaws. If that isn't clear, clarify it. Also, whether protected or not, a church should never offer its members any damaging information about a disciplined member without first seeking an attorney's counsel."[7]

One reason church membership is so critical is a concept called "informed consent." This means that if a member knows ahead of time and agrees (in writing) to abide by your church's policies and procedures relating to church discipline, then if a problem arises later his ability to bring a lawsuit is reduced. Much like clarifying boundaries and expectations with a teenager, clear communication of these policies is essential if the desired outcome is to be achieved.

But protection from a lawsuit is secondary. More importantly it is an essential component of biblical justice and love. Establishing, communicating, and applying biblical expectations for marriage and family are critical for exercising biblical justice and love in the local church. The best means for accomplishing this is through membership covenants presented in new-member classes and annual membership covenant-renewal ceremonies in the local church.

### Preach and Teach on Church Discipline

Since church discipline is a topic seldom touched on these days, church members need some in-depth instruction on the subject. And the information needs to flow formally and informally on an ongoing basis. Prepare the way, educate, persuade from Scripture. Make sure your people understand that this is God's idea. Ultimately Christians must "own" the truth that discipline is positive and for their good.

### Have Procedures for Church Discipline in Writing

Official guidelines for the process of church discipline must be stated in writing. To do church discipline haphazardly or impulsively raises the risk that the disciplined individual will not benefit spiritually. And it also increases the likelihood that the church and its leaders will face a lawsuit. Jay Adams comments, "Careful records of proceedings and decisions relating to all official discipline . . . should be kept. That is a part of good order. . . . All these records should be kept for the twofold purpose of safeguarding the church and protecting the brother or sister who undergoes discipline. If someone should raise a matter that has been officially set to rest by the church, the restored member ought to be able to point to the records to show that the matter is closed and that it is improper to bring it up again."[8]

### Seek Cooperation of Other Churches

The ability to conduct meaningful discipline is often compromised when an individual leaves a church and goes to another house of worship. In some communities churches are beginning to cooperate in disciplinary matters.

### Always Discipline In Love

Sometimes discipline turns into a power-and-control game. However, God's motivation for discipline is love, to make life better for the person under correction. That should be our goal too. Paul urged us to "forgive and comfort" such a person (2 Cor. 2:7). We need to help people get back on the right path; that is the essence of loving discipline. Jay Adams notes, "Converted Sauls must be welcomed with open arms and hearts, because they will need much help."[9]

### Celebrate Repentance

When the process ultimately results in a prodigal coming home, tell it to the church. This clears the slate of the person who has come back, and this helps congregants know how to relate to him or her better. But the public confession of sin also serves as a warning to the congregation to avoid violating Scripture.

*Establish an Environment for Expectations*

Expectations create results. If godly expectations in a family are established, clearly communicated, and lovingly enforced, family members will normally rise to the level established. It may be difficult to start, but establishing and maintaining biblical expectations (including consequences for unrepentant failure to abide by those expectations) is the critical first step to recovering biblical church discipline (both formative and corrective).

Discipline must be carried out carefully. That's why you need to seek out qualified assistance (including an attorney familiar with the laws of your state) as you build the right foundation to implement formative and corrective church discipline. We should seek to be both courageous and wise in fulfilling God's commands in this area.

## DISCIPLINE IN MARRIAGE AND FAMILY SITUATIONS

Without exercising church discipline on people who are breaking their marriage covenant, our efforts to save and restore families will be even more difficult.

Two important steps need to be made if church discipline is to strengthen marriages and families. First, before a couple is married, explain that they may experience difficulties at some point in their marriage and that the church wants to help them overcome those problems. Also explain that the church has the right and duty to initiate discipline on the husband and/or the wife.

A radical yet practical way of doing this is to ask the couple to sign a legally binding agreement that gives the church authority to provide help. What if every couple the church marries was asked to sign a marriage covenant, stating that if difficulties arise in the marriage, they agree to arbitration in the church? If churches began to refuse to marry couples who declined to sign such an agreement, this would be a great first step in restoring the dignity of the marriage covenant. Proper church discipline reestablishes the spiritual influence and jurisdiction of the church in handling disputes between Christians. Far too many Christians go to the non-Christian community for justice.

A second issue churches need to address through church discipline is covenant breaking. Each church should clarify its responsibility and authority to respond to those who are breaking their marriage covenant through emotional or physical abuse, neglect, adultery, sexual perversion, financial irresponsibility, or actions leading toward divorce. Repetitive covenant breaking should be viewed seriously and should invoke the loving arm of church discipline.

Concerning abuse of a spouse or a child, local churches should not be so quick to step aside and allow the civil government to take total responsibility for correction. Obviously civil authorities will often be involved, especially with child abuse. But why shouldn't the church also be involved in administering its own appropriate discipline? The church and state should play parallel roles in protecting children from harm.

On divorce a church needs to intervene as early as possible when relational difficulties begin to escalate. Discipline should be exercised before troubles mount, feelings overwhelm, and anger intensifies.

Many couples in our society, including some in our churches, are living with each other but aren't married. The church needs to provide some discipline in such situations and call on these couples to move apart or get married. Expectations for biblical marriage and family should permeate the church's life and message.

Gary Richmond, who has pastored thousands of single parents at the First Evangelical Free Church, Fullerton, California, agrees. "If we see that happening . . . we address it gently at first by saying, 'We need to tell you that we feel very uncomfortable with what you are doing on a biblical basis. This isn't moral; it is evil. We would like you not to do this.' If it should go on for another three or four weeks, then we would come back to them and say, 'On the basis of your choice to live in a situation that is not holy, we are asking you not to participate in our singles group.' Of course, we get accused of being judgmental and legalistic."[10]

Yes, confronting sin will cause conflict. But think of the holiness, peace, and spiritual health that will be the fruit of repentance and forgiveness.

## DO IT NOW

May I encourage you to initiate the process of recovering church discipline while you still can, before it's too late in our culture?

"I think the average church in America, if it does not get its house in order in this regard in the next five years ... it will be almost impossible—as time goes by—because there is such resistance to this concept of accountability," said Ken Sande. "I am urging churches: Now is the time before it is too late."[11]

God's ways are not always easy or popular, but His people will recognize and support what is right. Will you lead the way in restoring the blessing of church discipline to your church?

There's more at stake than many of us realize. Consider the following letter from a twelve-year-old boy who was asked to write what he thought of church discipline. "Belonging to a church that practices discipline means a lot to me. It makes me feel secure that someone is caring and watching out for me and tries to keep me from going astray. Just the fact that my brother and I get into so much conflict makes me realize that a church with a lot of members is apt to have conflict too. Resolving conflict with my brother makes me feel so good that we are reuniting. So in that sense I realize how vital church discipline is to the spiritual growth of a church and its members."[12]

Certainly if a twelve-year-old boy can catch the significance and meaning of church discipline, the rest of the congregation will as well.

## A PASTOR'S LOVING CORRECTION HELPS SAVE A MARRIAGE

We must remember that a primary goal of loving discipline in the body of Christ is to *help people*. If we continue to think that correction is just another word for punishment, we miss the point.

I once had the opportunity to interview Paul and Susie Luchsinger, a couple that were almost certainly destined for divorce. Even as they were involved in a music and speaking ministry (Susie is a singer, the sister of Reba McEntire; Paul is a rodeo rider) to local churches, Paul was abusing Susie. One time he pushed and shoved her from one end of their motor home to the other just before both went to share their testimonies and sing in a church. Like so many couples they knew, they were in trouble, but they did not know how to stop the downward spiral in their relationship. They needed help from someone on the outside.

Paul was not going to change his behavior and stop abusing his wife unless someone stepped in, confronted him, and held him accountable.

Susie first told another couple about Paul's abuse, and the husband stood up to Paul. Next a pastor, Ken Hutcherson, intervened. In Paul's words, "In April 1994, Hutch got in my face and said, 'If you ever do that again, I'm going to let you know how it feels.'" Paul learned later that the pastor really did not plan to beat him up but realized he needed to say something very strong to get the attention of a tough rodeo performer.

Paul then admitted that he needed help and became accountable. Pastor Hutcherson called Paul every Thursday to find out how he was doing. They became friends. Often they did not talk specifically about Paul's marriage or his abusive behavior, but Paul always knew this godly brother-pastor would be calling and helping him stay on the right path. In time God healed the marriage.

Now Susie comments, "Paul and I still have our struggles. At times we go head to head with things, but there has been no physical abuse in our family in the last four years. You know, when God gets hold of your life, and you're controlled by the Holy Spirit and you submit your life to Him every day, every moment of the day, it is hard to hit somebody whom you love."

That's the goal of godly church discipline—to be a tool God can use to save families and lives.

## RESOURCES

Adams, Jay. *Handbook of Church Discipline*. Grand Rapids: Zondervan Publishing House, 1986. Presents a basic overview for pastors, elders, and lay people, developed around five steps of corrective discipline based particularly on Matthew 18:15–17.

Sande, Ken. "Managing Conflict in Your Church." Audiotape series. Billings, Mont.: Peacemaker Ministries, 1997. Available at www.HisPeace.org. Training for church leaders on conflict resolution and redemptive church discipline. Explains how to reduce the potential of legal liability.

———. *The Peacemaker: A Biblical Guide to Resolving Personal Conflict*. 2d ed. Grand Rapids: Baker Book House, 1997. A thorough presentation of biblical principles to use in resolving personal, family, and corporate disputes in the body of Christ.

# IDEA INVENTORY

Since the amount of content in this book can seem overwhelming, I encourage you to list just one "memorable idea" from each chapter that really strikes you as applicable in your ministry.

After completing the book, pray over, sort, discard, select, prioritize, and schedule the ideas in this inventory. The result will be a set of action points that will clarify your vision and objectives for future ministry to families.

1. The Family Dunkirk

   _____
   _____
   _____
   _____

2. Big Idea 1: Minister to the "First Family" First

   _____
   _____
   _____
   _____

3. Big Idea 2: Reclaim the Covenant

_____

_____

_____

4. Big Idea 3: Remarket the Designer's Design

_____

_____

_____

_____

5. Big Idea 4: Make Your Church a Marriage-and-Family Equipping Center

_____

_____

_____

_____

6. Big Idea 5: Create a Church-wide Web

_____

_____

_____

7. Big Idea 6: Maximize Mentors

_____

_____

_____

8. Big Idea 7: Empower Parents as Faith Trainers

_____

_____

_____

_____

9. Big Idea 8: Follow the Life Cycle for Effective Family Ministry

_____

_____

_____

_____

10. Preparing for a Lasting Marriage: Family Life Cycle 1—Premarried

_____

_____

_____

_____

11. Honeymoon's Over: Family Life Cycle 2—Newly Married

_____

_____

_____

_____

12. Sleepless in Suburbia: Family Life Cycle 3—Full Nest 1

_____

_____

_____

_____

13. The Golden Years: Family Life Cycle 4— Full Nest 2

_____

_____

_____

_____

14. Encounter with Adolescence: Family Life Cycle 5—Full Nest 3

_____

_____

_____

_____

15. Free at Last: Family Life Cycle 6—Empty Nest 1

_____

_____

_____

_____

16. Sunset: Family Life Cycle 7—Empty Nest 2

_____

_____

_____

_____

17. The Adoptive Family

_____

_____

_____

_____

18. The Singles Ministry

_____

_____

_____

_____

19. The Single-Parent Family

_____

_____

_____

_____

20. The Stepfamily

_____

_____

_____

_____

21. Declaring War on Divorce

_____

_____

_____

_____

22. Church Discipline

_____

_____

_____

_____

# APPENDIX

## The Family Manifesto

In the early 1990s I concluded that if the Christian family was to endure intact and strong, its members needed to know God's plan for the family. Without a clear set of biblical beliefs, thinking would be muddy and behavior inconsistent—perhaps even contrary to God's Word.

The Lord impressed on me the urgent need for a written declaration of timeless *biblical* family values. As a result, in the fall of 1991 work began on a statement that came to be called the Family Manifesto. I asked Bill Howard, a friend, seminary graduate, and at that time a staff member of FamilyLife, to help me craft such a statement of beliefs.

Fifteen months later, after revisions by theological leaders, historians, professors, pastors, Christian leaders, and laymen, the Family Manifesto was complete. A number of public signings of the Family Manifesto occurred, and in the years since then, more than eight hundred individuals representing more than twenty-five countries have signed the original document at FamilyLife ministry headquarters in Little Rock, Arkansas.

As a new century begins, I am more convinced than ever that we need to rally around this clear, biblical statement about the family. Laypersons and church leaders alike need to know what the Bible teaches about the family.

I believe the Family Manifesto provides the clear statement the church needs.

(Note: Full-size, frameable copies of the Family Manifesto are available from FamilyLife. For more information call 1-800-358-6329.)

## THE FAMILY MANIFESTO

*Preface*

During the latter half of the twentieth century the American culture suffered an unrelenting decline. Although scientific and technological advances created an outer veneer of prosperity and progress, our inner moral values and convictions rapidly crumbled. Once, most Americans based their sense of right and wrong on Judeo-Christian principles, which provided them with a solid, biblical foundation for life. Today, a growing number of Americans see morality and ethics as relative and subjective and have developed their own version of "morality" with little regard to absolute standards.

This idea of moral tolerance has eroded the foundation of the American family and society. Many Americans today have little or no concept of how to maintain a successful marriage and how to raise children to become responsible adults. In addition, a growing number of educators, politicians, and members of the media are attacking and redefining the family, creating a vast amount of confusion about what a family is. Many people today proclaim that "family values" are important, but the gradual shift to moral relativism has led to a great debate about what "family values" ought to be.

Abraham Lincoln once said, "The strength of a nation lies in the homes of its people." It is our conviction that the family is the backbone of the Christian church and of society as a whole. History shows that, if any society wants to survive, it must uphold, strengthen, and continue to build upon the biblical institutions of marriage and family.

The Bible begins in Genesis with the marriage of a man and a woman and ends in the Book of Revelation with the marriage of Christ and His bride, the Church. In between, God provides timeless blueprints for family life, which, if followed in a spirit of humility and obedience, provide us with the only true way to maintain healthy family relationships.

The following document affirms this biblical model and challenges us to consider how we should live within the walls of our own homes. It is offered in a spirit of love and humility, not of judgment or contention. Furthermore, it is not intended to be a comprehensive doctrinal statement about what the Bible says about marriage, family, and related subjects.

Unquestionably, this document attempts to face critical cultural issues. We invite response from anyone who wishes to affirm the truths of marriage and family from the Scriptures. It is our hope that this document will serve to accurately represent the truth God has revealed to us in Scripture, will provide insight into what a biblical family looks like, and will show how we can honor and glorify Him in our family relationships.

We freely acknowledge that we, like all people, have often denied the biblical truths of family life by the way we live. We desire, however, to live by God's grace in accordance with the principles stated herein and to pass these principles on to future generations so that He will be honored and glorified as our families reflect His character.

## THE BIBLE

We believe the Bible was written by men who were divinely inspired by God the Holy Spirit, and we believe it to be authoritative and errorless in its original autographs. We believe the Bible contains the blueprints for building solid marriage and family relationships. It teaches principles for marriage and family life that transcend time and culture. We are committed to communicating biblical truth in order to strengthen and give direction to a marriage and family (2 Timothy 3:16; 2 Peter 1:20–21; Hebrews 4:12).

*Family*

We believe God is the originator of the family. It was established by God in His inaugural act of the marriage between a man and a woman. The Bible further defines the family through God's instruction for married couples to have children, whether by birth or by adoption. We believe the purpose of the family is to glorify and honor God by forming the spiritual, emotional, physical, and economic foundation for individuals, the church, and any society.

It is at home that children see manhood and womanhood modeled. It is at home that moral values are taught by parents and placed into the hearts of their children. It is at home that people see the reality of a relationship with Jesus Christ modeled. It is at home that people learn to live out their convictions. Therefore, we are committed to upholding the concept of family as God's original and primary means of producing godly offspring and passing on godly values from generation to generation. (Ephesians 3:14–15; Genesis 1:26–28; Romans 8:15, 23; John 1:12; Galatians 3:29; Psalm 78:5–7; Deuteronomy 6:4–9).

## MARRIAGE

We believe God, not man, created marriage. We believe marriage was the first institution designed by God. We believe the Bible teaches that the covenant of marriage is sacred and lifelong. The Bible makes it clear that marriage is a legally binding public declaration of commitment and a private consummation between one man and one woman, never between the same sex. Therefore, we believe God gives a wife to a husband and a husband to a wife, and they are to receive one another as God's unique and personal provision to help meet their mutual needs.

We believe God created marriage for the purpose of couples glorifying God as one flesh, parenting godly children, and enjoying sexual pleasure. As iron sharpens iron, we believe God uses marriage to sharpen a man and woman into the image of Jesus Christ. Just as the Trinity reflects equal worth with differing roles, we believe God created a man and a woman with equal worth but with differing roles and responsibilities in marriage.

Finally, we declare the marriage commitment must be upheld in our culture as that sacred institution of God in which men and women can experience the truest sense of spiritual, emotional, and physical intimacy, so that the two can become one (Genesis 2:18–25; Ephesians 5:30–33; 1 Corinthians 7:3; Matthew 19:4–6; Mark 10:6–9; 12:25; Proverbs 27:17; Romans 1:26–27, 8:29; Hebrews 13:4; Matthew 22:30; Deuteronomy 24:5; Song of Solomon).

## HUSBANDS

We believe God has charged each husband to fulfill the responsibility of being the "head" (servant-leader) of his wife. We believe God created a man incomplete, and as a husband, he needs his wife as his helper. We believe a husband will give account before God for how he has loved, served, and provided for his wife. We reject the notion that a husband is to dominate his wife. Likewise, we reject the notion that a husband is to abdicate his responsibilities to lead his wife. Rather, we believe his responsibility is to love his wife. This love is characterized by taking the initiative to serve her, care for her, and honor her as a gift from God. We believe his responsibility is to protect his wife and help provide for her physical, emotional, and spiritual needs.

We also believe a husband is to seek after and highly regard his wife's opinion and counsel and treat her as the equal partner she is in Christ. Therefore, we are committed to exhort and implore men not to abuse their God-given responsibilities as husbands, but rather to initiate a sacrificial love for their wives, in the same way Jesus Christ initiated sacrificial love and demonstrated it fully on the cross (Genesis 2:18–25; Ephesians 5:22–33; Colossians 3:19; 1 Peter 3:7; 1 Timothy 5:8).

## WIVES

We believe God has charged each wife to fulfill the responsibility of being her husband's "helper." We believe a wife will give account to God for how she has loved, respected, and given support to her husband. We uphold the biblical truth that she is of equal value with her husband before God. We reject the notion that a wife should assume the leadership responsibilities of her husband. Likewise, we reject the notion that a wife should passively defer to the dominance of her husband. We believe that her responsibility is to willingly and intelligently affirm, respect, and submit to her husband as the leader in the relationship and in his vocational calling. Therefore, we are committed to exhorting a wife to be in support of her husband by accepting and excelling in her responsibility as his helper (Genesis 2:18–25; Ephesians 5:22–33; Colossians 3:18; 1 Peter 3:1–6; Proverbs 31:10–12).

## SEXUAL UNION

We believe the Bible clearly states that marriage is the only context for sexual intimacy. We believe contemporary culture is pressing single people to engage prematurely in acts that are intended only for the context of marriage. Our culture has rejected God's plan for intimacy by promoting sexual promiscuity of various kinds and, as a consequence, has brought upon itself sexual diseases and relational dysfunctions. We believe in sexual purity and fidelity.

Therefore, we are committed to training parents to teach their children at an early age to respect their sexuality and to preserve their virginity and purity until marriage. We are committed to communicating the message to teenagers, single adults, and married couples that sexual intimacy is available only in the context of marriage (Genesis 1:24–25; Romans 1:24–27; 1 Thessalonians 4:3–8).

## FATHERS

We believe God has charged a father to execute the responsibilities of a family leader. He is accountable before God to lead his family by sacrificially loving his wife and children and by providing for their physical, spiritual, and emotional needs. We believe the greatest way a father can love his children is to love their mother. We believe children gain much of their concept of God from their fathers. We believe a father should teach his children, by instruction and example, truth from the Bible and how to apply it practically in daily life. Therefore, a father should spend a quantity of time, as well as quality time, with each child.

We believe a father should demonstrate godly character revealed in humility, tenderness, and patience toward his children. We believe a father should demonstrate love by practicing consistent discipline with each child. Therefore, we are committed to turning the hearts of fathers back to their children by emphasizing the importance of their role as "father." We are committed to exhorting every father to model a love for God and His Word, to model love for his wife, and to love his children (Malachi 4:6; Ephesians 6:4; Colossians 3:20–21; Deuteronomy 6:4-9; 1 Timothy 3:4–5; 5:8).

## MOTHERS

We believe God has uniquely designed women to be mothers. We believe the greatest way a mother can love her children is to love their father. We also believe God has created a woman with an innate and special ability to nurture and care for her children.

Therefore, we believe mothers are the primary people who execute the vital responsibilities of loving, nurturing, and mentoring children. We believe these responsibilities should be met before a mother contemplates any other duties. We believe our culture has devalued the role of a mother by placing greater significance on activities outside the home than on those inside the home.

We realize there are cases where a mother will find it necessary to work outside the home (e.g., financial distress, single parenthood); however, we also believe some couples have made career and lifestyle choices that result in de-emphasizing the mother's role as nurturer. Therefore, we are committed to presenting a biblical framework through which couples can rightly evaluate their priorities in light of a mother's role. We are committed to elevating motherhood by rightly assessing its exalted value in God's economy of the family. We are committed to exhorting mothers to model love for God and His Word, to model love for her husband, and to love her children (Titus 2:4–5; 1 Thessalonians 2:7; Proverbs 14:1, 31:1–31; Deuteronomy 6:6–9; 11:19; Ezekiel 16:44–45).

## CHILDREN

We believe children are the gifts of God and should be received and treated as such. We believe a child's life begins at conception. We believe children have a special responsibility to God in obeying and honoring their parents. We believe a child's identity and spiritual growth is either helped or hindered by his parents' devotion to God, to one another, and to him. Parents should see themselves as God's ambassadors, working to build strong character in the lives of their children through consistent godly living, nurturing, discipline, and teaching them right from wrong. We are committed to God's plan for passing His love down through the ages by encouraging parents to love their children "so the generations to come might know" the love and forgiveness of Christ (Ephesians 6:1–3; Colossians 3:20; Psalms 78:5–8; 127:3–5; 139:13–16; Proverbs 4:1; 6:20; Job 3:3).

## CHILDLESS COUPLES

We believe God has allowed some couples to be without biological children according to His sovereign plan in their lives. We believe couples without children are of no less value before God than those with children. We believe in encouraging childless couples to consider adoption as a family alternative. We are committed to encouraging childless couples to pass on a godly legacy through involvement with children in their immediate families, churches, and communities (Luke 1:6–7; Romans 8:28–29).

## GRANDPARENTS

We believe grandparents are to be honored as valued family members. We believe their wisdom in living should be sought and passed on to their children and their children's children. We also believe that grandparents have the responsibility of teaching and modeling to their grandchildren how to know Jesus Christ and grow in a relationship with Him as well as passing along biblical principles for godly living. The Old Testament is filled with examples of grandfathers and grandmothers who excelled in their roles of grandparenting.

Therefore, we are committed to giving honor to grandparents by encouraging their children and grandchildren to listen to their voices of wisdom. We are also committed to exhorting grandparents to pray for and become actively involved with children and grandchildren whenever it is possible (1 Timothy 5:4; Genesis 18:18–19; Proverbs 17:6; Psalm 78).

## CHURCH

We believe the family and the church are interdependent. A primary responsibility of the church is to help build godly families, and godly families also help build the church. We believe the family supplies the relational rudiments of the local church. We believe the local church is the spiritual home where families should corporately worship God. It is the place where the knowledge and love of God may be communicated to fathers, mothers, and children.

Therefore, we are committed to exhorting families to support the local church through their involvement. We are also committed to exhorting the local church to uphold the priority of helping build godly marriages and families (1 Timothy 3:15; Ephesians 5:22–33; Philemon 2; Colossians 4:15).

## DIVORCE

We believe God's plan for marriage is that it be a lifelong commitment between one man and one woman. We believe God hates divorce. We believe divorce brings harm to every person involved. Therefore, reconciliation of a marriage should be encouraged and divorce discouraged. We also believe that God allows for divorce in certain situations, not because He wills it, but because of the hardness of people's hearts. We believe the Bible teaches that God allows for divorce in the case of adultery and in the case where an unbelieving spouse has chosen to abandon the commitment of marriage.

We believe, however, that it is God's priority that marital oneness be restored and that, through the power of the gospel of Jesus Christ, forgiveness and reconciliation be experienced. We believe that in the unfortunate cases of abuse and abandonment, God has provided protection for an abused spouse and provision for child support through the church, civil law, godly counselors, prayer, and other practical measures. We believe God can restore broken people and broken marriages by His grace, by the power of His Spirit, and by His practical truths found in the Bible (Malachi 2:16; Matthew 5:31–32; 19:3–9; Mark 10:6–12; Luke 16:18; Romans 7:1–3; 13:1–5; 1 Corinthians 7:15).

## SINGLE PARENTS

We believe that, ideally, a child needs the influence of both a father and mother for healthy development in life and relationships. At the same time, we recognize that God's grace is sufficient and that He is a father to the fatherless and a husband to the husbandless. We also believe He is a guardian to children without a mother and a friend to a husband who has lost his wife.

We believe God, by His grace, can use the void left from a missing parent to accomplish His eternal purposes of building Christlike character in single parents and their children. We believe a single parent and his or her children are a family and that the Bible contains principles for them to grow as a family. We believe the local church should be a home for single parents, providing their children with godly people who serve as role models in place of the missing parent.

Therefore, we are committed to exhorting Christians within the local church to creatively help meet the needs associated with single-parent homes. We are committed to comforting and encouraging single-parent families by providing resources and developing biblical principles to assist those who struggle in the role of a single parent (Psalm 68:5–6; 1 Corinthians 7:32; James 1:27; 1 Timothy 5:3–16; Romans 8:28–29; Luke 18:3–5).

## BROKEN AND BLENDED FAMILIES

We believe God has allowed men and women, either by circumstance or by choice, to endure difficult and painful consequences in their marriages and family relationships. We also believe God gives abundant grace to the broken, blended, and single-parent families.

Therefore, we believe He can and does enable them to carry out His functions and principles for healthy family life. We are committed to comforting, encouraging, and teaching these families God's principles of marriage and family life. We are also committed to exhorting the local church to help with the burden of the broken family (James 1:27; 1 Timothy 5:16; Philippians 4:13).

## WORK AND FAMILY

We believe work is an important and necessary aspect of one's service to God and one's responsibility to provide for the needs of the family. We also believe security and significance cannot be found through pursuing career goals or financial achievement apart from one's responsibility to God and one's spouse and family. Instead, we believe those needs are best met in the warmth of a home where parents and children are experiencing harmony in their relationships with each other and with Jesus Christ. Therefore, we are committed to challenging any person or couple to rearrange their priorities so that over the course of a lifetime they can be successful at home and not merely successful in their careers (Revelation 3:14–22; Ephesians 6:7–8; Matthew 6:33; 1 Timothy 5:8; 1 Thessalonians 4:10–12).

## MENTORS

We believe in the biblical admonition for older men and women to teach younger men and women. We believe younger couples today should seek out older couples for their wisdom and counsel in matters of marriage and family. We believe older couples should be taught and encouraged to mentor younger couples, and we believe this is best accomplished through the local church. Therefore, we are committed to establishing a strategy for mentoring that the local church may implement and use to build strong marriages and families (Titus 2:3–5).

## MARRIAGE EDUCATION

We believe single adults who choose to marry should be taught the biblical principles of marriage. We also believe the education of a married couple does not end after the wedding ceremony is over, but continues throughout life.

Therefore, we believe that both premarital and postmarital education is helpful and essential in a couple's growth toward and in oneness. We are committed to elevating, establishing, and teaching the precepts of marriage by which single adults can rightly evaluate their relationships and equip themselves for marriage. We are committed to providing the teaching and training necessary to equip married couples to live a lifetime together as one. Finally, we are committed to showing couples how their marriages can be used by God to give others the hope found only in Jesus Christ (Titus 2; 2 Timothy 3:16–17; Acts 16:31–34; John 4:53).

## THE DECEIVER AND CULTURE

We believe there is a living devil who is God's enemy and whose nature and objective is to lie and deceive. We believe the devil has attacked God's plan for the family from the beginning of man until now. We believe he uses the various aspects of the culture to promote personal independence, distort the differences between men and women, confuse their roles, and elevate personal rights over marital responsibilities. We believe the devil seeks to persuade people to move away from God's plan for intimacy and oneness and toward isolation and divorce (John 8:44; Genesis 3; Isaiah 14:12–14; Ezekiel 28:12–18; 1 Peter 5:8; Ephesians 6:12; 1 John 2:15).

## GOD—THE CREATOR OF THE FAMILY

*Father*

We believe in the Fatherhood of God. The title "Father" implies that God is a relational being. The Bible reveals God has four primary relationships as Father: He is the Father of creation, of the nations, of the Lord Jesus Christ, and of all believers. We believe the Bible presents the title "Father" as one of the primary names Christians should use in addressing and relating to God. In doing so, Christians identify themselves as children who belong to the family of God. We are committed to proclaiming and demonstrating this truth about who God is and who we are, so that God will be glorified, and that He might use us to bring others into His family through a personal relationship with His Son (John 1:12; Exodus 3:14–15; Ephesians 3:16; Matthew 6:9; Romans 8:15; Acts 17:24–28).

*Son*

We believe God the Son, fully revealed in the person of Jesus Christ, was God's final sacrifice for the sins of man through the shedding of His blood on the cross and His resurrection from the dead. We believe He is the only way to know God the Father and to experience His plan for marriage and family. We are committed to introducing people to Jesus Christ in order that, by faith, they might personally receive Him, be born into the family of God, receive forgiveness and eternal life, and begin a relationship with God that is essential in marriage and family life (John 1:4, 12; 17:3; 1 John 2:23–24; Ephesians 2:19–22; Colossians 1:13–18; Hebrews 1:1–4).

*Holy Spirit*

We believe God the Holy Spirit is the agent and teacher of a godly marriage and family. We believe when Christian couples and their children consistently yield to His control and power, they will experience harmony in their marriages and families. Therefore, we are committed to sharing the ministry of the Holy Spirit with people so they may know God better, make Him known to others, and appropriate His power in fulfilling their duties in marriage and family relationships (John 14:26, 15:26, 16:5–15; Ephesians 5:18–21).

## COMMITMENT

In recognition of and in full agreement with these biblical principles regarding marriage and the family, I, by the grace of God, commit myself to adhere to, practice, and teach what God has made clear are my responsibilities within His design of marriage and the family.

# APPENDIX

## B

## Sample Marriage Covenants

*For additional information on marriage covenants, contact FamilyLife at 1-800-358-6329 or visit www.familylife.com.*

### BASIC COVENANT
*(Does Not Contain Binding Arbitration Wording)*

### OUR MARRIAGE COVENANT

Believing that God, in His wisdom and providence, has established marriage as a covenant relationship, a sacred and lifelong promise, reflecting our unconditional love for one another and believing that God intends for the marriage covenant to reflect His promise to never leave us nor forsake us, we, the undersigned, do hereby reaffirm our solemn pledge to fulfill our marriage vows. Furthermore, we pledge to exalt the sacred nature and permanence of the marriage covenant by calling others to honor and fulfill their marriage vows.

| | |
|---|---|
| *In the presence of God and these witnesses, and by a holy covenant, I,* | *In the presence of God and these witnesses, and by a holy covenant, I* |
| _____ | _____ |
| Husband's Name | Wife's Name |
| *joyfully receive you as God's perfect gift for me, to have and to hold from* | *joyfully receive you as God's perfect gift for me, to have and to hold from* |

*this day forward, for better, for worse, for richer, for poorer, in sickness and in health, to love you, to honor you, to cherish you and protect you, forsaking all others as long as we both shall live.*

*this day forward, for better, for worse, for richer, for poorer, in sickness and in health, to love you, to honor you, to respect and submit to you, forsaking all others as long as we both shall live.*

_____

Husband's Signature

_____

Wife's signature

Witnessed this day,_____

_____

Witness

_____

Witness

*Unless the Lord builds the house, its builders labor in vain. (Ps. 127:1, NIV)*

## COVENANT CONTAINING BINDING ARBITRATION WORDING

*Author and Publisher's Disclaimer*

*1. Biblical Basis.* We believe that the Bible provides thorough guidance and instruction for faith and life. Therefore, we base this proposal for a marriage covenant with a binding arbitration clause on scriptural principles rather than those of secular psychology or psychiatry. (For a description of the principles we embrace see question 17 in part I of the *Guidelines for Christian Conciliation* produced by the Institute for Christian Conciliation, a division of Peacemaker Ministries, http://www.HisPeace.org).

*2. Not Legal Advice or Representation.* Although this proposal for a marriage covenant with a binding arbitration clause may be used to resolve a legal dispute between a husband and wife, even so, reliance upon or utilization of the proposed covenant is not the legal advice or legal advocacy one would receive if he or she hired a personal attorney. Therefore, if you are concerned about your legal rights, you should consult with an independent attorney who is competent and able to advise you in regard to use of the covenant. Laws related to the legal effect of arbitration clauses vary from state to state. Therefore the proposed marriage covenant with binding arbitration clause might not satisfy the legal requirements in all states. Moreover, the marriage covenant is provided and proposed here with the understanding that neither the author nor the publisher is engaged in rendering legal or other professional advice. Therefore before utilizing, proposing the use of, or executing any such covenant, you should consult with an attorney to see how the law in your state would apply to it and, if necessary, how it should be modified to comply with the law of your state.

## OUR MARRIAGE COVENANT

Believing that God, in His wisdom and providence, has ordained and established human marriage as a covenant relationship intended to reflect the eternal marriage covenant established through the death, burial, and resurrection of His Son with His church, and therefore human marriage is a sacred and lifelong promise, reflecting our unconditional love for one another, and believing that God intends for the human marriage covenant to reflect His promise never to leave us or forsake us because of what He has done for us through His Son, Jesus Christ, we, the undersigned husband and wife, male and female, as image of God, do hereby affirm and reaffirm our solemn pledge to fulfill our marriage vows, so help us God; we furthermore pledge to exalt the sacred nature, glory, and permanence of God's eternal marriage covenant in His Son with the church through our marriage, by calling others to honor and fulfill their marriage vows; and we, upon full and informed consent and with full knowledge and understanding of this covenant to arbitrate, hereby irrevocably covenant and consent to submit any question concerning whether our marriage should be dissolved to binding arbitration in accordance with the Rules of Procedure of the Institute for Christian Conciliation, a division of Peacemaker Ministries, under the jurisdiction of _____ (name of local church) or any church which we or either one of us, might join hereafter, believing that any such issue is strictly a religious question to be resolved solely according to the standards set forth in the Holy Bible, and we do both hereby agree to submit to any arbitration decision made in accordance with the Rules of Procedure of the Institute for Christian Conciliation, a division of Peacemaker Ministries, as final and binding on the question of whether our marriage should be dissolved.

| | |
|---|---|
| *In the presence of God and these witnesses, and by a holy covenant, I,* | *In the presence of God and these witnesses, and by a holy covenant, I* |
| _____ | _____ |
| Husband's Name | Wife's Name |
| *joyfully receive you as God's perfect gift for me, to have and to hold from this day forward, for better, for worse, for richer, for poorer, in sickness and health, to love you, to honor you, to cherish you and protect you, forsaking all others as long as we both shall live.* | *joyfully receive you as God's perfect gift for me, to have and to hold from this day forward, for better, for worse, for richer, for poorer, in sickness and in health, to love you, to respect and submit to you, forsaking all others as long as we both shall live.* |
| _____ | _____ |
| Husband's Signature | Wife's signature |

Witnessed this day,_____

| | |
|---|---|
| _____ | _____ |
| Witness | Witness |

*Unless the Lord builds the house, its builders labor in vain. (Ps. 127:1, NIV)*

# APPENDIX

## A Sermon Outline on Divorce
## By Pastor Dan Jarrell*

### "THE DAY THE MUSIC DIED"

I. Introduction

   A. In 1971, singer and songwriter Don McLean released a song entitled "American Pie."

      1. The entire song was a tribute to Buddy Holly and a commentary on how rock and roll changed as a result of Holly's death.

      2. McLean seems to be lamenting the lack of "danceable" music in rock and roll during the early 70s and (in part at least) attributing that lack to the absence of Buddy Holly and the other musicians who died with him.

         a. Richie Valens ("La Bamba")

         b. The Big Bopper ("Chantilly Lace")

      3. McLean believed that Buddy Holly's death was the single most significant tragedy in the development and direction of rock and roll. It was a watershed event. When Holly died, the future of the music died with him.

      4. A death with culture-changing consequences.

   B. A much more significant kind of death with much greater consequences in our culture is occurring all around us each day. Yet it no longer even arrests our attention.

1. The death of marriages
2. The death of families
3. A death we have euphemistically called divorce.
   a. Divorce is now part of everyday American life.
      - Embedded in our laws, institutions, manners, mores, movies, television shows, novels, children's storybooks, and our closest relationships.
      - Divorce is so pervasive that most people assume it has seeped into the social and cultural mainstream over a long period of time. Yet this is not the case.
      - According to Barbara Dafoe Whitehead (*The Divorce Culture* [New York: Vintage, 1998]), "For most of the nation's history, divorce was a rare occurrence and an insignificant feature of family and social relationships." Divorce did not become commonplace until after 1960, according to Whitehead. She says, that divorce "doubled in roughly a decade and continued its upward climb until the early 1980s, when it stabilized at the highest level among advanced Western societies. As a consequence of this sharp and sustained rise," says Whitehead, "divorce moved from the margins to the mainstream of American life in the space of three decades."
   b. The consequent divorce culture means death for the American family.
   c. Our last thirty years define "The Day the Music Died."

C. What can we do about it?
   1. Understand and personally embrace God's design for marriage.
   2. Call divorce what it is: death.
   3. Feel the heartache of God over death of any kind.
   4. Choose life for yourself and for your family.

II. Body
   A. God designed marriage as a lifelong, life-giving relationship.
      1. Genesis 2:18–25

a. Not good for man to be alone.

b. A helper was needed.
   - Help to be fruitful and multiply.
   - Procreation (creating life) was the calling of the man and the woman. They were to pursue it together.

c. Woman was the helper "suitable" for man.
   - Suitable because together they could "create life."
   - Suitable because she was taken from the man. She was his completing part, taken from him and given back to him by God the Father.

d. Woman was crafted with the man in mind.
   - "Fashioned" implies "designed with a prototype in mind."

e. Together they were not two, but one.
   - "One flesh"—the most profound and deepest corporeal, emotional, and spiritual unity possible for humankind.
   - "The conjugal union is shown to be a spiritual oneness, a vital communion of heart as well as of body, in which it finds its consummation. This union is of a totally different nature from that of parents and children. . . . It is a holy appointment of God" (Keil and Delitzch, *Commentary on Genesis*, 1: 90–91).

f. Illustrations of "one-flesh" type of unity
   - Examples:
     Alloys of metal
     Chemical bonding in compounds or crystals
     Glue, which alters the nature of the surfaces being united.
     Computer network or any integrated system in which the nature of the whole depends on the parts, and the parts are affected by each other.
   - Separation cannot occur without destroying the nature of the item.

    2.  Matthew 19:1–6

        a.  God always intended one-flesh relationships to be permanent.

        b.  What God has united cannot be separated.

        c.  Separation may be physically possible but not without destroying what God has created.

B.  Divorce is a kind of death.

    1.  Death is separation rather than cessation.

    2.  Genesis 3

        a.  Adam and Eve were promised death if they ate the forbidden fruit.

        b.  They ate the fruit but did not die, at least not in a physical sense.

        c.  Genesis 4:1 in fact declares that they went on to have children.

        d.  In what sense did man and woman die? Or did they?

- Note the separations occurring in Genesis 3.
  Man from his wife (3:7)
  Man and woman from God (3:8)
  Man from the truth (3:9)—He didn't hide because of fear, but he did hide because of sin.
  Man from responsibility (3:12)
  Woman from her divine role and privileges (3:16)
  Man from his divine role and privileges (3:17)
- Note the separations, which continue in Genesis 4 and following.
- (Note: you need not use all these examples.)

        e.  Death is the tearing apart of things that God intended to remain joined.

- Physical death: the spirit torn from the body
- Spiritual death: our spirit separated from God's Spirit
- Divorce: the death of a marriage and family

    3.  (Illustration of death in a family due to divorce. This should be real and effective. Be sure neither to expose

anyone in your congregation nor to speak so as to reveal the family you are talking about. Help your congregation feel the death in divorce.)

C. God hates death, and therefore God hates divorce.
  1. Malachi 2:13–16
     a. Context refers to faithfulness to a covenant of unity.
     b. Men have "broken faith" with regard to this covenant and destroyed the "unity" established by God.
        • A unity designed to produce "godly offspring"
        • A faith breaking, which precludes the "birthing" of the life God desired to result from the union
     c. God hates divorce because it signifies the death both of a covenant relationship and the life that that covenant was designed to create.

(Note: If you wish to explain your congregation's specific views on divorce and remarriage, using Matthew 5:31–32 and 19:1–10, this is a good place in the sermon to do so.)

  2. The reaction of God to death
     a. John 11:35. Jesus burst into tears at the death of Lazarus, even though the Lord knew He would raise him from the dead.
     b. God would rather experience death Himself (as illustrated in the Cross) than to watch us experience it.
     c. Divorce is a kind of death, and God hates death.

D. We can choose life if we want to.
  1. The story of Hosea
     a. Even in the worst of circumstances God enabled a man and a woman to find unity. He restored their marriage, and gave life to children through them.
     b. Our marriages illustrate the covenant commitment God has given to His children. God is motivated to keep that commitment even as He did in the lives of Hosea and Gomer.
  2. The picture of Christ and the church
     a. Ephesians 5:25–33

      b.   The Holy Spirit is motivated to exalt the love Christ has for His bride. The Spirit will empower us to make our marriages work.

    3.   (Illustration: Tell the story of a couple whose marriage seemed hopeless and who committed themselves to choosing life instead of death. They worked through the issues, depended on God, sought His power, and learned to repent, forgive, restore, and be restored. Highlight the reward this couple has experienced and is experiencing. This will need to be a true story, and it is best if you are acquainted with the couple so that you can celebrate their success as you tell the story. End your illustration with a statement like this: "If God can breathe life into that marriage, He can breathe life into yours! Breathing life into dead things is God's deal!")

## III. Conclusion

A. On February 3, 1959, Buddy Holly, Richie Valens, and The Big Bopper died in a plane crash in Iowa. Many in our nation mourned.

B. Yet while people grieved the legends lost in that plane, greater catastrophes loomed on the horizon. The American family was starting to falter as her mothers and fathers chased individual fulfillment instead of the life-giving provision of covenant marriages. When the marriages died, we lost more than legends. We lost our legacy of life.

C. No one can go back and stop Buddy Holly from climbing on that plane. His loss is irreversible.

D. We can, however, reclaim what God intended for us to have in and through our marriages. We must embrace God's design for our union. We must get honest about the death we call divorce, and feel the heartache of God who gave us life and gave us marriage to enjoy. Regardless of what others choose, we must decide to pursue the sort of marriage, which is lifelong, and life-giving. It is not impossible. It begins with you and me . . . one marriage and one home at a time.

\* Dan Jarrell is a friend and former pastor of mine who now pastors Grace Community Church in Anchorage, Alaska. This outline is used with his permission.

# ENDNOTES

## CHAPTER 1—THE FAMILY DUNKIRK

1. Walter Lord, *The Miracle of Dunkirk* (New York: Viking, 1982), ix.
2. Carl Zimmerman, *Family and Civilization* (New York: Harper and Row, 1947).
3. "Living in Sin," *World*, 8 August 1998, 9.
4. "Demographics," *Atlantic Monthly* 284 (January 1998): 14.
5. "Sex on TV," *World*, 31 May/7 June 1997, 22.
6. "Where's Daddy? . . . And Who Cares?" *World*, 12 September 1998, 10.
7. David Popenoe and Barbara Dafoe Whitehead, "The State of Our Unions: The Social Health of Marriage in America," *The National Marriage Project*, June 1999, 2. Internet: www.marriage.rutgers.edu.
8. Ibid., 7.
9. "Divorce and Children," *In Focus*, Family Research Council, 6 May 1998.
10. "Till Death Do Us Part?" *Smart Marriages*, 25 March 2000. Internet: www.smartmarriages.com.
11. Roy Maynard, "Abortion: A Right That's Wrong," *World*, 16 January 1999, 15.
12. "Great Transitions: Preparing Adolescents for a New Century,"

*Carnegie Council of Adolescent Development,* abridged ed. (New York: March 1996), 11; and "Great Transitions," *Executive Summary,* 2.

13. "Newsweek.com Live Vote," *Newsweek,* 27 March 2000, 7.

14. Lord, *The Miracle of Dunkirk,* 25.

15. "Beginning in the 1980s social-science studies by Wallerstein, Hetherington, Bumpass, Popenoe, Weitzmann, McLanahan and Sandefur began to support the idea that divorce and single parenthood had, on average, negative consequences for both children and women" (Don S. Browning, "Practical Theology and the American Family Debate: An Overview," *International Journal of Practical Theology* 1 [1997]: 141). Browning's footnote 21 in his article cites the following references: Judith S. Wallerstein and Sandra Blakeslee, *Second Chances: Men, Women, and Children a Decade after Divorce* (New York: Ticknor and Fields, 1989); E. Mavis Hetherington, Martha Cox, and Roger Cox, "The Aftermath of Divorce," in *Mother-Child, Father-Child Relations,* ed. Joseph H. Stevens and Marilyn Matthews (Washington, D.C.: National Association for the Education of Young Children, 1978); Larry Bumpass, "What's Happening to the Family? Interaction between Demographics and Institutional Change," *Demography* 27 (November 1990): 483–98; David Popenoe, "American Family Decline, 1960–1990: A Review and Appraisal," *Journal of Marriage and the Family* 55 (August 1993): 527–41; Lenore J. Weitzman, *The Divorce Revolution: The Unexpected Social and Economic Consequences for Women and Children in America* (New York: Free, 1985); and Sara McLanahan and Gary Sandefur, *Growing Up with a Single Parent* (Cambridge: Harvard University Press, 1994). For an electronic version of Browning's article, go to http://uchicago.edu/divinity/family/browning_article.html.

Browning also writes that "family structure, seen in the 1960s and 1970s as a neutral factor for family well-being, was viewed by the early 1990s as highly relevant to the flourishing of children" (Browning, "Practical Theology," 141).

Browning's footnote 22 in his article cites Barbara Dafoe Whitehead, "Dan Quayle Was Right," *Atlantic Monthly* 279 (April 1993): 47–84. Within months liberal journalists such as Joan Beck, David

Broder, William Raspberry, and Clarence Page began acknowledging in their columns the seriousness of the family crisis.

Browning's footnote 24 cites the following references: Joan Beck, "Teenage Pregnancy Is an Issue That Crosses Party Lines," *Chicago Tribune,* 27 March 1994, sec. 4, p. 3; David Broder, "Family Values: Stop Arguing about Them and Start Changing Them," *Chicago Tribune,* 16 February 1993, sec. 1, p. 17; William Raspberry, "That Disturbing Charles Murray," *Washington Post National Weekly Edition,* 6–12 December 1993; and Clarence Page, "Wrong Target for Welfare Reform," *Chicago Tribune,* 11 May 1994. Reports of government-appointed groups such as The National Commission on Children (1991) and Families First: Report of the National Commission on America's Urban Families (1993) reversed the thinking of the Carnegie Council by reemphasizing the importance of intact families for child well-being (Browning, "Practical Theology," 141).

Browning's footnote 25 cites the following references: *Beyond Rhetoric: A New American Agenda for Children and Families* (Washington, D.C.: United States Government Printing Office, 1991); and *Families First: Report of the National Commission on America's Urban Families* (Washington, D.C.: United States Government Printing Office, 1993).

Browning also wrote, "The most definitive research was reported by Sara McLanahan and Gary Sandefur in their *Growing Up with a Single Parent* (1994). Using sophisticated statistical tools to analyze the data of four national surveys, MacLanahan and Sandefur concluded that children growing up outside of biological, two-parent families were twice as likely to do poorly in school, twice as likely to be single parents themselves, and one-and-a-half times more likely to have difficulties becoming permanently attached to the labor market. This was true when the data was controlled for the race, education, age, and place of residence of parents. Income reduced these disadvantages, but only by one half. Furthermore, this study showed that stepfamilies had no advantage over single parents; both were less successful in raising children than intact, biologically related families" (Browning, "Practical Theology," 142). This is so even though the average income of stepfamilies is higher than that of intact families, thereby challenging the idea that income rather than family structure is the chief predictor of child well-being (ibid., 143).

With the publication of the book by McLanahan and Sandefur the casualness of the 1960s and 1970s about family structure seems to be coming to an end. McLanahan, herself once a single mother, is surprised by what her own data suggests. She and Sanderfur write, "If we were asked to design a system for making sure that children's basic needs were met, we would probably come up with something quite similar to the two-parent family ideal. Such a design, in theory, would not only ensure that children had access to the time and money of two adults, it also would provide a system of checks and balances that promoted quality parenting. The fact that both adults have a biological connection to the child would increase the likelihood that the parents would identify with the child and be willing to sacrifice for that child, and it would reduce the likelihood that either parent would abuse the child" (*Growing Up with a Single Parent*, 38).

Some political liberals have begun to hear this changed message of the social sciences. It is precisely this kind of information that has turned some of them into neoliberals. On the other hand, there is little evidence that a similar shift is occurring in the liberal religious culture. Although Protestant evangelicals and Roman Catholics are inclined to believe these reports, they differ considerably in how they make use of such information within their practical theological positions (Browning, "Practical Theology," 143).

16. "Where's Daddy? . . . And Who Cares?" 10.
17. Family-Needs Survey, National Database, Overall Breakdowns, FamilyLife, March 2000, 3. For information on the Family-Needs Survey contact the Church Strategy Department at FamilyLife, 1-800-404-5052, ext. 2554.
18. Lord, *The Miracle of Dunkirk*, 39.
19. Ibid., 155.
20. Ibid., 278.

21. Ibid., 271.
22. Ibid., 270, 272.

## CHAPTER 2—BIG IDEA 1: MINISTER TO THE "FIRST FAMILY" FIRST

1. Ben Freudenburg and Rick Lawrence, "FamilyLife Today" radio interview by the author, "Becoming a Family-Friendly Church," 20–24 September 1999.
2. "Why Pastors Burn Out," *Discipleship Journal* 15 (March–April 1996): 29.
3. Fuller Institute of Church Growth, Fuller Theological Seminary, Pasadena, California, 1991; reported in "Family News from Dr. James Dobson," August 1998, 2.
4. H. B. London, interview by Bruce Nygren, 2 March 1999.
5. Lorna Dobson, *I'm More than a Pastor's Wife* (Grand Rapids: Zondervan, 1995), 102.
6. London, interview, 2 March 1999.
7. I thank all the wives of pastors who completed the questionnaire at the conference on "Building Strong Families in Your Church," March 2000, Dallas, Texas.
8. Dobson, *I'm More than a Pastor's Wife*, 106.
9. John H. Morgan, "What My Dad Did Right," *Leadership* 19 (spring 1998). Internet: www.christianityonline.com.
10. Lena Butler, "The Price of Living with a Great Pastor," *Leadership* 19 (spring 1998): 104. Internet: www.christianityonline.com.
11. Daniel L. Langford, *The Pastor's Family* (New York: Haworth Pastoral, 1998), 96.
12. London, interview, 2 March 1999.
13. H. B. London, Jr., and Neil B. Wiseman, *Your Pastor Is an Endangered Species* (Wheaton, Ill.: Victor, 1996), preface.
14. "Pastor Statistics," *Leadership* 13 (fall 1992): x.
15. London, interview, 2 March 1999.

## CHAPTER 3—BIG IDEA 2: RECLAIM THE COVENANT

1. "Generation 2000: A Survey of the First College Graduating Class of the New Millennium," conducted in 1997–98 by Louis Harris and Associates, for Northwestern Mutual Life Insurance Company, Milwaukee, Wisconsin, 8, 11.

2. "A Look at Statistics That Shape the Nation," *USA Today*, 13 April 1998. Internet: www.smartmarriages.com.

3. Pat Conroy, quoted in Wallerstein and Blakeslee, *Second Chances: Men, Women and Children a Decade after Divorce*, 20.

4. Barbara Dafoe Whitehead, *The Divorce Culture* (New York: Vintage, 1998), 6.

5. "Christians Are More Likely to Experience Divorce than Are Non-Christians," *The Barna Report* (October–December 2000): 9–11.

6. Kenneth Stevenson, *Nuptial Blessing: A Study of Christian Marriage Rites* (New York: Oxford University Press, 1982), 13.

7. Tertullian, *Ad Uxorem*, quoted in ibid., 17.

8. Stevenson, *Nuptial Blessing*, 82.

9. Barbeau, quoted in ibid., 75.

10. John Witte, Jr., *From Sacrament to Contract: Marriage, Religion and Law in the Western Tradition* (Louisville: Westminster John Knox, 1997), 7.

11. Stevenson, *Nuptial Blessing*, 197.

12. The following are organizations that initially joined the Covenant Marriage movement: American Association of Christian Counselors, Assemblies of God, Center for Marriage and Family Studies, Christian Men's Network, Covenant Keepers, CrossLife Ministries, FamilyLife, Family Foundations International, FOCCUS, Focus on the Family, Intimate Life Ministries, Jack Hayford Ministries, Journey to Intimacy, LifeWay Christian Resources, Marriage Ministries International, Marriage Plus Ministries, Marriage Savers, Moody Bible Institute, National Association of Marriage Enhancement, Promise Keepers, Smalley Relationship Center, Southern Baptist Association of Counseling and Family Ministry, Southern Baptist Seminary Department of Pastoral Care and Counseling, and Y.M.C.S. (Your Ministry Counseling Services).

13. Maggie Gallagher, "Marriage-Saving/A Movement for Matrimony," *National Review*, November 1999. Internet: www.smartmarriages.com.

14. Art Toalston, "Texas Baptists Counter Official Southern Baptist Stance on Marriage," *Baptist Press*, 1999. Internet: www.christianityonline.com.

15. *Smart Marriages*, 18 March 2000. Internet: www.smartmarriages.com.

16. If you want ideas on a covenant-signing event for your church or would like to order a printed covenant of your own, please contact FamilyLife at 1-800-FL-TODAY (1-800-358-6329) or www.familylife.com.

17. Jim Collins, quoted in Gayle White, "Religion in the News: Hundreds of Couples to Renew Vows Next Week," *Atlanta Journal and Constitution*, 4 January 1998, B5.

## CHAPTER 4—BIG IDEA 3: REMARKET THE DESIGNER'S DESIGN

1. The text of "Article XVIII. The Family" is available on the Internet at www.sbc.net.

2. "The Family Statement," Campus Crusade for Christ, 1999.

3. Mike Mason, *The Mystery of Marriage* (Sisters, Oreg.: Multnomah, 1985), 34.

4. John Piper, *What's the Difference? Manhood and Womanhood Defined according to the Bible* (Wheaton, Ill.: Crossway, 1990), 14.

5. Elisabeth Elliot, *Let Me Be a Woman* (Wheaton, Ill.: Tyndale, 1976), 127.

6. Robert Lewis, "FamilyLife Today" radio interview by the author, "Rocking the Roles," 27–31 December 1999.

7. Bob Lepine, *The Christian Husband* (Ann Arbor, Mich.: Servant, 1999), 91–92.

8. Debbie Moore, "Dorothy Patterson Speaks on Roles of Women in Ministries, Marriage," *Baptist Press*, 6 October 1999.

9. Piper, *What's the Difference?* 47–48.

10. Lawrence J. Crabb, *The Marriage Builder* (Grand Rapids: Zondervan, 1982), 35.

11. Wayne Grudem, "The Manhood-Womanhood Controversy," conference

on Building Strong Marriages in Your Church, Dallas, Texas, 20–22 March 2000.

## CHAPTER 5—BIG IDEA 4: MAKE YOUR CHURCH A MARRIAGE-AND-FAMILY EQUIPPING CENTER

1. "Churches Have Opportunity to Help Parents," Barna Research Online, 15 January 1998. Internet: www.barna.org.
2. Family Needs Survey, National Database, March 2000, 3. For further information on the Family Needs Survey, contact the Church Strategy Department of FamilyLife, 1-800-404-5052, extension 2554.
3. "Churches May Be Hindering—Not Helping—Family Growth," EP News Release, September 1998.
4. Ben Freudenburg and Rick Lawrence, "FamilyLife Today" radio interview by the author, "Becoming a Family-Friendly Church," 20–24 September 1999.

## CHAPTER 6—BIG IDEA 5: CREATE A CHURCH-WIDE WEB

1. Walter P. Wilson, *The Internet Church* (Nashville: Countryman, 2000), xi.
2. Christian Internet Initiative.
3. Jim Wolf, "Data Privacy Fears Haunt Internet," 5 October 2000. Internet: www.yahoo.com.
4. Christian Internet Initiative.
5. Barna Research, "The Cyberchurch Is Coming," 20 April 2000. Internet: www.barna.org.
6. Christian Internet Initiative.
7. *USA Today*, 27 October 1999.
8. Christian Internet Initiative.
9. Cal Thomas, "Selling Out a Heritage," *World*, 24 June 2000, 31.
10. Christian Internet Initiative.

## CHAPTER 7—BIG IDEA 6: MAXIMIZE MENTORS

1. James Patterson and Peter Kim, *The Day America Told the Truth* (New York: Prentice Hall, 1991), 230.
2. Survey conducted by Kevin Hartman, June 2000.
3. Interview by Kevin Hartman, June 2000.
4. Ibid.
5. Susan Hunt, "Older Women Mentoring Younger Women," Conference on Building Strong Families in Your Church, Dallas, Texas, 22 March 2000.
6. John Schmidt, "FamilyLife Today" radio interview by Bruce Nygren, 21 March 2000, Dallas, Texas.
7. Ibid.
8. Response to questionnaire given in the Conference on Building Strong Families in the Local Church, Dallas, Texas, 20–22 March 2000.
9. Hunt, "Older Women Mentoring Younger Women."
10. Ibid.
11. Wayne Younger, interview by Kevin Hartman, June 2000.
12. Hunt, "Older Women Mentoring Younger Women."

## CHAPTER 8—BIG IDEA 7: EMPOWER PARENTS AS FAITH-TRAINERS

1. Family Needs Survey, National Database, Breakdowns Overall, March 2000, 3.
2. George Barna, *The Second Coming of the Church* (Nashville: Word, 1998), 191.
3. Charles Swindoll, *Home Is Where Life Makes Up Its Mind* (Portland, Oreg.: Multnomah, 1979), 5.
4. "Churches May Be Hindering—Not Helping—Family Growth," *EP News Release*, September 1998.
5. Ben Freudenburg and Rick Lawrence, *The Family Friendly Church* (Loveland, Colo.: Group, 1998).

6. Ben Freudenburg and Rick Lawrence, "FamilyLife Today" radio interview by the author, "Becoming a Family-Friendly Church," 20–24 September 1999.

7. Howard G. Hendricks, *Heaven Help the Home!* (Wheaton, Ill.: Victor, 1990), 95–96.


## CHAPTER 9—BIG IDEA 8: FOLLOW THE LIFE CYCLE FOR EFFECTIVE FAMILY MINISTRY

1. Response to a questionnaire given in a conference on Building Strong Families in the Local Church, Dallas, Texas, 20–22 March 2000.

2. Jerry Daley, interview by Kevin Hartman, June 2000.

3. Response to a questionnaire given in a conference on Building Strong Families in the Local Church, Dallas, Texas, 20–22 March 2000.


## CHAPTER 10—PREPARING FOR A LASTING MARRIAGE

1. Survey conducted at a conference on Building Strong Families in Your Church, Dallas, Texas, 20–22 March 2000.

2. See the data available through www.marriagesavers.com.

3. "Christians Are More Likely to Divorce Than Are Non-Christians," *Barna Research Group*, 21 December 1999.

4. Survey conducted by Kevin Hartman, June 2000.

5. Ibid.

6. Tom Elliff, "FamilyLife Today" radio interview by the author, "Ten Questions Every Husband Should Ask," 12–13 June 2000.


## CHAPTER 11—HONEYMOON'S OVER

1. Aviva Patz, "Will Your Marriage Last?" *Denver Post,* 1 May 2000, F1.

2. Survey conducted at a conference on Building Strong Families in Your Church, Dallas, Texas, March 20–22, 2000.

3. Patz, "Will Your Marriage Last?", F6.

4. Visit their website at www.HisPeace.org. Ken Sande's book, *The Peace-*

*maker: A Biblical Guide to Resolving Personal Conflict* (Grand Rapids: Baker, 1997), is an excellent work on biblical conflict resolution.

## CHAPTER 12—SLEEPLESS IN SUBURBIA

1. For an excellent treatment of the topic of childlessness see William Cutrer and Sandra Glahn, *When Empty Arms Become a Heavy Burden: Encouragement for Couples Facing Infertility* (Nashville: Broadman & Holman, 1997).
2. Survey conducted at a conference on Building Strong Families in Your Church, Dallas, Texas, 20–22 March 2000.
3. On early childhood conversions see Roy B. Zuck, *Precious in His Sight: Childhood and Children in the Bible* (Grand Rapids: Baker, 1996), 18–21, 240–41.

## CHAPTER 13—THE GOLDEN YEARS

1. Survey of pastors, FamilyLife, 1998.

## CHAPTER 14—ENCOUNTER WITH ADOLESCENCE

1. Survey taken at a conference on Building Strong Families in the Local Church, Dallas, Texas, 20–22 March 2000.
2. Survey of pastors, FamilyLife, 1998.

## CHAPTER 15—FREE AT LAST

1. George Barna, *Baby Busters* (Chicago: Northfield, 1992), 15.

## CHAPTER 16—SUNSET

1. See the four-part series on aging and retirement by Howard G. Hendricks, "On the Edge of Eternity: A Conversation about Aging," *Bibliotheca Sacra* 157 (January–April 2000): 3–14; (April–June 2000): 131–40; (July–September 2000): 259–70; (October–December 2000): 387–96.

## CHAPTER 17—THE ADOPTIVE FAMILY

1. "Adoption by the Numbers," Scripps Howard News Service, 4 June 1999. Internet: www.familynews.com.
2. "The State of the Children," Institute for Children, 1999. Internet: www.forchildren.org.
3. Roy Maynard, "No Place like Home," *World*, 6 December 1997, 12.
4. FY Orphan Visa Statistics, Joint Council on International Children's Services, 2000. Internet: www.jcics.org.
5. "Adoption by the Numbers."
6. Quoted in Lynn C. Franklin with Elizabeth Ferrer, *May the Circle Be Unbroken* (New York: Harmony, 1998), 132.
7. Ibid., 135.
8. Ibid., 223.

## CHAPTER 18—THE SINGLES MINISTRY

1. Albert Hsu, *Singles at the Crossroads* (Downers Grove, Ill.: InterVarsity, 1997), 14.
2. Dick Purnell, "Single Adults: Why They Stay and Why They Stray," Conference on Building Strong Families in Your Church, 20–22 March 2000, Dallas, Texas. Audiotape available from Audio Mission International, 1-800-874-8730.
3. Barna Research, "Church Attendance," 6 September 2000. Internet: www.barna.org.
4. Jim Talley, "FamilyLife Today" radio interview by the author, "Putting Your Marriage Together," 18–20 January 1999.
5. Nancy Leigh DeMoss, *Singled Out for Him* (Buchanan, Mich.: Life Action Ministries, 1998), 16.
6. Steve Woodrow, interview by Bruce Nygren, 26 April 2000.
7. Purnell, "Single Adults: Why They Stay and Why They Stray."
8. Talley, "Putting Your Marriage Together," 18–20 January 1999.
9. Woodrow, interview , 26 April 2000.
10. DeMoss, *Singled Out*, 40.

11. Woodrow, interview, 26 April 2000.
12. Susie Shellenberger and Michael Ross, *Adventures in Singlehood* (Grand Rapids, Zondervan, 1996), 46–48.
13. Purnell, "Single Adults: Why They Stay and Why They Stray."
14. Woodrow, interview, 26 April 2000.

## CHAPTER 19—THE SINGLE-PARENT FAMILY

1. Popenoe and Whitehead, *The State of Our Unions: The Social Health of Marriage in America*. Internet: www. marriage.rugers.edu. See also Zuck, *Precious in His Sight*, 28.
2. Lynda Hunter, "FamilyLife Today" radio interview by the author, "Parenting on Your Own," 4–12 January 1999.
3. Gary Richmond, *Successful Single Parenting*, rev. ed. (Eugene, Oreg.: Harvest House, 1990), 69.
4. Purnell, "Single Adults: Why They Stay and Why They Stray."
5. Catherine Marshall, *Meeting God at Every Turn* (Carmel, N.Y.: Guideposts, 1980), 143.
6. Lynda Hunter, "FamilyLife Today" radio interview by the author, "Parenting on Your Own," 4–12 January 1999.
7. Gary Richmond, "FamilyLife Today" radio interview by the author, "Successful Single Parenting," 17–20 May 1999.
8. Correspondence with David Sims.
9. Mike Yorkey, *The Christian Family Answer Book* (Wheaton, Ill.: Victor, 1996), 208.
10. Richmond, "Successful Single Parenting," 17–20 May 1999.
11. Ibid.
12. Ron Deal, interview by Bruce Nygren, 3 March 2000.
13. Richmond, "Successful Single Parenting," 17–20 May 1999.
14. Marshall, *Meeting God at Every Turn*, 142.

## CHAPTER 20—THE STEP-FAMILY

1. Letter to FamilyLife, edited and altered slightly to protect anonymity. Used by permission.

2. "Till Death Do Us Part?" *Smart Marriages*, 19 March 2000. Internet: www.smartmarriages.com.

3. "Notes for Remarriage and Stepparenting." 2 March 2000. Internet: www.uakron.edu/hefe/court/note19.

4. "Step-families: 'You Get to Love More People, You Know!'" 2 March 2000. Internet: www.montana.edu.

5. Edward Douglas and Sharon Douglas, *The Blended Family* (Franklin, Tenn.: Providence House, 2000), 2.

6. Larry L. Bumpass, "The Changing Character of Stepfamilies," 1994, quoted in "The Statistics Are Staggering," Stepfamily Foundation. Internet: www.stepfamily.org/statistics.

7. J. Larson, "Understanding Stepfamilies," *American Demographics* 14 (1992): 360.

8. Ibid.

9. Family-Needs Survey, National Database, Overall Breakdowns, March 2000, 34. For more information, contact FamilyLife Church Strategy Department, 1-800-404-5051, ext. 2554.

10. Deal, interview, 3 March 2000.

11. Quoted in James D. Eckler, *Step-by-Stepparenting* (White Hall, Va.: Betterway, 1988), 7, 29.

12. "Notes for Remarriage and Stepparenting," 2 March 2000. Internet: www.uakron.edu/hefe/court/note19.

13. Quoted in Eckler, *Step-by-Stepparenting*, 67.

14. Deal, interview, 3 March 2000.

15. Douglas and Douglas, *The Blended Family*, 9.

16. Eckler, *Step-by-Stepparenting*, 54.

17. Talley, "Putting Your Marriage Together," 18–20 January 1999.

18. Eckler, *Step-by-Stepparenting*, 76.

19. Ibid.

20. Ibid., 90–91.

21. Quoted in Jay Kessler, "Fearing Unfaithfulness, a 'Co-ed' Wife and Stepfamily Tensions," *Marriage Partnership* (spring 1999). Internet: www.christianityonline.com.

22. Deal, interview, 3 March 2000.

23. William J. Doherty, *The Intentional Family* (Reading, Mass.: Addison-Wesley, 1997), 175.

24. Deal, interview, 3 March 2000.

25. Catherine Marshall, *Meeting God at Every Turn* (Lincoln, Va.: Chosen, 1980), 195–96, 198–99.

26. Patricia L. Papernow, *Becoming a Stepfamily: Patterns of Development in Remarried Families* (San Francisco: Jossey-Bass, 1993).

## CHAPTER 21—DECLARING WAR ON DIVORCE

1. Ariel Levy, "No Joy in Splitsville," *New York Magazine*, 12 May 1997. Internet: www.smartmarriages.com.

2. Jack C. Smith, James A. Mercy, and Judith M. Conn, "Marital Status and the Risk of Suicide," *American Journal of Public Health* 78 (1988): 78–80, quoted in Glenn T. Stanton, *Why Marriage Matters: Reasons to Believe in Marriage in Post-Modern Society* (Colorado Springs: Piñon, 1997).

3. Lee Robins and Darrel Regier, *Psychiatric Disorders in America: The Epidemiologic Catchment Area Study* (New York: Free, 1990), 334. These statistics, of course, do not clarify whether a person gets divorced because he or she is mentally or emotionally unstable, or whether divorce causes the instability.

4. Based on statistics presented in Robins and Regier, *Psychiatric Disorders*, 64.

5. Robins and Regier, *Psychiatric Disorders*, 103. Here too the statistics do not tell whether the divorce causes the alcoholism or whether the alcoholism causes the divorce.

6. Sara McLanahan, "The Consequences of Single Motherhood," *American Prospect* 18 (1994): 48–58.

7. Paul R. Amato and Alan Booth, *A Generation at Risk* (Cambridge, Mass.: Harvard University Press, 1997), 10.

8. Deborah A. Dawson, "Family Structure and Children's Health and Well-Being: Data from the 1988 National Health Interview Survey on Child Health," *Journal of Marriage and the Family* 53 (1991): 573–84.

9. Cynthia C. Harper and Sara S. McLanahan, "Father Absence and Youth Incarceration," paper presented at the annual meeting of the American Sociological Association, San Francisco, 1998.

10. Larry L. Bumpass and James A. Sweet, "Cohabitation, Marriage and Union Stability: Preliminary Findings from NSFH," NSFH Working Paper No. 65 (Madison, Wis.: Center for Demography and Ecology, University of Wisconsin-Madison), 1995.

11. Nicholas Zill and Charlotte A. Schoenborn, "Risk of Maltreatment of Children Living with Stepparents," in *Child Abuse and Neglect: Biosocial Dimensions*, ed. R. Gelles and J. Lancaster (New York: de Gruyter, 1987), 215–36.

12. David Popenoe, *Life without Father: Compelling New Evidence that Fatherhood and Marriage Are Indispensable for the Good of Children and Society* (New York: Free, 1996).

13. Sara McLanahan and Gary Sandefur, *Growing Up with a Single Parent: What Hurts, What Helps* (Cambridge, Mass.: Harvard University Press, 1994), 41.

14. Ibid., 53.

15. Ronald Brownstein, "Promise of Reducing Poverty May Be Found inside Marriage Vows, *Los Angeles Times*, 6 October 1997. Internet: www.smartmarriages.com.

16. Steve Grissom, "FamilyLife Today" radio interview by the author, 31 August–4 September 1998.

17. Barbara Dafoe Whitehead, "Ending the Church's Silence on Divorce," *Christianity Today*, 17 November 1997, 53.

18. Ibid.

19. Jan Johnson, "How Churches Can Be Truly Profamily," *Christianity Today*, 6 February 1995, 35.

20. Ibid.

21. William Raspberry, "Marriage Mentors," *Washington Post*, 15 February 1999. Internet: www.washingtonpost.com.

22. Amato and Booth, *A Generation at Risk*, 220.

23. Jeff Atkinson et al., *The American Bar Association Guide to Family Law* (New York: Times, 1996), 62–63.

24. Some details are altered.

25. M. A. Strauss and R. J. Gelles, *Physical Violence in American Families* (New Brunswick, N.J.: Transaction, 1990), quoted in National Violence against Women Prevention Research Center. Internet: www.violenceagainstwomen.org.

26. Talley, "Putting Your Marriage Together," 18–20 January 1999. Contact Dr. Talley at www.drtalley.com.

27. Grissom, radio interview, 31 August–4 September 1998.

28. Michele Weiner Davis, *Divorce Busting* (New York: Summit, 1992).

29. For an excellent book on counseling by both laypersons and professionals see Jeffrey Watson, *Biblical Counseling for Today: A Handbook for Those Who Counsel from Scripture*, Swindoll Leadership Library (Nashville: Word, 2000).

30. Armond M. Nicoli II, "Fractured Family: Following It into the Future," *Christianity Today*, 25 May 1979, 10–15.

31. Amato and Booth, *A Generation at Risk*, 10.

32. Used by permission.

33. Used by permission.

## CHAPTER 22—CHURCH DISCIPLINE

1. Jay E. Adams, *Handbook of Church Discipline* (Grand Rapids: Zondervan, 1986), 11–12.

2. Ken Sande, interview by Bruce Nygren, 22 March 2000.

3. Ken Sande, *Managing Conflict in Your Church: Seminar Workbook* (Billings, Mont.: Peacemaker Ministries, 1993), 45.

4. Ibid., 40.

5. Sande, interview, 22 March 2000.

6. Sande, *Managing Conflict in Your Church*, 77. See also Ken Sande, *The Peacemaker* (Grand Rapids: Baker, 1997).

7. "Church Discipline in Court," *Your Church*, July/August 1999, 8. Internet: www.christianityonline.com.

8. Adams, *Handbook of Church Discipline*, 87.

9. Ibid., 95.

10. Gary Richmond, "Successful Single Parenting," 17–20 May 1999.

11. Sande, interview, 22 March 2000.
12. Ken Sande, "Church Discipline: God's Tool to Preserve and Heal Marriages," Conference on Building Strong Families in the Church, Dallas, Texas, 20–22 March 2000. Used by permission. Audiotape available from Audio Mission International, 1-800-874-8730. Ken Sande can be reached at www.HisPeace.org.

# SCRIPTURE INDEX

# SUBJECT INDEX

Time pressure, and Internet, 66
Turner, Ted, 27

**—U/V/W—**

Unmarried couples, 2
We Stand With You, 41, 42–48
Web site. *See* Church Web site
Wedding vows, 36, 103.
    *See also* Marriage
Wenger, Carl, 75
Wesley, John, 262
White, Reggie, 261
Whitehead, Barbara Dafoe, 28, 245
Wiccan, on Internet, 65
Widowhood, 187–89
Wife
    Family Manifesto view, 285
    role in Christian marriage, 54, 56.
    *See also* Marriage; Women
Wilson, Walt, 63
Witte, John, 31
Women
    mentoring younger women, 75–76

role of women, 40–49.
    *See also* Marriage; Wife
Woodrow, Steve, 207, 209, 210, 211
Word of God. *See* Jesus Christ; Scripture
Work, Family Manifesto view, 290–91
World Wide Web. *See* Internet

**—X/Y/Z—**

Yorkey, Mike, 219
Young children, 132. *See also* Young
    families
Young families, 127–40
how to assist them, 128–32
mentoring ideas, 133–34
poor role models, 128
resources, 136–40
stress from children, 128–29.
    *See also* Families
Young people, views on marriage, 4.
    *See also* Teenagers
Younger, Wayne, 77
Youth pastor, and parents, 162–63
Zimmerman, Carl, 1–2